A geography of
Britain

A. R. TOLSON

and

M. E. JOHNSTONE

OXFORD UNIVERSITY PRESS
1972

Oxford University Press, Ely House, London W.1

GLASGOW NEW YORK TORONTO MELBOURNE WELLINGTON
CAPE TOWN IBADAN NAIROBI DAR ES SALAAM LUSAKA ADDIS ABABA
DELHI BOMBAY CALCUTTA MADRAS KARACHI LAHORE DACCA
KUALA LUMPUR SINGAPORE HONG KONG TOKYO

First published 1970
Second edition—metric 1972

Photoset in Great Britain by
BAS Printers Limited, Wallop, Hampshire
and printed in Hong Kong by
Lee Fung Printing Co. Ltd.

Contents

Ordnance Survey Maps

Since the Ordnance Survey maps are not metricated it has not been possible to metricate the references to these maps.

Acknowledgments

We should like to thank the following for permission to reproduce photographs and other figures: Aerofilms Ltd., Figs. 20, 65, 69, 71, 86, 87, 89, 90, 92, 98, 105, 109, 111, 116, 125, 154, 169, 173, 193, 196, 213, 227, 232, 235, 240; Airviews M/C Ltd., 171; John Armitage, 133, 137; C. F. Barber, 158, 159, 160, 161, 162, 163, 164; Bellwood Photography Ltd., 150; British Leyland, 200; British Petroleum, 231, 233; British Steel Corporation, Scunthorpe Division, 34; British Travel Association, 4, 12, 28, 35, 36, 80, 189, 239, 244; Burrow and Co. Ltd., 166; J. Allan Cash, 3, 33, 43, 44, 51, 52, 67, 68, 70, 75, 82, 88, 99, 100, 107, 108, 115, 117, 119, 120, 121, 134, 135, 138, 140, 165, 195, 202, 218, 220, 224; Central Electricity Generating Board, 205; Cumbernauld Development Corporation, 6; Crowda Premier Oils Ltd., 174; Elsam, Mann and Cooper Ltd., 168; *Farmer and Stockbreeder*, 55, a, b, c, d, f; Geological Museum, 113; Geological Survey, 27, 106; *Geomorphology* by B. W. Sparks, Longmans, 10; Henry Grant, 5, 64, 176, 197; Harland and Wolff, 249; I.C.I. Fibres Ltd., 155; Institute of Geological Studies, 132; London Brick Company, 37; Mansell Collection, 151; Patrick McCullagh, 192; M. C. Morris, 131; National Coal Board, 144, 145, 181; Northern Ireland Government Office, 241; Northern Ireland Tourist Board, 242, 248; Ordnance Survey, 83, and colour sections between pp. 24–5, 192–3, 208–9; Penrhyn Quarries, 217; G. R. Roberts, 14, 15, 17, 30, 32, 130, 177, 178, 187; *The South East Study*, H.M.S.O., 81; C. G. Stanford, 79; *A Strategy for the South East*, H.M.S.O., 78; J. K. St. Joseph, 57b, 209, 212; Susan A. Tempest, 94a; *The Times*, 8; Richard Thomas and Baldwin Ltd., 184; John Topham, 55e; United Kingdom Atomic Energy Authority, 146.

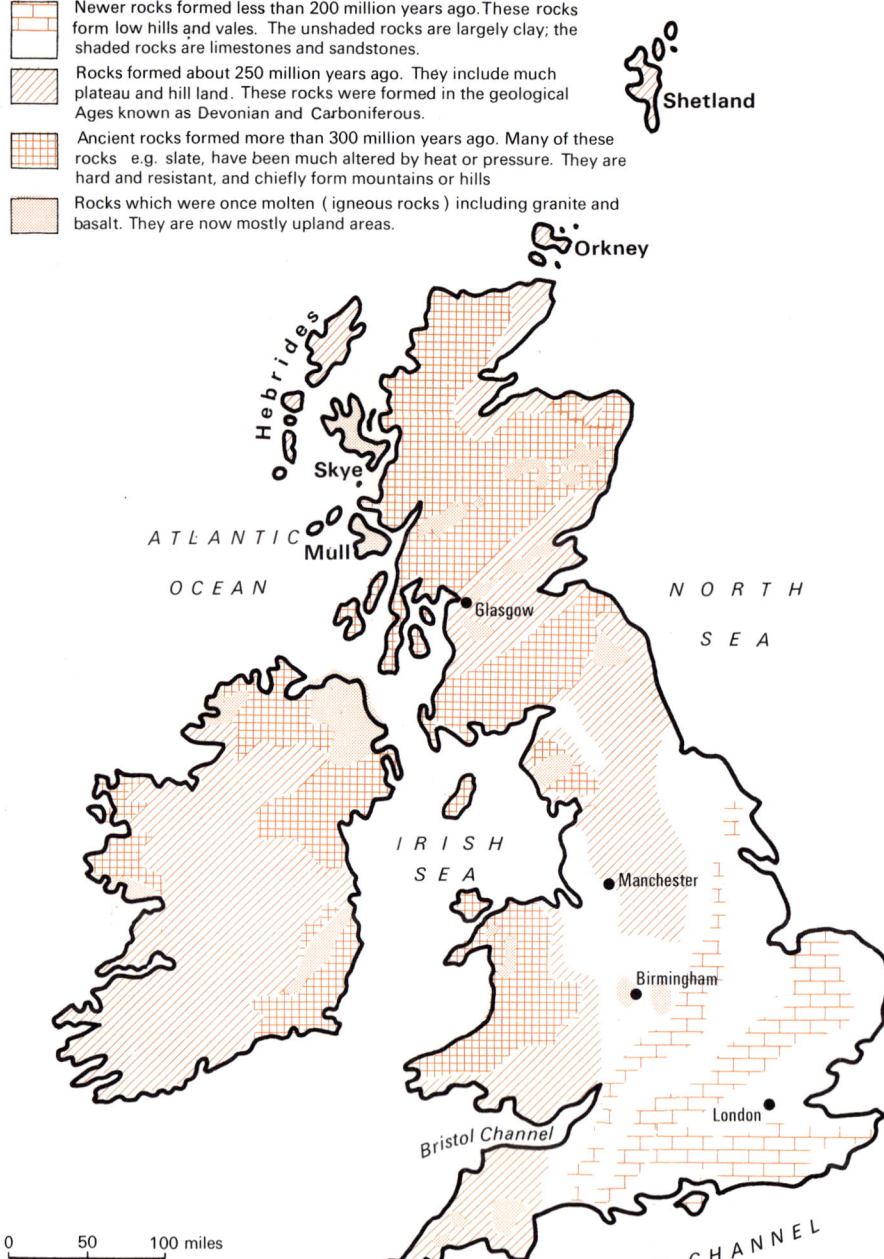

Newer rocks formed less than 200 million years ago. These rocks form low hills and vales. The unshaded rocks are largely clay; the shaded rocks are limestones and sandstones.

Rocks formed about 250 million years ago. They include much plateau and hill land. These rocks were formed in the geological Ages known as Devonian and Carboniferous.

Ancient rocks formed more than 300 million years ago. Many of these rocks e.g. slate, have been much altered by heat or pressure. They are hard and resistant, and chiefly form mountains or hills

Rocks which were once molten (igneous rocks) including granite and basalt. They are now mostly upland areas.

Fig. 1   The Structure of Britain.

6

Introduction

The oldest parts of Britain are in the north and west, in Ireland, Scotland, Cumberland, Wales, and Devon and Cornwall. Some of the rocks which form these lands were once molten, and cooled and solidified to become part of the earth's crust. Others were once muds and sands which collected at the bottom of ancient seas. The scale of geological time is very different from the scale of historical time. The ancient rocks were formed more than 400 million years ago. During their long history they have been so altered by heat or pressure that they no longer have their original properties. The old rocks are hard and resistant, and most of them form mountains or hills.

The mountains were built when the rocks were subjected to tremendous pressure, so that they were crumpled and folded over each other. Over millions of years the ancient mountains have been worn down by rivers, ice, waves, the wind, and exposure to extreme changes of temperature. The highest mountains in Britain today are around 1200 m above sea level.

At a later period, about 250 million years ago, the 'Carboniferous' rocks of the Pennines, South Wales, and much of Central Scotland were formed. These sandstones, limestones and coal measures are also relatively hard, and much of the land which they form is higher than 300 m above sea level.

Most of the eastern and southern parts of Britain are made of 'newer' rock, dating from about 200 million years ago. This part of the country was then covered by the sea. From the high mountains to the west, rivers carried sands and muds into the sea which built up layers hundreds of metres thick. Earth movements caused the sea bed to be uplifted so that it became part of the land. The sandstones, clays and limestones which form eastern England were all once part of a sea bed. They are softer rocks, and have been worn down to form low hills and vales. The highest parts are lower than 300 m above sea level.

The climate of Britain has changed many times in the course of geological history. The salt deposits of the Cheshire plain were dried out from lakes when the climate was as dry as it is today in the Sahara. The coal measures were formed from decayed forests which grew in a climate like that of the Amazon basin. More recently, during the time known as the Ice Age, the climate became as cold as in Polar regions. Ice covered the land as far south as the valley of the Thames, and scooped out deep valleys in the mountains and spread mud and sands over the lowlands. At the end of the Ice Age, water from the melting ice swamped the land. The seas rose and

Shetland

Orkney

Hebrides

Skye

ATLANTIC

Mull

OCEAN

NORTH SEA

Glasgow

IRISH SEA

Manchester

Birmingham

London

Bristol Channel

ENGLISH CHANNEL

0   50   100 miles

0   80   160 km

Fig. 2   Population distribution.

8

Fig. 3   The sparsely populated highlands, a view in upper Teesdale, on the Yorkshire–Durham borders.

Fig. 4   The agricultural lowlands, a view near Devil's Dyke, north of Brighton in Sussex.

flooded the coasts, making Britain an island, separating her from the continent of Europe.

The climate of Britain today is mild. The northern tip reaches 60° N. latitude, only 6° south of the Arctic Circle; the southern tip is 50° N. latitude, yet the average winter temperatures are above freezing point and are as high as 8 °C in Cornwall. Warm winds often blow from the warm currents of the north Atlantic, and they moderate the temperatures.

Britain has been inhabited for centuries, and no part is still in its natural state. The forests of oak and beech which once covered the lowlands have been cut down. Even the bleak moorlands were once largely wooded, but have been cleared and are now kept clear by grazing sheep.

Fifty-five million people live in Britain. Villages, towns, roads, railways, mines, quarries are as much a part of the scenery as the hills and valleys. Geology and climate have made the structure; the people have made the landscape.

The map, Fig. 2, shows the distribution of population in the United Kingdom, and a division into four different types of landscape. It is a generalized map, so within each area there are exceptions to the general rule.

The sparsely populated highland regions are composed mostly of old hard rocks. The soils are thin, the slopes are steep, the climate is wet, travel from one part to another is difficult, and arable farming and manufacturing industries are almost impossible. The empty hills provide the wildest landscapes in Britain, and some of them are now National Parks.

Most of the agricultural areas are found in the lower lands which have been formed from softer rock. Although Britain is primarily a manufacturing land, 80 per cent of the land is used either as pasture or for arable farming. The land

9

Fig. 5 The rooftops of Manchester, nineteenth-century housing in one of the older manufacturing areas.

Fig. 6 The new town of Cumbernauld near Glasgow

has been farmed for hundreds of years, and most of the countryside is divided into a pattern of fields separated by hedges or stone walls. Within the agricultural areas are scattered small and large towns which have been market centres in the past and today have usually some manufacturing industries as well.

The older manufacturing areas are in the north and midlands. During the nineteenth century Britain became the most prosperous manufacturing nation in the world. Britain was rich in coal, and coal provided power for manufacturing industry. Large towns grew up near the coalfields. Often it is difficult to tell where one town ends and another begins, for they have sprawled out and joined together forming several conurbations. The older manufacturing towns made Britain prosperous in the nineteenth century but they have many problems today, and much new building is going on to replace the hectares of older housing.

South-eastern England is dominated by London. London has spread its influence far beyond the actual boundaries of the Greater London Council area. It has affected the farming, the growth of towns and communications, manufacturing and service industry over a wide area. In the twentieth century, the south-east has been the most prosperous part of Britain. There has been little unemployment, and there has been more new building.

Physical changes in the land are slow, but economic changes are rapid, especially today. It is impossible to be up-to-date with all the changes. But it *is* possible to see where some of the changes are taking place, and to suggest what kind of changes to look for. The following list is of changes which have begun, and which are likely to accelerate in the next decades.

INTRODUCTION

1. The population is growing. It is estimated that the population of the United Kingdom will be 61 558 000 in 1981.

2. The distribution of population is changing. The population is becoming less in the highlands, in many rural areas, and in regions of declining manufacture. The towns are growing, especially in the midlands and in southern England, but the centres of large towns are losing population.

3. Agricultural land is being lost to housing, roads, industrial plant, airports. But more is being produced per hectare from the farmland, so as yet there is no loss in the total amount produced from farms.

4. Fuel and power supplies are changing. Less coal is being used. Some nuclear power is now used and in the future, natural gas may be a large source of supply. Much more petroleum is now used, and imports of petroleum have enormously increased.

5. Imports of major raw materials, especially petroleum and iron ore, are increasing. Much new manufacturing industry is being established along the coasts, particularly along the estuaries. The use of the shores of the estuaries for industrial development is likely to increase.

6. Some older industries are likely to employ fewer people and to produce less, notably coal mining, cotton and wool textiles, railway engineering.

7. Other industries are likely to continue their expansion, notably electronics (e.g. telecommunications) and chemicals.

8. The number employed in 'service' industries is increasing, and is likely to go on increasing. Service industries are listed as: gas, electricity and water services; transport and communication; distributive trades; insurance, banking and finance; professional and scientific services; public administration and defence.

9. Changes in organization are likely to continue so that business enterprises, including farms, will be run in larger units. There will be more take-over bids and mergers.

10. Official influence—by government departments and local authorities—on the location of industry, location of new housing, and rural preservation is likely to increase.

1. Rivers

Almost any landscape in Britain is one of hills and valleys. Most valleys have been made by rivers. As a river flows continuously over the same path, it carries away mud, gravel, and even larger rocks, so that bit by bit it cuts into the land. The wearing away of land is called erosion, and although there are other agents of erosion, such as the sea or glaciers, rivers are the main agents of erosion in Britain.

The map opposite shows the rivers and hills of England and Wales. The lower lands have been eroded by the rivers gradually over thousands of years, and the hills have been left as higher land between the valleys. Soft rocks are more easily eroded than hard rocks. Most of the lower lands have been eroded out of relatively soft rock, whereas the harder rocks remain as hills.

The beginning of a river is called a *source*. The river flows downhill from its source until it reaches the sea. The stretch where it reaches the sea is its *mouth*. Many of the river mouths in Britain, like the Thames or the Mersey, are wide and scoured by the tides, and are called *estuaries*. Smaller rivers which join a main river are *tributaries* and the point where the tributary meets the main stream is a *confluence*.

A river with all its tributaries carries water away from the land, or *drains* it, and the area it drains is called the *drainage basin*. The drainage basin of the river Thames is outlined on the map. All the rain falling in this area which is not evaporated or used by plants or man eventually finds its way to the Thames and out to the North Sea. The line dividing one drainage basin from another is the *watershed*. This is higher ground between two drainage basins—sometimes only very slightly higher. On one side of the watershed the water flows one way, in this case towards the Thames; on the other side it flows another way—to the English Channel or Bristol Channel.

---

1. Name the rivers which flow into the Wash, the Humber, the Bristol Channel, the Solent.

2. In what hills are the sources of the rivers Trent, Severn, Mersey, Thames, Tyne?

3. What hills form the watershed between (a) the Mersey and Don (b) the Thames and Severn?

4. Draw a map to show the drainage basin of either the Trent or the Severn.

5. Some main watersheds are lower than 150 m. Find two of these, and name the drainage basins they separate.

12

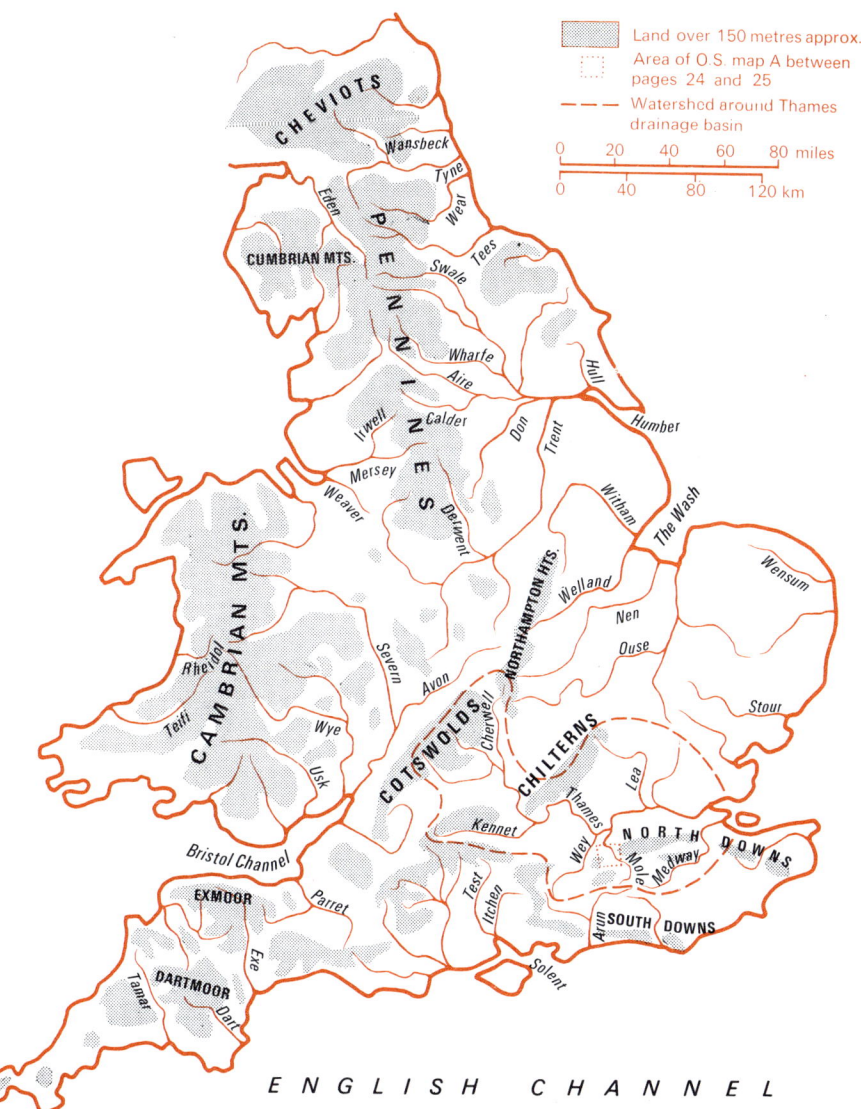

Land over 150 metres approx.

Area of O.S. map A between pages 24 and 25

Watershed around Thames drainage basin

0	20	40	60	80 miles
0	40		80	120 km

Fig. 7   The hills and valleys of England and Wales.

6. Name two rivers which flow largely through high hills. Name two which flow almost entirely through lowland.

7. Look at your atlas. What towns are at the confluence of the Mersey and Irwell, the Severn and Avon, the Aire and Calder, the Thames and Cherwell, the Thames and Kennet?

Fig. 8　The river Lyn, North Devon, after the flood in 1952. The river in flood was able to carry huge boulders and to tear down trees.

How rivers erode valleys

Rivers get their supply of water from the rain which falls on to the land. Fig. 9 shows what happens to the rainwater. The source of a river is often a marshy region on the top or side of a hill, or it may be a spring of clear water seeping or bubbling from the ground. Springs come from water collecting underground. Large rivers have more than one source. Each source supplies a tributary, and the tributaries are gathered by one main river which flows to the sea.

A river erodes the land partly because as it flows away downhill it cuts its bed deeper into the land. It does this in several ways. It carries away soil and rock particles. It rolls pebbles along the bed of the stream and this can, in course of time, wear down the solid rock. Pebbles are washed into hollows and swirl around enlarging the hollows into pot holes so that the bed of the stream is pitted. After heavy rain, the stream swells to a powerful torrent, and then it can undermine a large part of its banks, dislodge large rocks, and shift them downstream. The larger rocks are slowly battered down, and the smaller particles of sand and mud are carried downstream. During flood, a river's power to erode becomes much greater than it normally is, and large rocks may be carried a long way. The river Lyn in North Devon, shown in the photograph, is quite a small stream which flooded

14

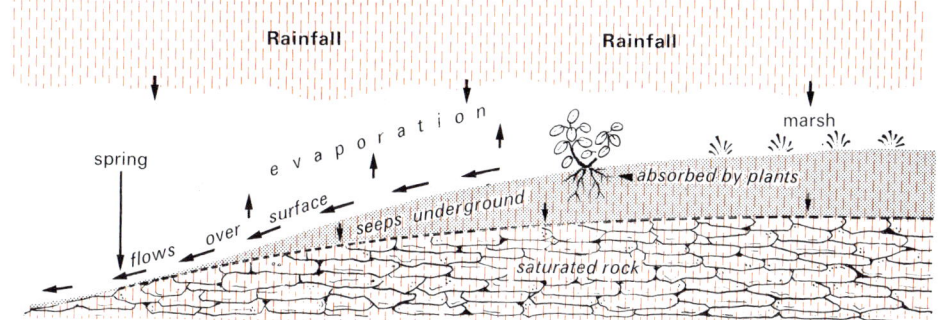

Fig. 9   What happens to rainwater.

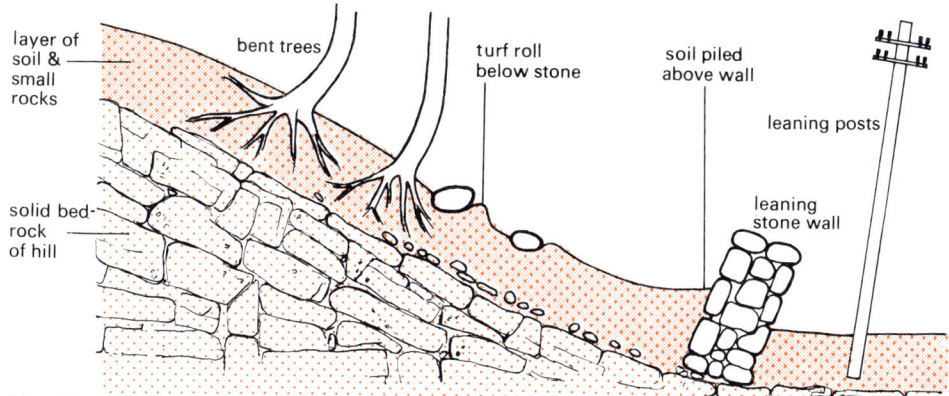

Fig. 10   Soil creep on a hillside.

disastrously in 1952, when it became strong enough to carry boulders weighing more than ten tonnes.

Valley widening

As a river deepens its bed it is said to be 'downcutting'. If this were the only erosion taking place, the river would flow through a narrow, steep-sided trench. But the sides of a river valley widen out and become sloping so that the valley is V-shaped. There are often tributary rivulets which make minor gulleys on the valley sides. Erosion of the valley sides, however, is not all concentrated on grooves, but is a mass movement taking place over the whole of the valley slopes.

Rocks on the valley sides are exposed to 'weathering'. Moisture and weak acids from the atmosphere help to dissolve them, and frost helps to break them up. The loosened material on the valley sides can gradually move downhill. Rain helps to wash loose material down towards the river, a surface movement called 'rainwash'. Rain water also acts as a lubricant at greater depths, and the diagram Fig. 10 above shows how a slope is affected by 'soil creep'. There may also be more sudden landslips on the valley sides. Weathering, rainwash, soil creep, and landslips are part of the widespread erosion which takes place more easily where rivers have

15

1. RIVERS

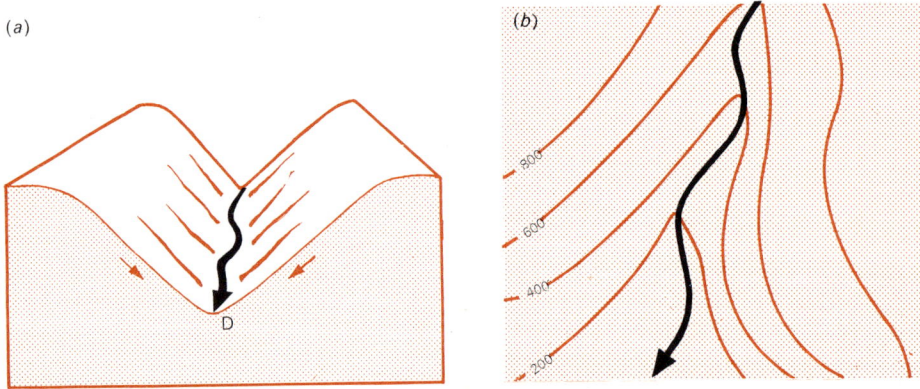

(a)

(b)

Fig. 11 A steep-sided, V-shaped valley. Downcutting takes place at D. Weathering, rainwash, soil creep, and landslips widen the valley sides.

made an initial groove in the land. They cause valleys to be V-shaped, like the example shown in the photograph of the Badgeworthy valley.

Some valleys are more obviously V-shaped than others. The diagrams above show a straight, steep-sided valley with no flat land beside the river.

Figure 13 shows a river winding through the hills, cutting symmetrical shoulders called interlocking spurs. Compare these diagrams with the photographs Fig. 12, and Fig. 15.

Fig. 12 The Badgeworthy valley, North Devon. Draw a sketch of the photograph, and label river downcutting, slopes widened by weathering, rainwash, soil creep, and landslips. There is almost no level land beside the river. You can just pick out the outline of interlocking spurs in the background.

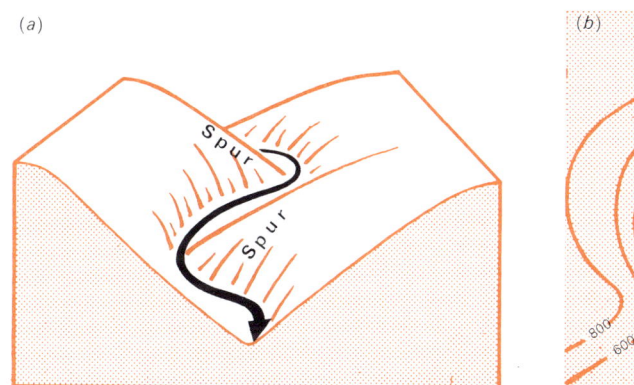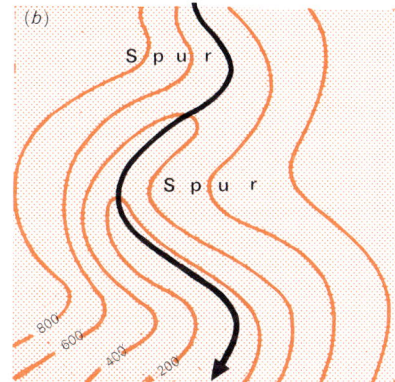

(a)

(b)

Fig. 13   A winding, steep-sided, V-shaped valley with interlocking spurs.

The flood plain

The diagrams overleaf show a different valley shape, for here the central part of the valley is flat, but there are steep slopes along the edge. The flat part in the centre has been formed by 'deposition'. The river is depositing sand, mud and coarser material, and is building level land called a 'flood plain'. The flood plain widens out partly because the river cuts into the foot of the slopes at each edge.

There are many valleys which have flat flood plains edged by steep hills. The photograph of Box Hill shows part of the flood plain of the river Mole, and the

Fig. 14   Box Hill. This view is taken with the camera pointing eastwards towards Box Hill across the Mole Valley. On the left, bare white patches of chalk show through the trees. This is a steep river cliff called 'The Whites'. Find it on the Ordnance Survey Map A opposite p. 24. In the foreground is the flat flood plain of the river Mole.

Fig. 15   A river valley with flood plain between steep slopes (South Wales). Draw a sketch of the photograph and label the flood plain and steep wooded slopes. What evidence is there that the river has changed its course?

(a)
(b)

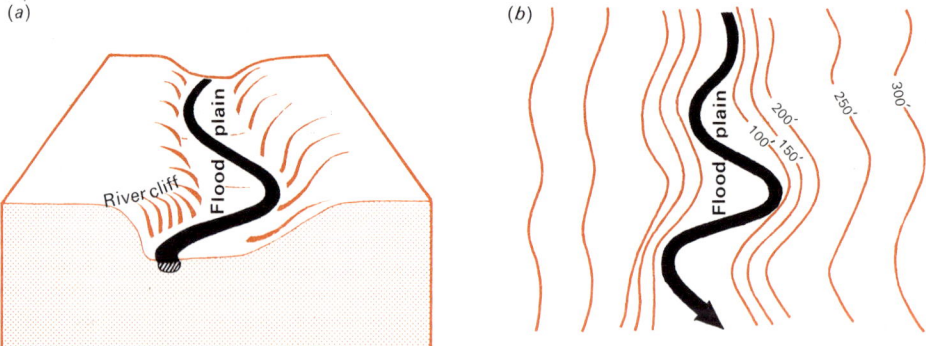

Fig. 16   A flood plain edged by hills.

steep hills rising immediately beside the flat land. Fig. 15 also shows a river which has built up a flood plain between steep slopes.

Erosion and deposition work side by side. Water flowing round a curve is deeper on the outside of the curve and flows more quickly than it does on the inside. The river erodes its banks powerfully on the outside of the curve, cutting a steep bank of rock and mud. Where the river touches the foot of the hills, a high precipitous slope is formed called a river cliff, and the hills are cut back, making a valley like the one in Fig. 16.

At the same time the river deposits some of the material it carries. On the inside

18

Fig. 17   The river Mole at Swanworth farm north of Dorking. The river is both eroding and depositing. Find a river bank being undercut, deposits on the inside of a meander curve with plants growing on them. Notice the differences in speed of the river.

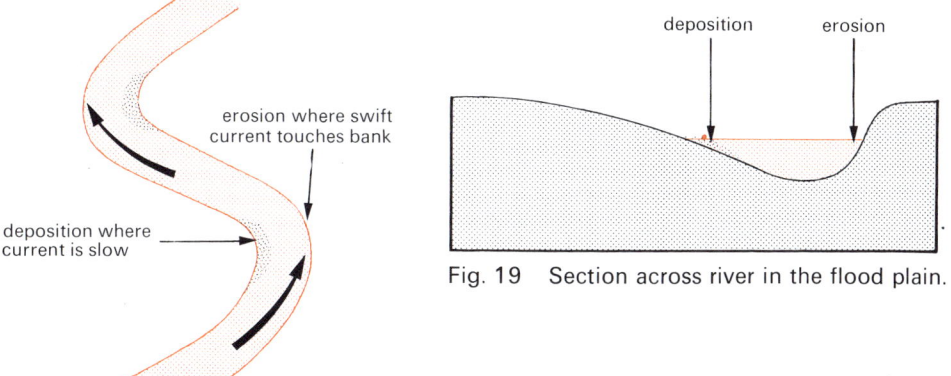

erosion where swift
current touches bank

deposition where
current is slow

deposition   erosion

Fig. 19   Section across river in the flood plain.

Fig. 18   Erosion and deposition in the flood plain.

of the meander the current is slow, and some of the pebbles, sand and mud carried by the river are not moved forward but are deposited. They collect on the river bed and the water becomes shallow. Gradually the deposits make the water shallow enough for plants to grow.

First reeds grow; then mud is trapped around their roots, especially during flood. Eventually the river bed is built higher until it is above the normal water level. At this stage grass is able to grow. The flood plain is therefore made out of the deposits brought down by the river. The photograph of the river Mole above shows a detail of the river at work, eroding and depositing in its flood plain.

19

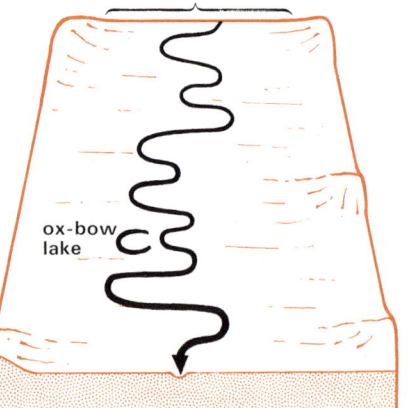

Fig. 21   A wide flood plain.

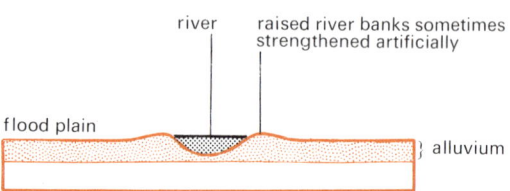

Fig. 20   The flood plain of the river Thame near Aylesbury, in the Oxford clay vale.

Fig. 22   Section across the flood plain.

The flood plain is not always enclosed between hills. As the diagram above shows it may be very wide and if there are hills they can hardly be distinguished. In a wide flood plain, the river is usually broad, and swings in wide meanders across the plain. During flood, the water is able to spread a long way over the level land. The river is full of fine deposits of mud and it spreads these over the plain, building up deep layers of alluvium (mud deposited by rivers). Near the river the deposits are thicker, so that the actual banks of the river may rise like low walls above the plain. These banks are often strengthened artificially.

The river continues to erode the outside curve of the meander more rapidly than the inside. Sometimes the meanders are cut through and ox-bow lakes are formed (Fig.23). During flood the river becomes powerful enough to break its banks where they nearly touch. The ox-bow lake is stagnant water and eventually is clogged by plants and dries up.

The flood plain may not be completely flat. Often there are steps in the plain which are called terraces. These can be seen very clearly in the flood plain of the river Mole (Fig. 24). There are also terraces beside the Thames. Terraces are formed

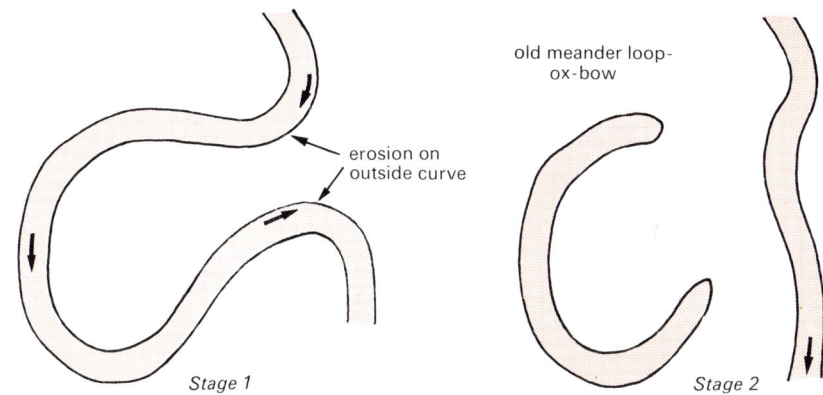

erosion on
outside curve

old meander loop-
ox-bow

Stage 1

Stage 2

Fig. 23   Formation of an ox-bow lake.

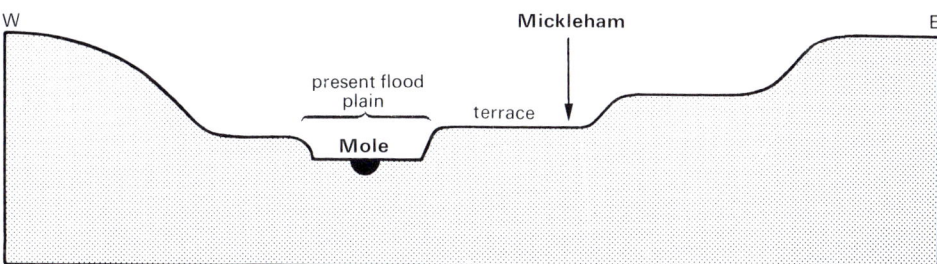

W

Mickleham

E

present flood
plain

terrace

Mole

Fig. 24   Terraces in the Mole flood plain.

when the river erodes a deeper valley into the deposits it laid down at some earlier period. This may happen if there is a change of climate, so that rainfall becomes heavier and makes the streams more powerful; or when there is a change in the level of the land and sea so that the river has a steeper drop between its source and the sea. The result is that the river is given new power to cut down. It forms a new flood plain below the old one, cutting a step in the land, and the level land of the old flood plain becomes a terrace. Terraces are often composed of gravel and may form the only firm, well drained building land for houses and roads in the flood plain.

Several factors affect the shape of a valley at any one place. One is whether or not the rock which the river flows over is resistant to erosion. A river flowing over a resistant rock tends to make a steep-sided valley, because erosion is concentrated on the bed of the river and downcutting is active, but the valley sides cannot be easily widened by weathering, rainwash, soil creep, or landslips. On the other hand, if the rock is not resistant, erosion can take place over a wide area. Valleys tend to widen out, and rivers form broad flood plains, where the rock is non-resistant. The river Thame shown in the photograph flows over soft, easily eroded clay for much

21

of its course. Many rivers flow through more than one type of rock and the valley shape changes from place to place.

Another factor affecting the shape of the valley is the gradient of the river. Even quite a small river may cut a deep valley if the gradient is steep.

Other factors influencing the shape of a river valley are climate, the vegetation of the slopes, glaciation, and any change made by man, e.g. quarrying and damming.

Generalizations about river valleys, however, are not satisfactory and may be misleading. Each valley must be looked at on its own to see how the different factors at work have interacted.

The Valley of the River Mole

The Ordnance Survey $2\frac{1}{2}$ in. Map A, opposite p.24, shows part of the valley of the river Mole and one of its tributaries, the Pipp Brook.

The main feature shown on the Ordnance Survey map is the gap in the hills where the Mole flows between the steep slopes of the North Downs. The North Downs are composed of chalk which is soft enough to be cut into easily by a river. However, chalk is not easily eroded by surface rainwash, because rain water quickly soaks into the chalk and does not flow over the surface. The edges of the Mole valley have therefore remained steep.

The Pipp Brook is quite a small stream, which has cut a steep-sided valley. It has a steep gradient, and the sandstone (greensand) over which it flows is fairly resistant to erosion, so the valley sides have not widened out much.

Follow the valley from where the Pipp Brook enters the map in the south (1545) northwards until it joins the river Mole. Then follow the river Mole northwards until it leaves the area shown on the map. Notice the differences in the width of the flat land beside the rivers.

8. Draw a section (a) across the Pipp Brook valley from 134473 to 138479. What type of valley does this section show? (b) across the Mole from Camilla Lacey (164520) to Box Hill (178514). Label the river, river cliff, motorway, railway, flood plain. (See p. 126 for an example of how to do it.)

9. Draw a contoured sketch map to show the Pipp Brook valley between the bridge at 134484 and the southern edge of the map. Draw the course of the stream, and the contour lines 300 ft., 350 ft., 400 ft., 450 ft.

10. Draw a contoured sketch map to show the river Mole and its valley between Burford Bridge (172519) and northing 54. Include land within about $\frac{1}{2}$ mile of the river. Draw the river Mole, the 150 ft. contour line, and three other contours. Shade the area of the flood plain.

11. (a) How many feet does the Pipp Brook drop from the point where it enters the map to its confluence with the Milton Brook? (b) What is the height of the river Mole above sea level at the railway bridge at 164537? (c) Measure the distance along the Mole from Burford Bridge (172519) to the bridge north of Mickleham. (d) In what ways and where has the drainage been altered artificially?

12. Draw an enlarged map of square 1652 and label a river cliff, steep slope, spur, railway cutting, railway embankment, dual carriageway, ox-bow lake (this one was formed artificially).

13. Look at Fig. 154 p. 142. Draw a sketch of the photograph and label the flood plain, a meander loop, a filled-in ox-bow lake, a river terrace. Find the river Weaver on Fig. 7.

14. What is 'downcutting'? How does a river lower its bed?

15. What are rainwash and soilcreep? What effect do they have on the shape of a river valley?

16. Describe the following, and explain how each was formed: pot hole, river cliff, ox-bow lake, flood plain, river terraces.

Headward erosion and river capture

Besides wearing away the land it flows over, a stream also cuts back at its source. Fig. 9 shows how a spring emerges on a hillside where the underlying rock is saturated. The land behind the spring may be slowly undermined, so that the source of a river gradually cuts back into the hillside. The process of cutting back into the hills at the source is called 'headward erosion'.

Often one river carries out the process of headward erosion more quickly than its neighbour. The stronger river may collect the water of the neighbouring stream into its own stream, and river capture takes place. A small scale example of river capture is shown on the Ordnance Survey map, and is illustrated in Figs. 25 and 26.

The Pipp Brook has captured the headwaters of the Milton Brook. The Pipp Brook was more powerful than the Milton Brook, and therefore headward erosion took place more rapidly. The Pipp Brook cut back until its source was as deep as the

Fig. 25   The Pipp Brook and the Milton Brook. Compare these diagrams with Fig.26.

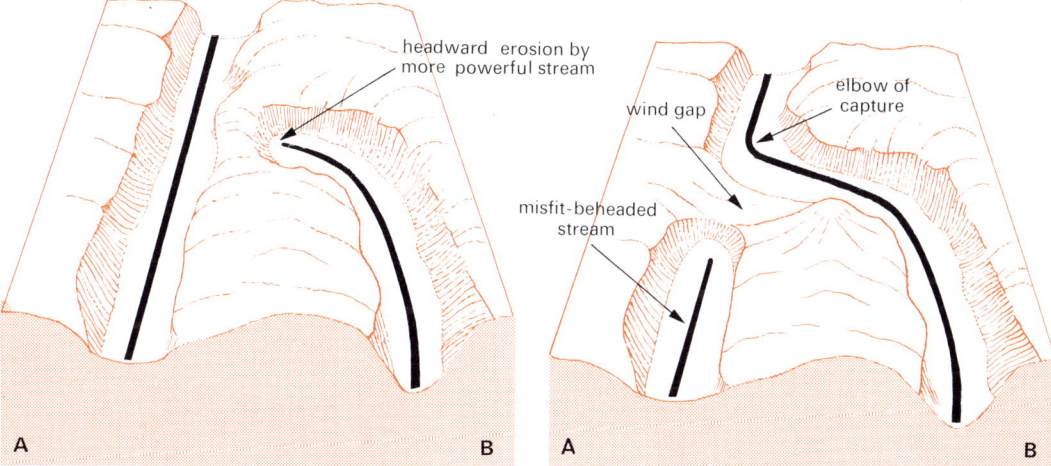

Stage 1.

Stage 2, today.

23

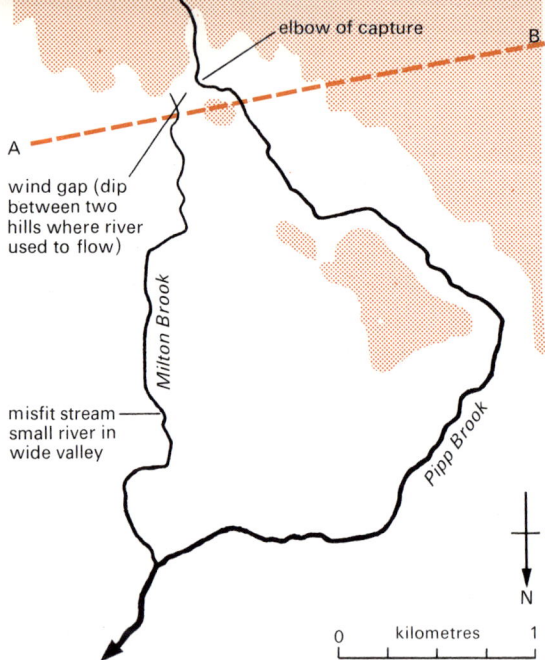

elbow of capture

B

A

wind gap (dip between two hills where river used to flow)

Milton Brook

misfit stream — small river in wide valley

Pipp Brook

N

0   kilometres   1

Fig. 26 Pipp Brook Capture. Compare this map with the Ordnance Survey Map A opposite p. 24

valley of the Milton. Then the water which used to follow the Milton valley began to take a new course, and flow down the Pipp Brook. The point of capture is marked by a sharp bend called an elbow of capture. The small dry pass where the old Milton Brook used to flow is called a wind gap. The wind gap can be seen on the Ordnance Survey map at 148468. The Milton is now a very small stream, but it still flows through the valley it made when it was bigger, so it is called a misfit stream. The process of river capture takes a long time.

There are many other examples of river capture. One is that of the Blyth by the North Tyne in Northumberland; another that of the Teifi by the Rheidol in Wales. The map at the beginning of this chapter (Fig 7) shows the drainage which rivers have been able to achieve so far. If they continue their work without interruption, they may be able to make larger drainage basins and alter the pattern which we see today.

17. The river Mole flows through a gap in the North Downs. What other rivers flow through gaps in (a) the North Downs (b) the South Downs (c) the Chilterns?
18. Name four rivers which have broad flood plains shown on Fig. 7. What is the type of rock where the flood plain is at its widest? (Fig. 1.)

How to give grid references from Ordnance Survey Maps

The vertical lines are EASTINGS and the horizontal lines NORTHINGS. A four figure reference defines a square. To refer to a place within a square, estimate tenths eastwards and northwards. Give the easting first. On the Dorking map, 1649 contains most of Dorking; 163494 refers to a school.

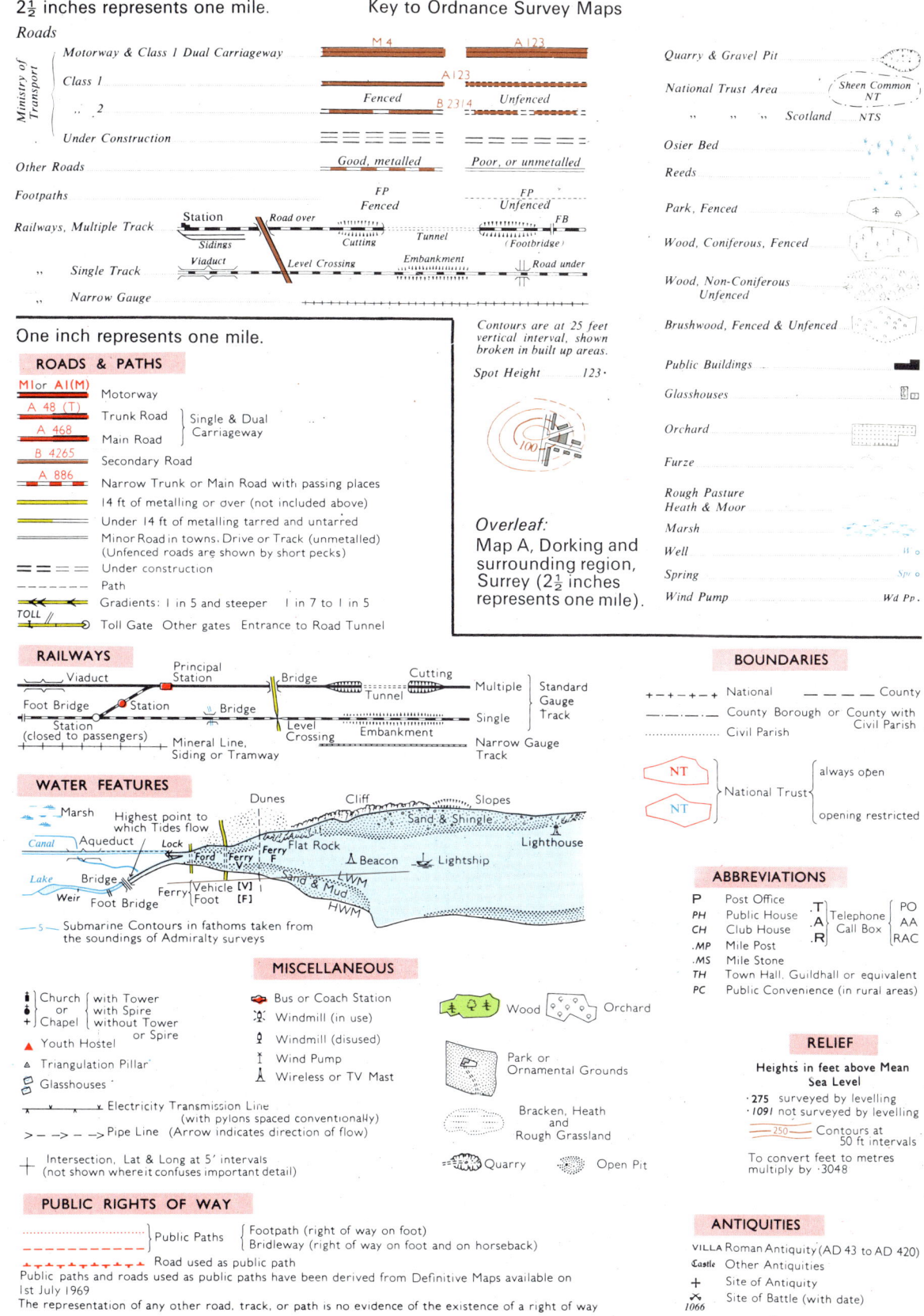

Key to Ordnance Survey Maps

2½ inches represents one mile.

Roads

Motorway & Class 1 Dual Carriageway	M 4	A 123
Class 1	A123	
„ 2	Fenced / B 2314	Unfenced
Under Construction		

Ministry of Transport

Other Roads — Good, metalled / Poor, or unmetalled

Footpaths — FP Fenced / FP Unfenced

Railways, Multiple Track — Station / Road over / Cutting / Tunnel / FB (Footbridge)
Sidings
„ Single Track — Viaduct / Level Crossing / Embankment / Road under
„ Narrow Gauge

Quarry & Gravel Pit
National Trust Area — Sheen Common NT
„ „ Scotland — NTS
Osier Bed
Reeds
Park, Fenced
Wood, Coniferous, Fenced
Wood, Non-Coniferous Unfenced
Brushwood, Fenced & Unfenced
Public Buildings
Glasshouses
Orchard
Furze
Rough Pasture Heath & Moor
Marsh
Well
Spring — Spr
Wind Pump — Wd Pp.

One inch represents one mile.

ROADS & PATHS

M1or A1(M)	Motorway
A 48 (T)	Trunk Road — Single & Dual Carriageway
A 468	Main Road
B 4265	Secondary Road
A 886	Narrow Trunk or Main Road with passing places
	14 ft of metalling or over (not included above)
	Under 14 ft of metalling tarred and untarred
	Minor Road in towns. Drive or Track (unmetalled) (Unfenced roads are shown by short pecks)
= = = =	Under construction
- - - - -	Path
	Gradients: 1 in 5 and steeper / 1 in 7 to 1 in 5
TOLL	Toll Gate Other gates Entrance to Road Tunnel

Contours are at 25 feet vertical interval, shown broken in built up areas.

Spot Height 123·

Overleaf:
Map A, Dorking and surrounding region, Surrey (2½ inches represents one mile).

RAILWAYS

Viaduct — Principal Station — Bridge — Cutting — Multiple | Standard Gauge Track
Foot Bridge
Station — Bridge — Tunnel — Single |
Station (closed to passengers) — Level Crossing — Embankment — Narrow Gauge Track
Mineral Line, Siding or Tramway

WATER FEATURES

Marsh
Highest point to which Tides flow — Dunes / Cliff / Slopes / Sand & Shingle
Canal — Aqueduct — Lock — Flat Rock — Lighthouse
Ford — Ferry F — Beacon — Lightship
Lake — Bridge — LWM
Weir — Foot Bridge — Ferry — Vehicle [V] / Foot [F] — Sand & Mud — HWM

5 Submarine Contours in fathoms taken from the soundings of Admiralty surveys

MISCELLANEOUS

Church or Chapel { with Tower / with Spire / without Tower or Spire
Youth Hostel
Triangulation Pillar
Glasshouses

Bus or Coach Station
Windmill (in use)
Windmill (disused)
Wind Pump
Wireless or TV Mast

Wood — Orchard
Park or Ornamental Grounds
Bracken, Heath and Rough Grassland
Quarry — Open Pit

Electricity Transmission Line (with pylons spaced conventionally)
Pipe Line (Arrow indicates direction of flow)
Intersection, Lat & Long at 5′ intervals (not shown where it confuses important detail)

PUBLIC RIGHTS OF WAY

Public Paths { Footpath (right of way on foot) / Bridleway (right of way on foot and on horseback)
Road used as public path

Public paths and roads used as public paths have been derived from Definitive Maps available on 1st July 1969
The representation of any other road, track, or path is no evidence of the existence of a right of way

BOUNDARIES

+ - + - + - National
— — — — County
—··—··—··— County Borough or County with Civil Parish
·················· Civil Parish

NT
NT } National Trust { always open / opening restricted

ABBREVIATIONS

P	Post Office	T.A.R	Telephone Call Box	PO
PH	Public House			AA
CH	Club House			RAC
.MP	Mile Post			
.MS	Mile Stone			
TH	Town Hall, Guildhall or equivalent			
PC	Public Convenience (in rural areas)			

RELIEF

Heights in feet above Mean Sea Level
·275 surveyed by levelling
·1091 not surveyed by levelling
——250—— Contours at 50 ft intervals
To convert feet to metres multiply by ·3048

ANTIQUITIES

VILLA Roman Antiquity (AD 43 to AD 420)
Castle Other Antiquities
+ Site of Antiquity
⚔ Site of Battle (with date)
1066

Map B, Coast near Braunton, North Devon (one inch represents one mile).

2. The Scarplands

The scarplands are alternating hills and vales which extend from Yorkshire in the north to Devon in the south. The hills are called escarpments. The most characteristic feature of an escarpment is the steep slope which rises abruptly from the plain. The steep slope is the 'scarp'. The other side of the escarpment is usually much gentler, and is called the 'dip' slope. Some of these hill ranges are low, and the scarp can hardly be distinguished; but often the scarp forms a striking landmark for miles. Between the escarpments, there are broad vales. The escarpments and vales form the pattern of the country over most of south and east England.

The chalk escarpments

The main chalk escarpments are shown on Fig 29. Those with the most clearly marked scarps are the Yorkshire Wolds, the Chilterns, the Berkshire and Marlborough Downs, the North and South Downs.

Chalk scenery is easy to recognize. The picture below shows the scarp slope of the Marlborough Downs. The summit is a long, level plateau, about 200 m high. Below the plateau is a steep, smooth slope. The chalk does not show through the covering of short grass. You can also see smooth, concave hollows scooped out of the slope. Fig. 28 shows that the scarp of the chalk downs in Sussex is very similar.

Fig. 27   The Marlborough Downs.

Fig. 28   Part of the South Downs. The village in the foreground is Poynings, north of Brighton.

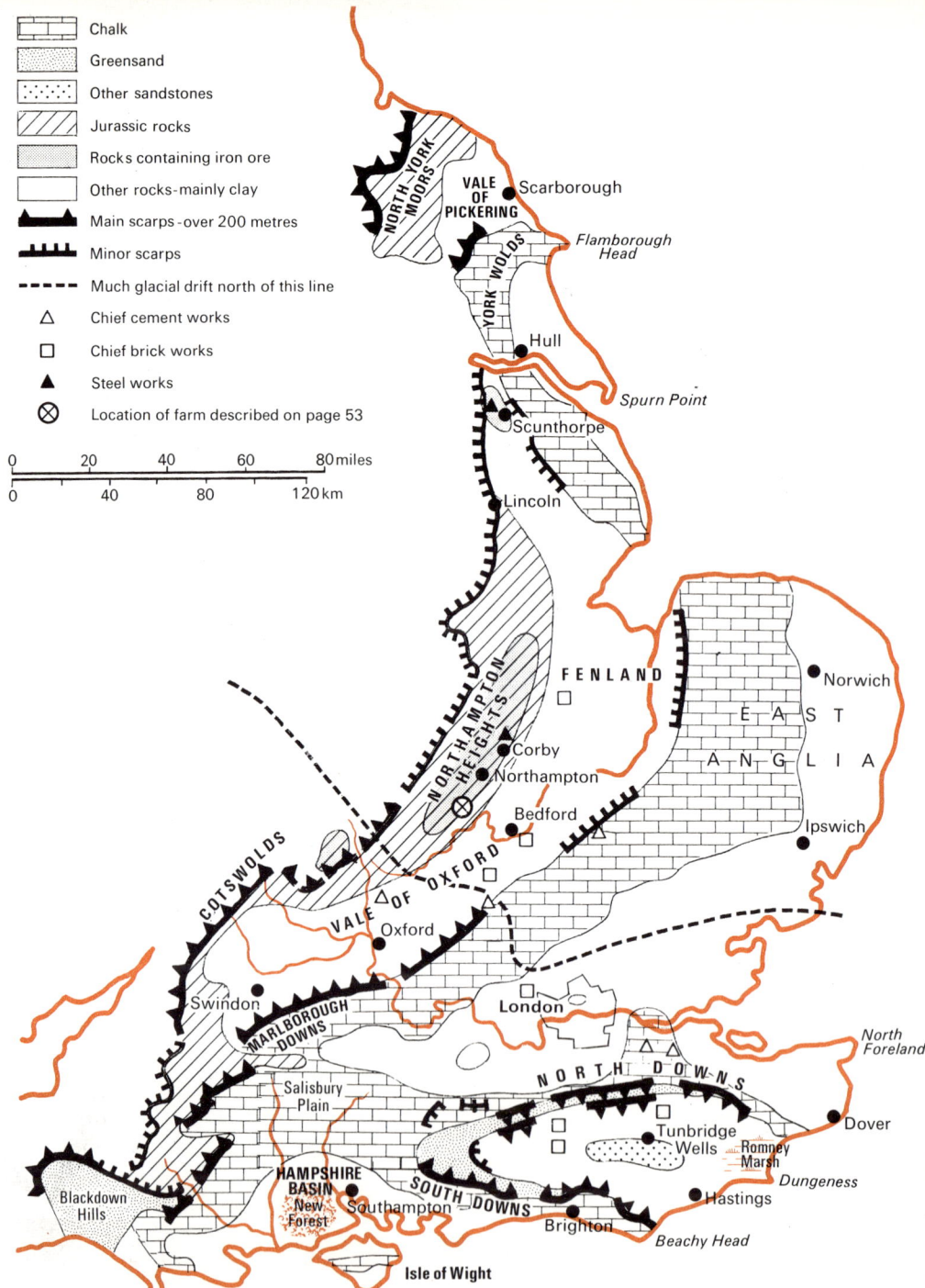

NORTH YORK MOORS

VALE OF PICKERING

Scarborough

Flamborough Head

YORK WOLDS

Hull

Spurn Point

Scunthorpe

Lincoln

FENLAND

Norwich

EAST ANGLIA

NORTHAMPTON HEIGHTS

Corby

Northampton

Bedford

Ipswich

COTSWOLDS

VALE OF OXFORD

Oxford

London

Swindon

MARLBOROUGH DOWNS

NORTH DOWNS

North Foreland

Salisbury Plain

Tunbridge Wells

Romney Marsh

Dover

Dungeness

Blackdown Hills

HAMPSHIRE BASIN

New Forest

Southampton

SOUTH DOWNS

Hastings

Brighton

Beachy Head

Isle of Wight

Fig. 29   The scarplands of England.

26

Fig. 30   A dry valley in the chalk at Box Hill. It is shown on the Ordnance Survey Map A opposite p. 24, in the north-east corner of square 1751. The sharp bend in the road at 177519 can just be seen. Find on the map the two branches of the dry valley and the spur between them. How high is the highest land shown in the picture? How high is the lowest land?

On the gentler dip slope the land is rolling, but the surface is broken by deep steep-sided valleys. There are no rivers in the valleys, which are therefore dry valleys, and the hills are dry. The picture of a dry valley at Box Hill (above) shows the shape of a typical chalk dry valley.

Chalk is a permeable rock, that is, a rock through which water passes. When rain falls onto chalkland, it sinks quickly into the ground. As the water soaks away underground, it fills up the lower layers of the chalk until they are saturated. The top of the saturated layer is called the water table. If it rains heavily for a few days, the water table rises. There is always water underneath the surface of the chalk, and deep wells can be dug to reach this (Fig. 31).

Although small streams cannot flow for long over the chalk, many larger rivers cross the chalk where there are gaps in the hills; they are able to keep flowing because the water table in the gaps is high enough. An example is the river Mole north of Dorking (O.S. Map A, opposite p. 24). Even the dry valleys may have temporary streams in them after heavy rain. The dry valleys are shaped like river valleys. It is not known exactly how they were formed, but it seems likely that they were formed by running water; the water table must have been higher at one time

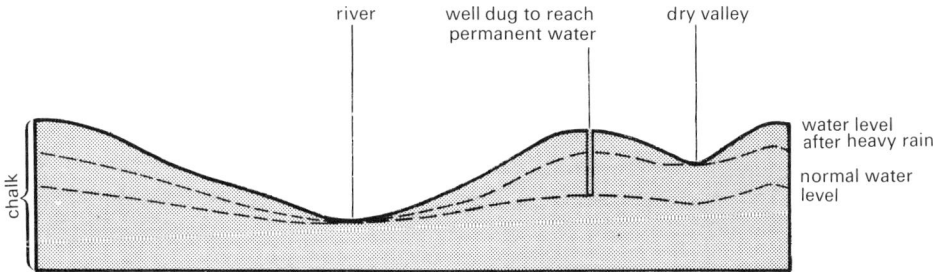

Fig. 31   The water table.

than it is today.

Chalk is composed of the skeletal remains of sea organisms, which accumulated at the bottom of a sea earlier in geological times. The calcium carbonate of which it is largely composed is dissolved by rainwater, so chalk is eroded chemically. In this way, it has been estimated that each square mile of English chalk country loses 140 tonnes of matter each year. In places the chalk is covered with a shallow layer of clay. On many parts of the Chilterns and North Downs there is a covering known as clay-with-flints. This clay holds water and woodlands of beech and oak grow on it.

North of the line shown on the map much of the land is covered with clay and sand deposited on top of the chalk during the ice age. It was a deposit which was collected at the bottom of ice sheets, and is called a glacial drift deposit (see p. 85). When the underlying rock is covered in this way, the scenery is different. In East Anglia the East Anglian Heights form a low chalk escarpment but there is so much glacial drift it is difficult to tell where the chalk begins. The rolling, humpy agricultural land looks very much the same as large areas of the Midlands which are also covered with glacial drift.

One way of telling what the underlying rock is, is by looking at churches and other old buildings. Embedded in chalk are hard nodules called flints. These can be seen in bands across chalk cliffs or quarries. Flints can be split in a certain way so that they have a shiny surface, and are called knapped flints. Flints are used as a building stone in chalk country, and the vast mediaeval East Anglian churches, built of flint, are evidence of the underlying chalk. Most of the pebbles on the beaches of the south and east coasts are flints which have been rounded as they roll against each other in the sea, and they, too, are used in building.

The chalk hills were some of the first parts of Britain to be settled. The burial grounds of ancient Britons—tumuli and long barrows—form humps which are recorded on Ordnance Survey maps. Ancient camps and fortifications are also marked. When England was forested, the chalk formed more open country than the wet clay lowlands. It was easier to move from place to place on the chalk. Many of the earliest roads, such as the Pilgrims Way marked on Ordnance Survey Map A, opposite p. 24, lead directly along chalk ridges, although even on the chalk the woodland was probably much thicker than it is today. Sheep grazing on the hills over the years have kept trees and shrubs down.

For centuries, the chalk lands were valuable because they were sheep pastures, but today relatively few people live on the chalk hills. Since World War II, in spite of the thin dry soil, much of the chalk land has become arable farmland. There are ploughed fields where the whiteness of the chalk shows through the soil, and through the green shoots of wheat and barley. Dairy cattle too are raised on some of the chalk hills, especially in the hills around the Hampshire Basin. Some of the downs are still open grassland where sheep graze, and occasional clumps of trees break the smoothness of the skyline.

28

2. THE SCARPLANDS

Not many houses are built on the higher parts of the downs. The old villages are usually in the sheltered valleys or at the foot of the scarp. At the scarp foot there is often a line of springs or water seepage which provides a water supply. Villages at the foot of the scarp are near both chalk and clay rocks, and this gives a variety of soils, making it easy to farm the land in a variety of ways. Where a river breaks through a gap in the hills, there is often a gap town. Gap towns commanding route-ways have grown larger than scarp-foot villages.

On the whole, because of its dryness and height, chalk is not of great agricultural value, and it is partly for this reason that many famous race-courses, such as Goodwood, Epsom, and Newmarket, use the rolling contours of the downs. There are military training grounds, too, on Salisbury Plain.

One very important use to which the chalk is put today, however, is in making cement. The tall chimney of a cement works trailing smoke across the vale is a common sight at the foot of the chalk scarps. Cement requires both chalk and clay, and thus at the foot of the scarp the works are ideally located. Chalk provides calcium carbonate, which is combined with the alumina, iron, and silica of the clay to form cement. The equipment needed to manufacture cement—excavators, crushers, kilns, storage tanks—is large, and cement making is a heavy industry. The cement industry has become extremely important in recent years, because cement is the essential ingredient in concrete which is now widely used in building —in the construction of bridges, docks, runways, offices, schools, farm buildings, as well as in smaller objects like lamp standards and fence posts. Concrete reinforced with steel is now a major building material.

1. What is meant by: saturated rock, dry valleys, scarp-foot villages?

2. Draw a sketch of Fig. 27. Label scarp slope, plateau top, farmland at foot of scarp, concave hollow in scarp.

3. Use Ordnance Survey Map A, opposite p. 24, which shows part of the North Downs north of Dorking. (a) Locate the area of the map on Fig. 7. (b) Look at the northern half of the map. Follow the line of the scarp from square 1349 eastwards to square 1850. The scarp is broken by the gap made by the river Mole. How high is the bottom of the scarp slope in square 1850? About how high is the top of the scarp in square 1551? (c) The dip slope is broken by many steep-sided dry valleys. Give the names of three roads or buildings in the bottom of dry valleys. Name two spurs between the dry valleys. (d) Draw a section across the chalk escarpment from the marking F.P. at 184535 to Deepdene Bridge 187503. Label a dry valley, scarp slope, dip slope, crest of escarpment. (See p. 126 for an example of how to do it.) (e) Compare the positions of Warren farm and Birchingrove farm. (f) List the evidence of early settlement on the map. What other facts show that most of the land north of northing 51 is made of chalk? (g) Draw a contoured sketch map of the escarpment between the river Mole and the eastern edge of the map. Include the 200 ft., 400 ft., 600 ft. contour lines and the river. Label the dry valleys.

29

Fig. 32   Part of the dip slope of the Cotswolds near Chippenham, showing the plateau-like surface, arable farmland on thin soils, and dry stone walls.

Fig. 33   The market place at Stow-on-the-Wold, a small town in the Cotswolds. Both walls and roofs are built with local stone.

The Jurassic escarpments

The main Jurassic escarpments are shown on Fig. 29. The word 'Jurassic' is used to describe all rocks formed during a particular time in geological history. The Jurassic hills of England are made of limestones, ironstones, and sandstones.

There are three main types of limestone found in Britain. Limestone is a general name given to calcareous rocks (i.e. containing lime and formed largely of skeletal remains). Chalk is one type—a white powdery rock, fairly easily dissolved, but harder than the clays which surround it. Jurassic limestone is granular and yellowish, and splits easily into blocks. A third type is Carboniferous limestone—an older and harder rock, grey in colour, which forms large parts of the Pennines.

The Cotswold hills are made of Jurassic limestone. The scarp rises steeply above the Severn plain. The Cotswolds reach 300 m and are higher than any of the chalk hills. The scarp slope is steeper, and scarred here and there with patches of bare rock. The summit of the escarpment is an open rolling plateau, like the land shown in Fig. 32. The limestone is a permeable rock, so there are numerous dry valleys. But there are also many streams on the surface, although they often disappear for short distances underground before reappearing.

The Cotswolds are farmlands for sheep, barley, wheat, and some cattle. On the hills the fields are often separated by stone walls. Jurassic limestone makes a good building stone, as it is harder than chalk and splits in a regular pattern. It is used in most of the village buildings. Many of the villages like Chipping Camden and Stow-on-the-Wold were prosperous market towns during the Middle Ages, when farmers

Fig. 34 Open cast mining of iron ore. A thick mantle of waste is removed before the ore-bearing rocks are reached.

and merchants made money out of the wool trade. Some of their profits helped to build large stone churches.

North-east of the Cotswolds, the Northampton Heights form a lower, less obvious escarpment. The hills are largely covered with glacial drift. In the Lincoln Edge, the hill-forming rock is not so thick, and the hills are a narrow ridge. The city of Lincoln, built in a gap in this ridge, is a perfect example of a gap town. Its mediaeval cathedral overlooks vales on each side of the ridge.

The Jurassic rocks contain iron ore, especially on the eastern side of the Northampton Heights and in the Lincoln Edge. About one-third of the iron ore smelted in Britain comes from these iron-bearing rocks. There is hardly any other home supply of iron ore today.

The mining of this iron ore is open-cast (Fig. 34). The ore-bearing rocks are fairly close to the surface, so shafts do not have to be dug. The top layers are removed by excavators. The top soil is preserved carefully so that it can be used again after the ore has been removed. Up to 40 m of 'overburden' is excavated before the ore is reached.

The chief mines are close to the two towns of Corby and Scunthorpe. The mine at Frodingham, near Scunthorpe, is the largest in the country. Corby and Scunthorpe both have large iron and steel works, and do not use as much imported ore as other iron and steel towns. The locally mined iron ore does not have a high iron content—only between 20–30 per cent—whereas the best imported ores have an iron content of over 60 per cent, so it is easier to smelt the ores close to the places where they are mined. Coal for the furnaces is brought from the Yorkshire coalfield. Some of the iron ore is also sent to blast furnaces on Teeside, the Sheffield area, and the Midlands.

The North Yorkshire moors also contain iron ore. For many years the Cleveland mines supplied iron ore to the furnaces of Middlesbrough, but the ore is now nearly worked out, and the last mine was closed in 1964. The North Yorkshire Moors differ from all the other escarpments. They are much higher, reaching nearly 450 m, and are true open moorland, with grass and heather growing over the hills, and sheep grazing. The Jurassic rocks here are mainly sandstones which are very resistant to erosion, though the rivers have in many places cut through to the underlying clay to form beautiful dales such as Rosedale.

The sandstone hills

Sandstones are made of small grains of sand, worn originally from older rocks. The sands collected at the bottom of a sea and were gradually cemented together. Apart from the Jurassic sandstones, there are three main types of sandstone in the scarplands.

The Hastings sandstones in the Weald do not form an escarpment. This is the central part of south-east England marked on the map at the beginning of the chapter. It is hilly, up and down country, difficult to cross. There are no open plateau lands as there are on the chalk. Most of the rivers of south-east England rise in these hills. They are swift-flowing streams near their source and erode their beds rapidly, making steep-sided valleys separated by narrow ridges. The hills are called the Forest Ridges, a reminder that 'Weald' meant 'wood' in Saxon times. A lot of the hills are still wooded, and the scenery of woodland interspersed with pasture for sheep and cattle is typical of the central Weald. Orchards of fruit trees and fields of hops vary the landscape. The wood in mediaeval times was burned to make charcoal for smelting the iron ore which used to be mined in the Weald. There are still some deposits of ore but they are not big enough to be worth mining today.

Another sandstone is 'greensand' which forms a clearly marked escarpment in south-east England, south of the North Downs. The highest point is Leith Hill. Part of the greensand escarpment is shown on Ordnance Survey Map A. The largest area of greensand is found in the Blackdown Hills, at the western rim of the scarplands. Here the rocks level out to form a steep-edged plateau.

Besides the Hastings sands and the greensand, there are also patches of sandstone in the London and Hampshire Basins. They form such well known areas as the Aldershot common, Hampstead Heath and the New Forest.

The clay vales

The chalk and limestone are permeable, so rainwater seeps through them and there is not much water flowing over the surface to erode the rock. These rocks are therefore resistant to erosion by running water and remain as hills. Clay, on the

Fig. 35 The Pantiles, Tunbridge Wells, Kent. Many of the houses in the Weald of Kent and Sussex, which was once much more wooded than it is today, are partly timbered 'frame' buildings. Tunbridge Wells grew as a resort after the chalybeate springs were discovered there in 1606. It became especially fashionable during the eighteenth century.

Fig. 36 Abingdon, a small market town in the clay vale of Oxford. The line of the Thames can just be seen in the distance.

other hand, is impermeable. Water does not pass through it, but flows over the surface. Clay is easily eroded by running water, and is worn down over large areas by weathering, rainwash, or soil creep. The clay lands have been gradually worn down to form lowlands. The scarplands form a series of hills and vales because they are made up of these alternating bands of resistant and non-resistant rocks.

The clay vales are below 100 m. Near the rivers, there is flat land in the flood plains sometimes forming a meadow land which has to be artificially drained. Normally the scenery is gently undulating. The watersheds are not obvious, and the divide between the Thames and Ouse drainage might be passed unnoticed on a journey from Oxford to Northampton.

The scenery of the clay is green farmland, often pasture for cattle, although more and more is now being used for crops of wheat and barley. There are plenty of trees to be seen, in patches of woodland, or scattered in the fields and hedgerows, and hedges rather than walls mark the field boundaries.

2. THE SCARPLANDS

Fig. 37   The Stewartby brick factory in the clay vale near Bedford.

The clay itself is a raw material for bricks. Quarries for brick works and forests of tall chimneys from the brick kilns break the rural landscape. More than half the bricks made in Britain come from the Oxford clay vale.

In many places in the clay vales there are terraces of gravel beside the rivers. Water drains away more easily from gravel than from clay, so these terraces form firm, drier land and are sites of villages and towns. Gravel (now widely used in making concrete) is also dug in many places, and huge water-filled gravel pits are often seen near the rivers. (See p. 21.)

In the Oxford clay vale, the main towns are the county towns—Northampton, Bedford, Oxford—which have served as markets for centuries, and which now also employ many people in manufacturing industries. Oxford and Northampton have populations of over 100 000. Swindon, which started as a railway junction, is rapidly becoming a large town with many growing manufacturing industries, changing the rural character of the southern part of the clay vale.

The structure of the scarplands

All the rocks of the scarplands are composed of small particles which have been cemented together. For example chalk is composed mainly of the shells and skeletons of sea organisms; clay is composed of mud; sandstone, of sand grains. All these particles collected at a time when the sea covered nearly all of what is now England. It is difficult to imagine the length of time necessary for so much to accumulate, or the depth of rock which was thus formed.

34

2. THE SCARPLANDS

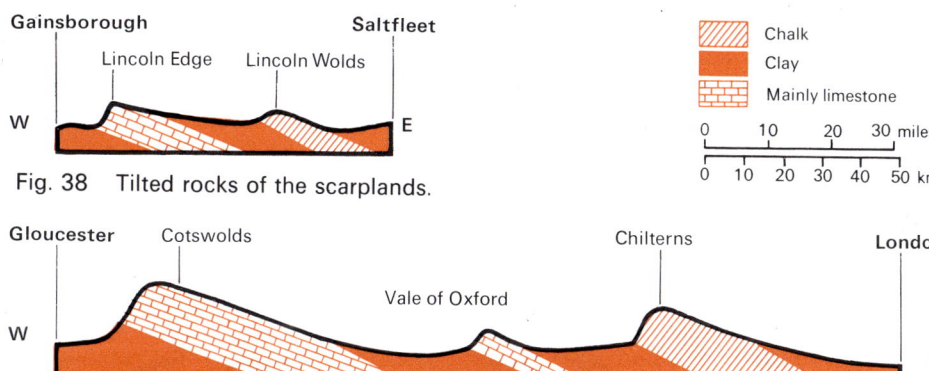

Fig. 38   Tilted rocks of the scarplands.

Chalk
Clay
Mainly limestone

0   10   20   30 miles
0 10 20 30 40 50 km

Fig. 39   Tilted rocks of the scarplands, dipping down gently to the east.

Because these rocks are composed of sediments, they are called 'sedimentary' rocks. Sedimentary rocks lie in layers, one on top of the other. The oldest rock formed the first layer at the bottom of the sea. Gradually the younger ones were deposited on top. In the scarplands, the Jurassic rocks of the Cotswolds are the oldest, and the London clay the youngest. A key to a geological map shows the oldest rocks at the bottom, the newest at the top.

The rocks are found in layers called strata, and each of these is itself formed in layers. Thus within the chalk or greensand there are harder and softer layers. The different layers within each major division are called beds, and are separated by 'bedding planes'.

The rocks are not horizontal. They were deposited on a sea bed which sloped down towards the east. They have also been gently tilted as a result of earth movements, so that there is a general dip of the rocks down to the east. These tilted rocks, with their alternating layers of resistant and non-resistant rocks at the surface, form the scarplands.

The structure of the scarplands is illustrated in the sections, Figs. 38, 39 and 41. These should be compared with the map, Fig. 29.

The general dip eastwards has been complicated by folding. During the Alpine mountain building period, the rocks a long way from the Alps were disturbed, and gently folded into domes and hollows. The upward folds are called anticlines, and the downward folds synclines. South-east England (Surrey, Kent, Sussex) is an

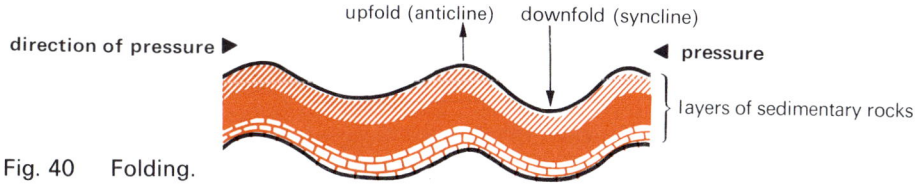

Fig. 40   Folding.

35

anticline. The central part has been worn away, because the top of an anticline is always an area of weakness, as the rocks are stretched. Rivers were easily able to erode it. The Hampshire Basin and the London Basin are both synclines.

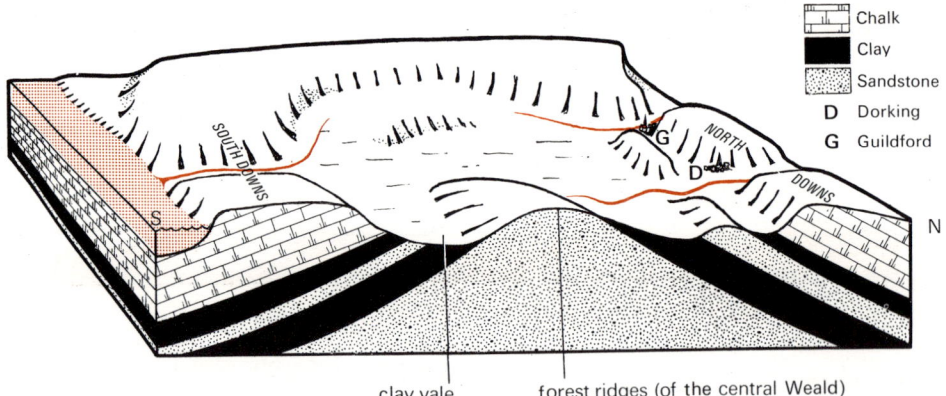

Fig. 41   Anticline of south-east England. The rocks have been folded up into a dome, the weaker top of the dome has been eroded away.

4. What differences are there between chalk and clay? Mention composition of rock, height of land, permeability, farming, sites of towns and villages.

5. Mining and quarrying are extractive industries. List the extractive industries of the scarplands and name the other industries associated with each.

6. Describe the changes of scenery you would encounter on a journey from London to Gloucester.

7. Explain with examples the terms sedimentary rock, strata, anticline, syncline.

3. Weather and Climate

When we describe the weather as raw, muggy, or crisp, we are describing the feel of the air around us. This depends partly on the season, and partly on where the air has come from, and the route by which it has travelled to Britain. Britain receives a great variety of air. Its position on the west side of the vast Eurasian land mass, and bordering the Atlantic, means that both maritime and continental air reach Britain. Also, because of its latitude, between 50° and 60° north, both polar and tropical air reach Britain. Air moving over Britain from one of these directions is called an 'air stream'. The air streams which affect the weather of Britain are shown on Fig. 42.

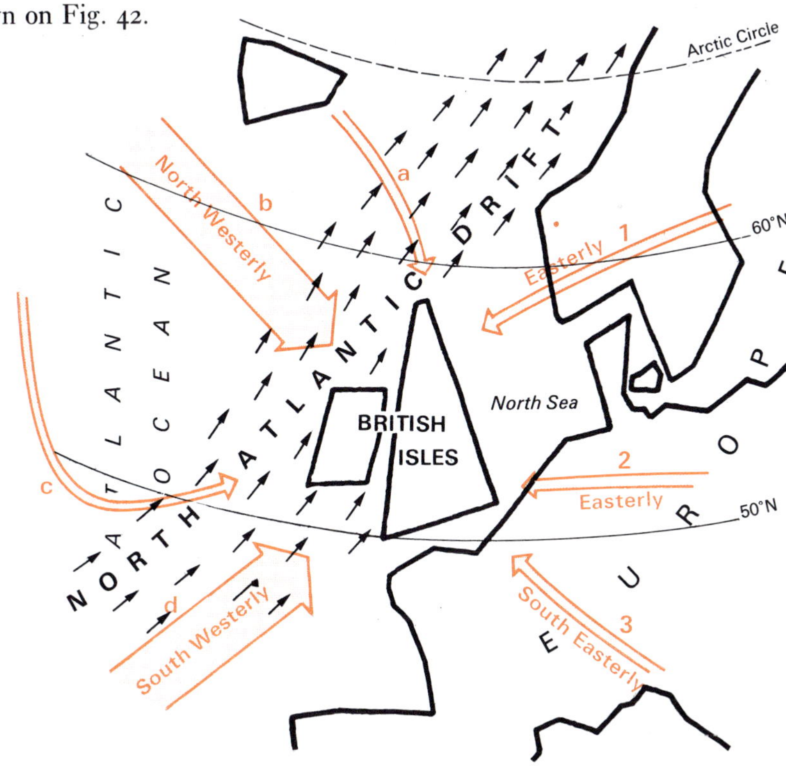

Fig. 42   Air streams which affect Britain. The width of the arrows indicates approximately how frequently the different air streams affect Britain.

Fig. 43   Cumulus cloud near the mouth of the River Torridge in Devon.

Air from the west is damp because it has spent a long time over the Atlantic Ocean. If it comes from the north it is also cool. When a north-westerly air stream (*a*, *b*, and *c* on the map) crosses the British Isles, the air is fresh and clear with good visibility. Winds are strong and gusty. Big fluffy 'cumulus' clouds are blown quickly across the sky leaving patches of clear blue between them. The weather is unsettled, alternately bright and showery. The 'bright periods and scattered showers' of the weather forecasts occur with this kind of air. The showers do not last long, but may be heavy, with large rain drops, and are sometimes accompanied by thunder or hail.

In winter, north-westerly air tends to be cold and raw with a temperature of about 7 °C in the middle of the day, and sometimes frost at night. In summer, north-westerly air streams bring cool days with temperatures reaching about 18 °C in the middle of the day, and 10 °C at night.

If the air approaches from due north (route *a* on the map), it is usually colder than if it comes from the north-west or west. Showers of sleet or snow may fall in the winter, especially over the hills in the north.

Air coming from the south is usually warm. South-westerly air streams (route *d* on the map) bring the milder days of winter, with day time temperatures up to 12 °C. The temperature does not change much from day to night. In summer south-westerly air streams may bring hot, fine days with temperatures of about 20 °C.

38

Fig. 44 When the skies are clear, air close to the ground often becomes colder than air higher up. Water vapour near the ground condenses to form mist or fog, especially near rivers. This scene is in the Wye Valley, Herefordshire.

Coastal fog is common when south-westerly air crosses the country. This fog does not usually persist far inland, but the air is damp and muggy, and visibility is poor. Rain may fall over hilly districts, but elsewhere the weather is usually overcast, but dry.

Easterly air streams (1 and 2 on the map) do not reach Britain as often as westerly air streams. In winter, most of the Eurasian land mass becomes extremely cold. Sometimes air from the continent spreads across Britain. Easterly air streams bring the coldest winter weather, with temperatures often below freezing point even at midday, and bitterly cold, frosty nights.

Easterly air which has passed over a mass of land and only a few miles of sea (route 2 on the map) is dry. When the air stream comes from due east the skies are clear and cloudless and the weather is bright and crisp. If the air approaches from the North-east, however, it picks up moisture crossing the wider part of the North Sea. This gives unpleasant raw weather. Fog quite often develops at night and may persist all day. It is cold and gloomy.

Occasionally in summer hot, dry air coming from a south-easterly direction (route 3 on the map) brings a spell of weather when day time temperatures may reach 30 °C and may not drop below 20 °C at night. South-easterly air streams bring the hottest summer weather. The sky is cloudless, hazy and pale in colour. Sometimes, however, huge cumulus clouds build up in the afternoons, and there may be thunderstorms.

3. WEATHER AND CLIMATE

Changeability is the main characteristic of the British climate. The weather changes as one type of air gives way to another. Weather changes occur in rapid succession when a 'depression' crosses the country.

A depression is a vast swirl of air about 800 km across. Warm damp air from the south is drawn into cold northern air. Fig. 45 shows this diagramatically. Over

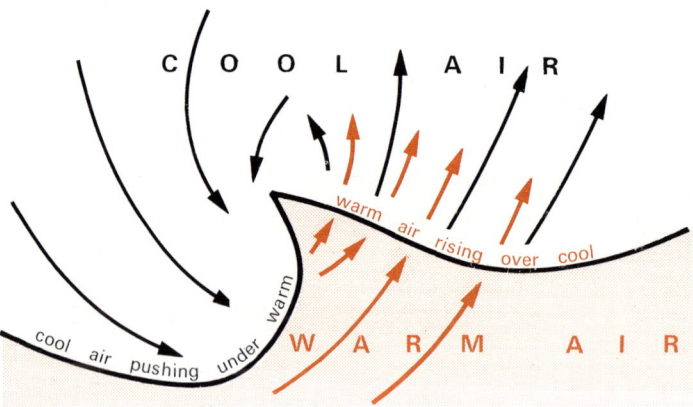

Fig. 45   The swirl of air of a depression.

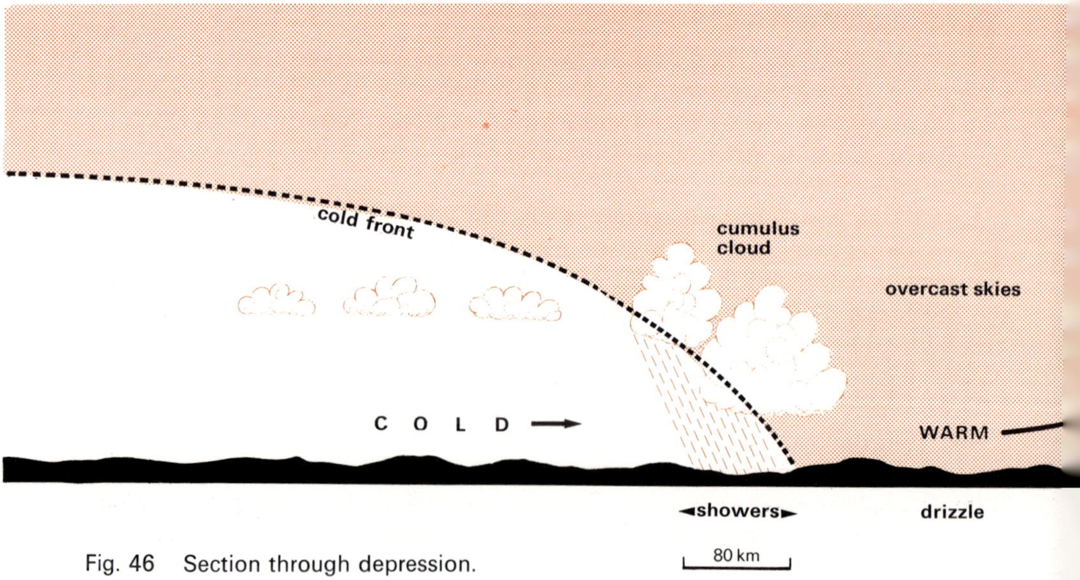

Fig. 46   Section through depression.

Britain the air swings in an anticlockwise direction. As a depression moves east-wards across the country, cool weather is succeeded by the mild, damp conditions of the warm air sector. The cooler, showery conditions of the north-westerly air then follow.

The meeting of the warm and cold air is called a front. On the east side of the warm sector lies the 'warm front', shown on Fig. 46. The warm air is less dense than the cold air. At the warm front, warm air is rising gently over the cold air as they both move eastwards. On the west side of the warm air sector, cold air is pushing underneath the warm, and lifting it off the ground. This is the 'cold front'.

As the air rises along the fronts it cools and some of the water vapour (invisible water in the form of a gas) it contains condenses into water droplets, forming cloud. The droplets may coalesce and fall to the ground as rain. As a front passes over Britain, rain often falls. Rain occurring with the passage of fronts is called 'frontal rain'. At the warm front, the air rises gently and slowly over the cold for a long distance, and thick layers of grey cloud result. This gives steady rain over a belt as much as 300 km wide. At the cold front, the air is forced to rise quickly, and billowing cauliflower shaped cumulus clouds result, which give shorter heavy showers of rain.

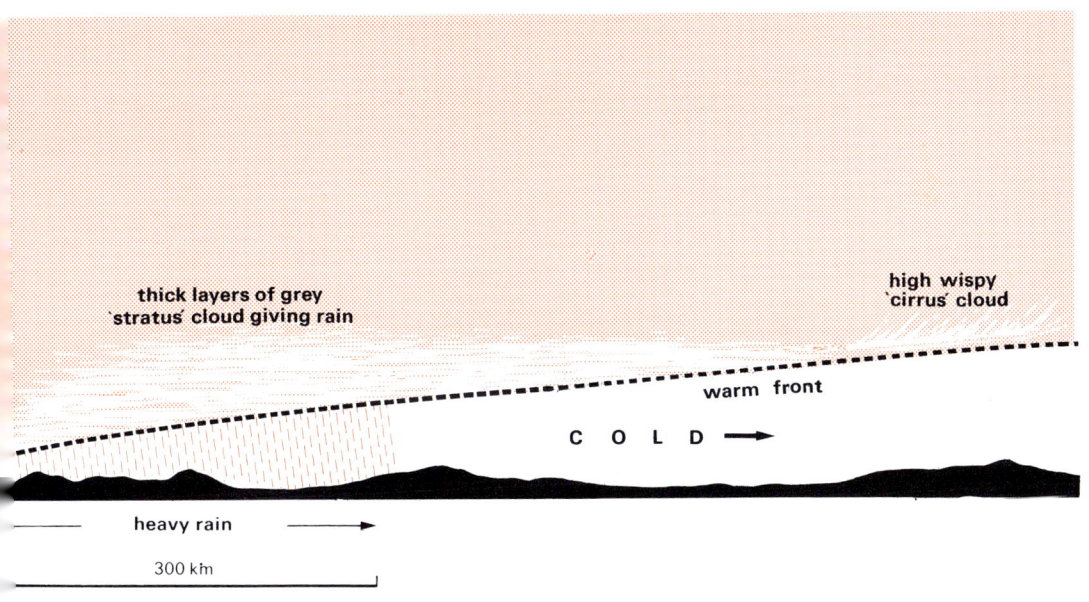

thick layers of grey
'stratus' cloud giving rain

high wispy
'cirrus' cloud

warm front

C O L D →

heavy rain →

300 km

3. WEATHER AND CLIMATE

Depressions cross the country from west to east, and take two or three days to pass right over. About thirty depressions cross Britain in the course of a year. The weather map below shows a depression over Britain.

1. (a) Copy Fig. 42 and beside each arrow write notes about the weather conditions the air stream brings to Britain in both winter and summer. (b) Write in bold letters on the map near the source of the arrows Cold Polar Air, Warm Tropical Air, Continental Air.

2. Look at the weather map (Fig. 47). (a) Describe the weather conditions which are being experienced at the four places A (East Anglia), B (London), C and D (Atlantic weather ships). (b) Explain the differences in weather between A and B. (c) Use Fig. 46 and state what type of cloud you would expect to find at D, E and F. (d) Draw a rough sketch of the British Isles like the one in Fig. 42. Add to your sketch the fronts shown on the weather map. Draw arrows to represent wind direction. Shade the cooler air in blue and the warm air sector in red. Add symbols to show where rain is falling. (e) Compare your map with the section shown in Fig. 46. Where are the conditions the same and where are they different?

Depressions are centres of low atmospheric pressure and rising air. Anticyclones,

Fig. 47 A depression over Britain.

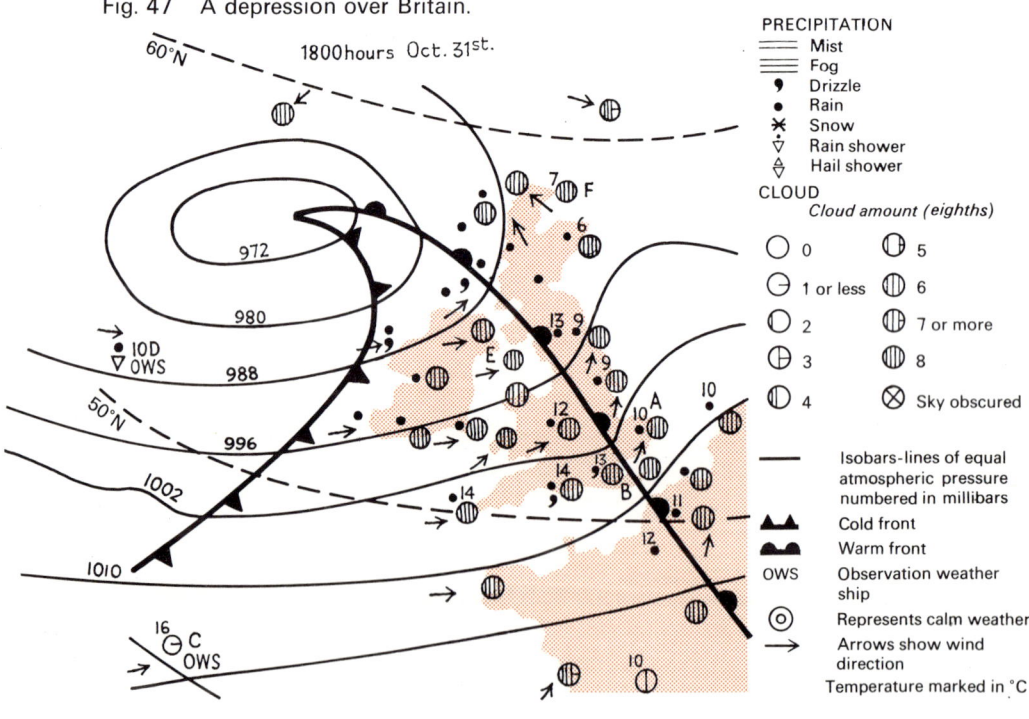

however, are centres of high atmospheric pressure and descending air. The weather map (Fig. 48) shows an anticyclone over Britain. In an anticyclone the air moves slowly in a clockwise direction. Anticyclones are usually composed of mild air from the south-west and bring calm, settled weather. As they are much bigger than depressions, often over 1500 km across, and move slowly, the settled weather may last for a week or ten days.

In summer, anticyclones bring clear skies and hot sunny days. In winter, they often give inland fog, and dull overcast weather known as anticyclonic gloom. Anticyclones affect the south of Britain more frequently than the north.

A great variety of atmospheric conditions therefore affect Britain, and account for the day to day changeableness of the weather. There are also variations from year to year. Averages of temperature and rainfall for a place are worked out over a period of thirty years, as the record for one year only would not necessarily give a true picture of its climate. Each day the average of the maximum and minimum temperatures of a weather station is worked out. The daily averages are totalled and divided by the number of days in each month to find a monthly average. These monthly averages are again averaged over a period of thirty years. The word 'climate' is used to describe average conditions. The graphs of temperature and rainfall

Fig. 48   An anticyclone centred over Britain.

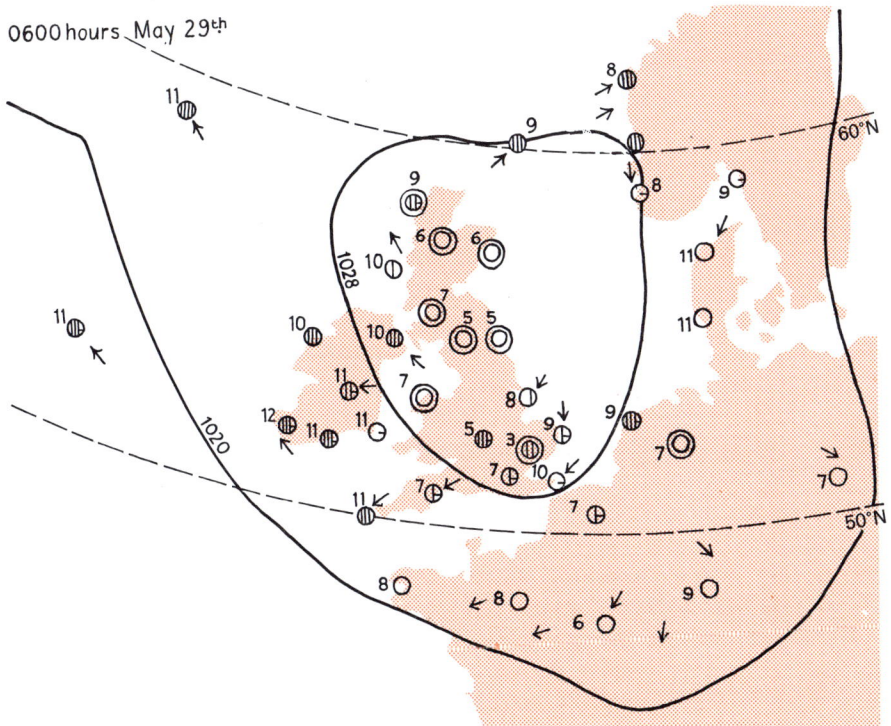

43

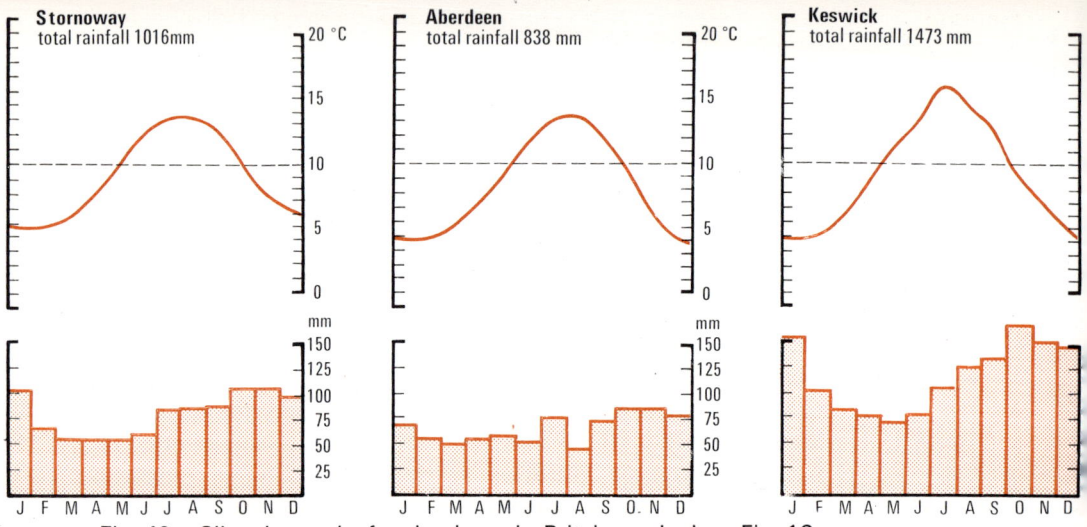

Fig. 49 Climatic graphs for six places in Britain marked on Fig. 13.

given above for six places in Britain show average, or 'mean', conditions for the twelve months of the year. It is clear from the graphs that there are marked differences in climate between the different parts of the country.

The questions below refer to the graphs.

3. Find the six places for which graphs are given. They are located on Fig. 50. Look in your atlas, and find the six places on a relief map of Britain. Write a few sentences about each place to describe its position, e.g. latitude, position in relation to sea and mountains.

4. Study the graphs and notice the differences in total rainfall, seasonal distribution of rainfall, annual range of temperature (difference between the summer maximum and winter minimum).

5. Draw a rough sketch map to represent the British Isles (as in Fig. 42). Mark the six places for which graphs are given. Beside each place (a) write 'under 1000 mm annual rainfall' or 'over 1000 mm annual rainfall'; (b) write the maximum and minimum temperatures and the annual range of temperature.

6. Complete the following sentences: (a) The rainfall is ...... in the west of Britain than in the east. (b) In the west, the wettest season is .... (c) The range of temperature is ...... in the west than in the east. (d) The temperatures are ...... in the north than in the south. (e) The warmest winters are experienced in the .... (f) The warmest summers are experienced in the ....

The graphs show that the western places—Stornoway and Penzance—have only a small difference in temperature between the warmest and the coldest months: that is, they have a low annual range of temperature. The air streams which affect the western places most often come from the west, from over the Atlantic Ocean.

In winter, air over the sea is warmer than air over the land. Even in the east, seaside towns are warmer than places inland in winter. The sea off Britain's west coast is kept especially warm by a drift of warm water called the North

44

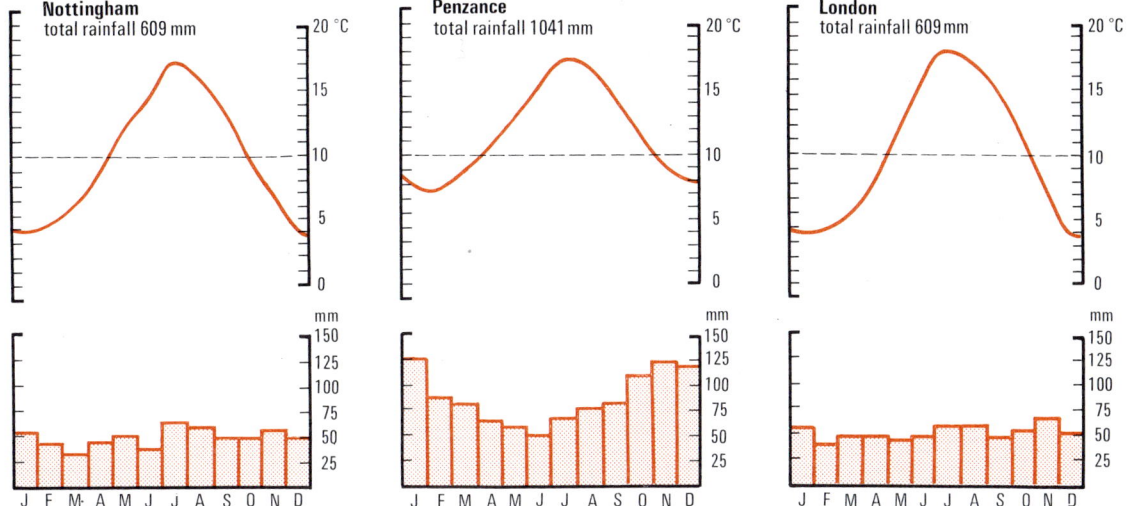

Atlantic Drift (Fig. 42). Propelled by westerly winds, this carries the warm water from the south-west across the Atlantic and past the west shores of Britain. Air coming off the Atlantic in winter is therefore mild, because it has been warmed by its contact with the warm sea. In summer, air coming off the ocean is cooler than air over the land. Therefore westerly air streams tend to raise the temperatures in winter and lower them in summer.

Because Britain receives more air streams from the west than from the east, the winters are rather warmer and the summers rather cooler than is usual for the latitude. There is a low annual range of temperature and the climate is said to be moderate. The moderating effect of the westerly air streams is greatest in the west of the country. The annual range of temperature is only 8 °C in Stornoway and 9 °C in Penzance. However, places on the east side of the country have a greater range of temperature. In London it is 14 °C, in Nottingham 13 °C, and in Aberdeen 10 °C. To reach these places air from the west has to cross the land. In winter the air gets colder as it moves eastwards over land. In summer the air gets warmer as it moves eastwards.

The easterly places are also more often affected by easterly air streams which have come from the Eurasian continent and which bring spells of cold weather in winter. Aberdeen, Nottingham, and London therefore have colder winters. The south-east of England is also affected more often by the south-easterly air streams which bring spells of hot weather in summer. This is one of the reasons why London records the highest summer temperatures.

Throughout the year Stornoway is colder than Penzance. This is partly because Stornoway receives cool north-westerly air streams more frequently, and also, of course, because it is further north. The sun's rays reach the ground more obliquely in the north than in the south and give less intense warmth. Even mild south-westerly air is cooled on its journey north to Stornoway.

It is clear from the graphs that places in the west of the country have more rainfall than places in the east. On the west side of the country, air from the west is coming straight off the sea, and contains a great deal of water vapour. The highest land in Britain is also on the west side of the country. The damp air is forced to rise over the high land; it becomes cool as it rises, and the water vapour it contains condenses to form first cloud, then rainfall. Rain which falls as damp air rises over mountains is called 'relief rainfall'. The wettest parts of Britain are the mountain regions. Keswick, in the English Lake District, has an annual rainfall of 1473 mm because it lies in a mountain region on the west side of the country.

The east of the country is drier because there is less moisture left to fall as rain. Moreover many eastern places are in the lee of mountains which act as rain-catchers.

In Stornoway, Keswick, and Penzance the heaviest rainfall is in winter. Depressions, bringing belts of frontal rain, are more active in winter. In the east, the rainfall is more evenly distributed. At Nottingham and London there is a slight increase in rainfall in July and August. Both these places become hot during summer days. The warm air rises forming convection currents. As it rises it is cooled. Some of the water vapour it contains condenses into water droplets, forming cumulus clouds which may eventually give rain showers, sometimes with thunder.

The average temperature and rainfall conditions for the British Isles are shown in the maps on pp. 46 and 48. The average yearly rainfall over the country is shown by an isohyet map. Isohyets are lines of equal rainfall. Isotherms are used to show

Fig. 50   Rainfall.

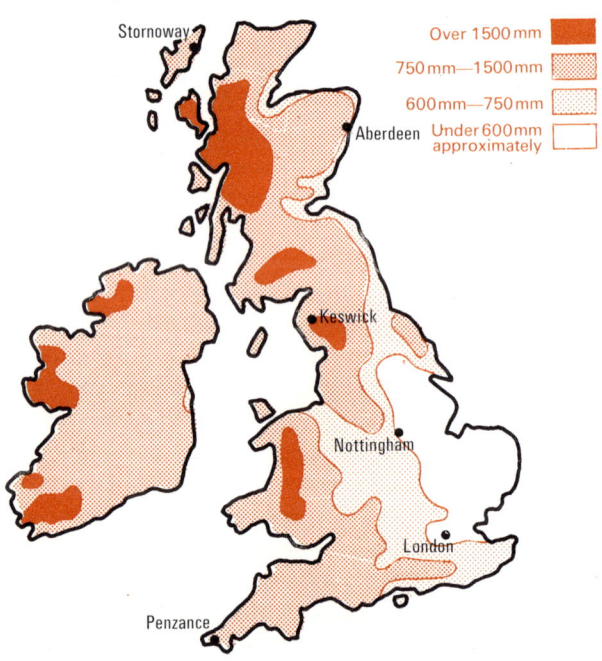

Fig. 51 Snow on Box Hill. When water vapour condenses below freezing point it forms tiny ice crystals. These join together and fall to the ground as snow. On average, snow falls on about 14 days a year in Cambridge, 6 days a year in Exeter, and 23 days a year in Harrogate. How do you account for these differences?

Fig. 52 Frost. When air close to the ground becomes cold, water vapour condenses to form droplets of water. These droplets are dew. In freezing weather, ice crystals are formed. This gives frost. Dew and frost are usually seen after a cloudless night, when heat has escaped quickly from the earth. Clouds act as a blanket to keep warmth near the ground at night, and cloudy nights are usually warmer than clear ones.

47

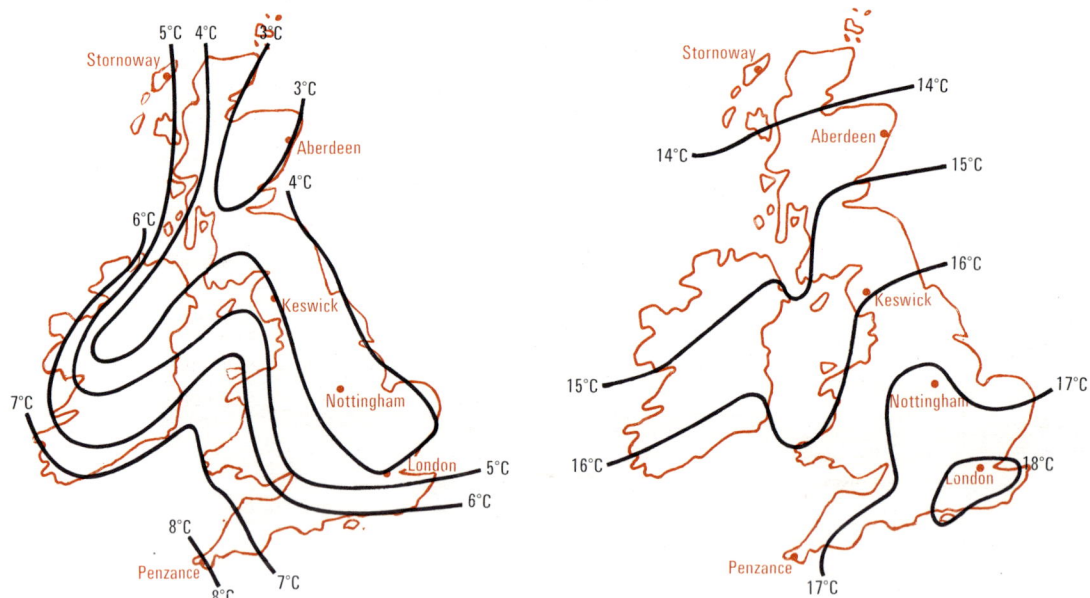

Fig. 53   Isotherms for January.   Fig. 54   Isotherms for July.

average temperature conditions over the whole country. For example, in July the warmest part of the country is the south, centred on London. This area is encircled by the isotherm 18 °C.

Before an isotherm map is drawn, all temperatures are 'reduced to sea level'. Temperature decreases with height so that if the actual average temperatures were plotted the isotherms would correspond with contours and the effect of anything but height on temperature would not be seen.

7. How is the weather brought by anticyclones different from that brought by depressions?

8. What are (a) frontal rainfall (b) relief rainfall (c) convectional rainfall?

9. Describe the climates of the following regions of Britain: The south-west, the north-west, the south-east, the north-east. Explain the main characteristics you mention.

10. How is the climate of a place in Britain affected by its position being (a) by the sea (b) a long way inland (c) in the mountains (d) in the lowlands in the lee of the mountains (e) in the north (f) in the south?

11. How do you explain the following: (a) The Scilly Isles are the warmest part of Britain (average annual temperature 11·5 °C); (b) Braemar, Aberdeenshire, is the coldest weather station (6·5 °C); Stretham (Isle of Ely, Cambridgeshire) is the driest (annual average rainfall 506 mm); Styhead Tarn at 488 m in Cumberland is the wettest (4394 mm)?

12. The climatic statistics given below are for Blackpool, Luton, and Inverness. (a) Draw graphs for each station. (b) Say which station each is, and give reasons for your answer.

	J	F	M	A	M	J	J	A	S	O	N	D	Total Rainfall
Temp °C	3	4	6	8	11	14	17	16	14	10	6	4	
Rainfall mm	61	43	41	48	48	41	61	58	51	61	69	56	638
Temp °C	3	4	5	7	9	12	14	14	12	8	6	4	
Rainfall mm	69	48	38	46	53	51	74	79	66	74	64	58	720
Temp °C	4	4	6	8	11	14	16	16	13	11	7	5	
Rainfall mm	86	58	51	48	64	56	76	94	89	99	89	84	894

13. The following climatic records are not a true guide to climate in Britain. Why not, and what do they show about British weather? The highest temperature recorded is 38·1 °C at Tonbridge, Kent, in July 1868. The highest monthly record of rainfall was 1435 mm at Llyn Llydassy, Caernarvonshire, in October 1909. The driest year was at Margate, in 1921, when 235 mm of rainfall was recorded.

4. Farming

This chapter describes farming, shown opposite, in the scarplands south of the Humber, and in the London and Hampshire basins. The structure of these regions is explained in chapter 2. Farming in other parts of Britain is described in other chapters, but much of what is said here, especially about mixed farming and modern changes in farming, applies to other regions as well.

Most of the farms in the lowlands of the south and east of England are mixed farms. On each farm some of the land is used for crops, and some is used as pasture for animals. Few farms specialize entirely in either crops or livestock.

Farming which involves ploughing the soil and growing crops is called arable farming. The chief crops grown, apart from market gardening crops, are illustrated in Fig. 55. If the crops are to grow well, the soil must be cared for, and there are two main ways in which the farmer can make sure the soil stays fertile:

1. By planting crops in rotation, so that different crops are grown in a field in successive years. Usually wheat, barley and a root crop form part of the rotation. It is common also to grow grass for two or more years before ploughing the land again. This grass, which is different from permanent pasture, is called a 'temporary ley', and is used to feed livestock. Some plants benefit the soil. This is true of leguminous crops like clover, or peas, which restore nitrogen to the soil.

2. A second way of restoring goodness to the soil is by adding artificial fertilizers or animal manure. When animals are fed in the fields, either on root crops or on temporary leys, natural manure benefits the soil. Thus when farmers use the land for both arable farming and livestock, practising mixed farming, they help to preserve the fertility of the soil.

Fig. 55 Some crops grown in Britain.

a. wheat   b. barley   c. oats

4. FARMING

Ploughing is done in the autumn. The plough is used to turn over the soil, to allow frost to reach it, and to prepare it for sowing. Some wheat is sown in the autumn and forms small green shoots during the winter. Some is sown in the spring. The two kinds are therefore called winter wheat and spring wheat. Grain harvest is usually in August, and hay is usually cut twice during the summer. Root crops are harvested or fed to animals throughout the autumn months.

The following section describes a fairly large farm in the scarplands of central England. It is typical of farming over a large part of the English lowlands in the variety of produce, the way the work is organized, and the equipment used.

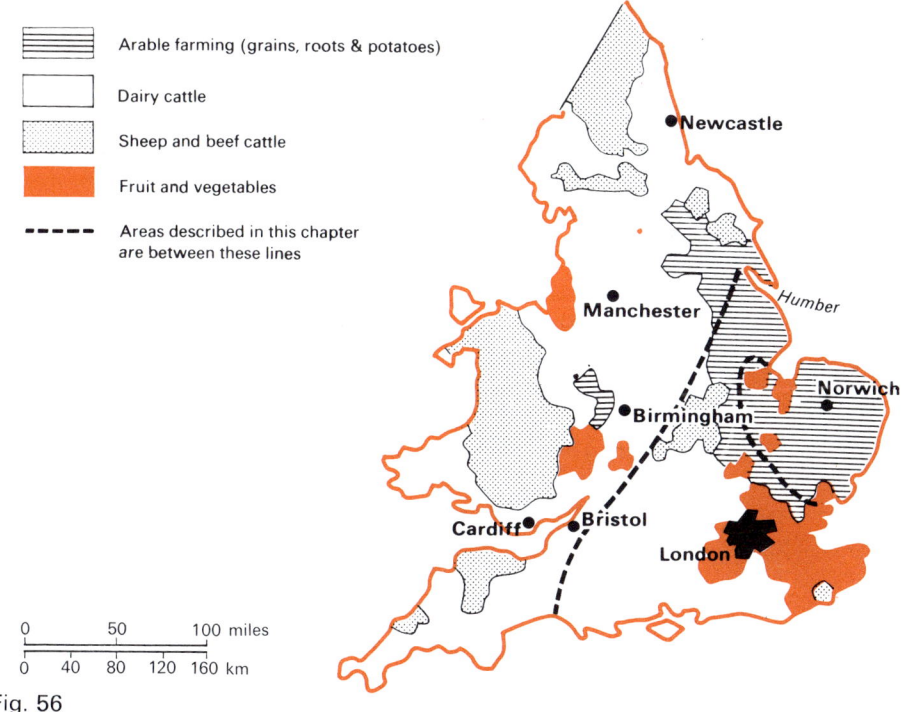

Arable farming (grains, roots & potatoes)

Dairy cattle

Sheep and beef cattle

Fruit and vegetables

Areas described in this chapter are between these lines

Newcastle

Manchester

Humber

Birmingham

Norwich

Cardiff

Bristol

London

0   50   100 miles

0   40   80   120   160 km

Fig. 56

d. rye grass and clover

e. hops

f. sugarbeet

4. FARMING

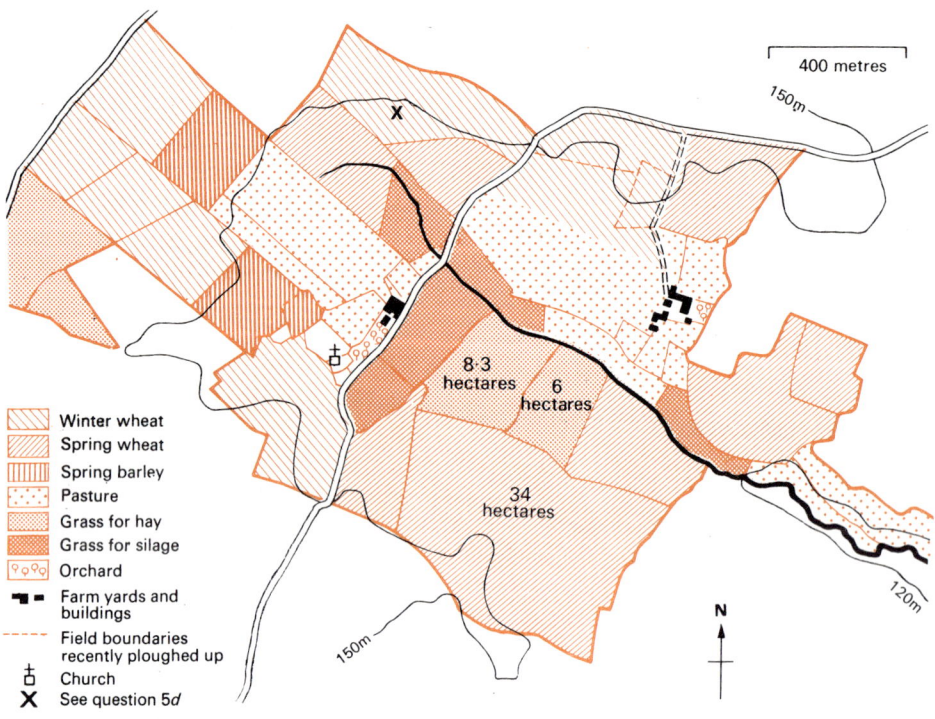

Winter wheat
Spring wheat
Spring barley
Pasture
Grass for hay
Grass for silage
Orchard
Farm yards and buildings
Field boundaries recently ploughed up
Church
See question 5*d*

400 metres

150m

150m

120m

8·3 hectares

6 hectares

34 hectares

X

N

Fig. 57a   Manor House Farm, a mixed farm in Northamptonshire.

Fig. 57b. Manor House Farm. Compare the photograph with the map (Fig. 57a). Find the farm buildings, the orchard, the course of the stream. In which direction was the camera pointing? Find the southern boundary of the farm on the photograph.

A mixed farm in Northamptonshire

Manor House Farm and Oakley Bank Farms, about 16 km south-west of North-ampton, are worked together as one. The size of the two farms is 252 hectares. They lie in undulating country, between 120 and 150 m. The underlying rock is ironstone[1] which gives a rusty tinge to the local buildings, but it is covered with a thick layer of boulder clay.[2]

There are three main enterprises on this mixed farm. Wheat is the main crop. 146 hectares of wheat are grown; 61 are winter sown wheat, which gives a good yield in the summer, but is sometimes damaged by a very cold or wet winter. The rest is spring sown wheat, which gives a lower yield but is less likely to be damaged. The rolling land is well drained. Most of the wheat is grown on the higher parts of the farm.

Second in importance is dairying. About seventy milking Friesian cows are kept, and one Friesian bull. There is a modern milking parlour with a row of stalls. Each cow stands on a raised concrete block, so that the cowman can walk round her easily. The cows are milked, six at a time, by machine. The milk flows into glass containers beside each cow so that the amount can be measured. It then flows along pipes to a large steel tank. A milk tanker comes each day from Northampton to take the milk to a central dairy.

The cattle need a variety of food, and throughout the summer they can pasture out of doors. Much of the land is used as pasture. In winter they also eat hay and silage. Silage is made chiefly from grass which is cut young and stored in a barn, then left to ferment. (This is not the only way of making silage; it may even be made under a tarpaulin in a field.) The first cut of grass is put down in June. Another cut is added in August, and it is ready for the cattle in October. It ferments slowly and has a strong smell like compost. It looks black and flaky like a mass of tobacco. The diet of cattle is varied with barley, and 16 hectares of spring sown barley are planted. The cattle may also be given potatoes if they happen to be cheap. Silage gives a good quantity of milk, but for quality other ingredients must be added to the diet.

Beef cattle are also raised. The Friesian bull calves are kept to sell as beef, and there is also a small herd of about thirty Herefords which are beef cattle. They take from eighteen months to two years to fatten. When they are ready, they are taken to the market at Banbury. Raising beef cattle as well as dairy cattle enables the farmer to make the best use of his land. Near the farm are a number of small fields which cannot be used for crops. However, they provide good pasture for calves, especially in the spring. As the calves grow, they can be moved into larger fields, after the hay has been cut. Beef cattle can also be pastured in the long narrow fields beside the streams.

[1]One of the Jurassic rocks, see page 31.
[2]A type of glacial drift, see page 85.

4. FARMING

Another way in which the farmer uses his land to the full is by buying lambs in August. These lambs, born in March, can be fed on stubble fields after the wheat or barley has been harvested. They provide good extra income for the farmer, they make use of the land, and manure the fields. About 500 lambs are bought, and most are sold for meat before Christmas.

Machinery used on the farm includes a combine harvester, five tractors, plough, seed drill, harrow, and a forage harvester for cutting silage; in the barns are a grain drier, and a mill to make cattle food from barley. Five men are employed, including two cowmen.

This farm illustrates many of the changes which have taken place in farming over the last thirty years. First, a large amount of machinery is now used. Few labourers are employed, and these are skilled cowmen or mechanics. One way of solving the problem of how to pay for the expensive machinery and labour which a modern farm needs is by making the farms larger. On a large farm, the equipment is used more of the time and is not lying idle. Because labour and machinery are put to their full use, large farms are more profitable. This is one reason why, as in the case just described, neighbouring farms may join together. Large farms need a lot of organization and are run more like businesses: much farm work is now done in an office, arranging for produce to be sold, ordering feed and equipment, or applying for grants for improvements or farm subsidies.

Another way of making farming more profitable is by intensifying the agriculture, making each hectare produce more. The description of the Northamptonshire farm showed the care which is taken to get the maximum use from the land. Today much more food is produced from the land, both in crops and livestock, than thirty years ago. This is possible partly because more land is now used for crops rather than pasture. Fig. 58 shows changes in land use. During World War II much land was ploughed for the first time, especially on poorer soils like the chalk downs. The government encouraged the change by paying grants of money, or subsidies, to farmers to plough up their permanent pasture. The country needed to grow as

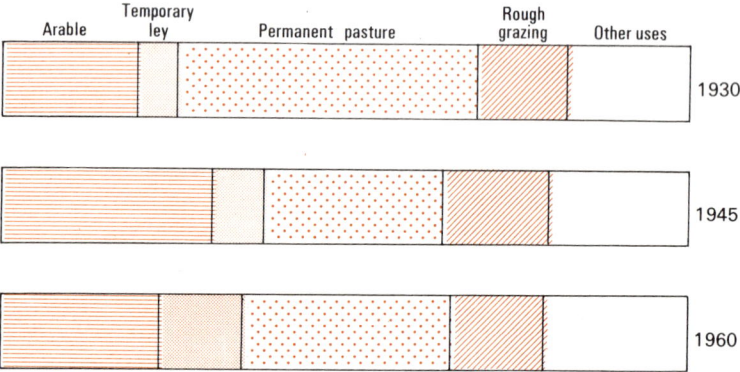

Fig. 58   Land use in England and Wales.

54

much of its own food as possible. Much of the land which was first ploughed during the war has remained arable ever since.

There has also been an enormous increase in the use of artificial fertilizer. Artificial fertilizers have made it possible to grow good crops on rather poor soil. They have also made it possible to obtain higher yields per hectare, and to grow the same crop several years running without using a rotation.

Although there is now less permanent pasture, far more cattle are raised than formerly. They are raised on land which was traditionally sheep pasture, like the Hampshire Downs or the Cotswolds. Water can now be pumped up to the top of these dry hills easily and more temporary ley is now grown. New types of grass, such as Italian rye grass, have been introduced, and these grow well with artificial fertilizers, giving a high yield per hectare. Temporary ley is cut for silage which is fed to cattle. Because the yield per hectare is high, more cattle can be kept.

The changes which have taken place in farming methods have occurred throughout the country; but whereas in south and east England the land ploughed during the war has remained arable, in the north and west country more land has reverted to its former type of farming.

1. Many changes have been brought about because of government subsidies paid to farmers. What arguments can be used (a) in favour of and (b) against the payment of farm subsidies?

2. How have (a) the use of artificial fertilizers (b) the use of machinery helped to change farming in Britain?

3. Write definitions of: arable farming, temporary ley, silage, spring and winter wheat.

4. Use your atlas and Fig. 29 to locate the farm described on page 53. Draw a map to show its position. Include the Northampton Heights, Oxford Clay Vale and Chiltern Hills; the rivers Nen, Cherwell and Thames; the towns Northampton, Banbury and Oxford.

5. Use the description of a mixed farm p. 53 and Fig. 57. (a) The farm buildings are centrally placed. Why is this an advantage? (b) What advantages are there in running the two farms as one unit? (c) Why have some field boundaries been ploughed up? (d) Describe a year's work in field X. (e) An average rotation used on the farm is: two years winter wheat, one year spring wheat, one year barley undersown with grass, two years grass for silage. Draw a map of the farm to show a possible use of the fields in the following year.

Distribution of crops

Most farms in the scarplands—and indeed most farms in England—are mixed farms. The type of farming described in the account of the Northamptonshire farm is typical of much of the Oxford Clay vale. The position of the farm is shown in the map of the scarplands on p. 26. It is roughly in the centre of England. The enterprises are fairly evenly balanced between arable and livestock.

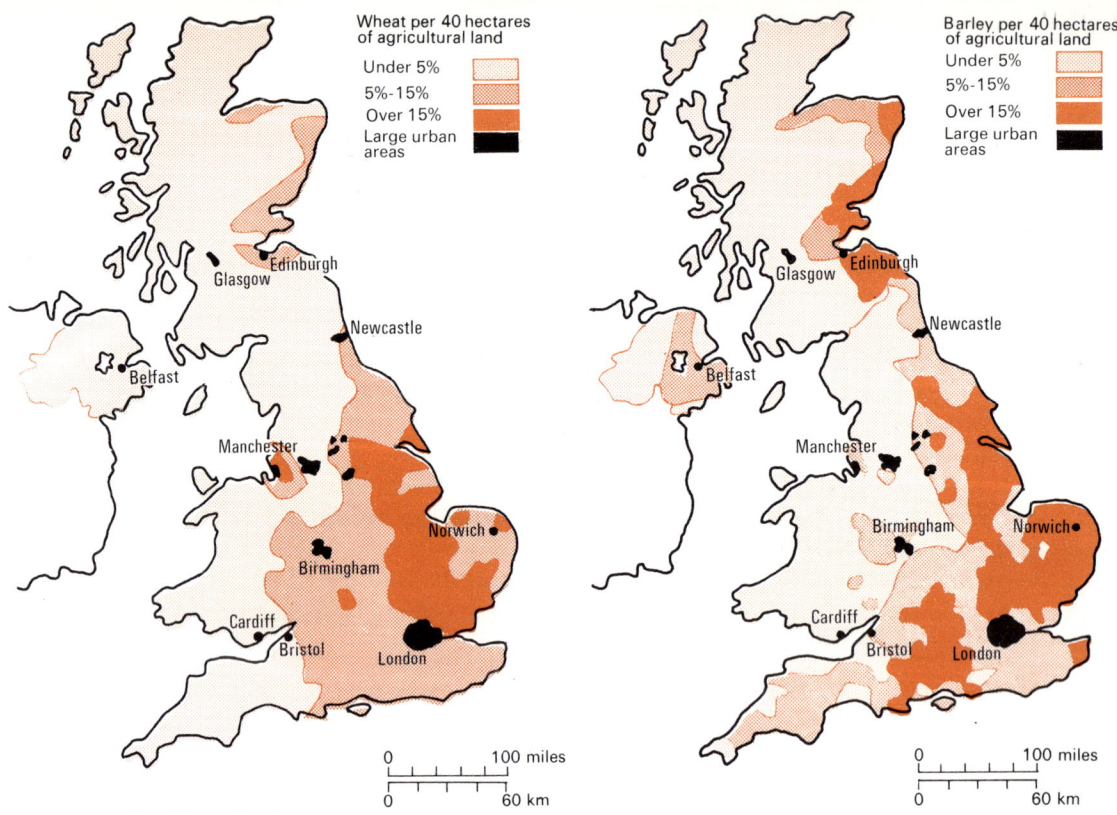

Fig. 59   Distribution of wheat.   Fig. 60   Distribution of barley.

If you go east or west from here, however, the emphasis changes.

The main reason for this change is the change in climate. The east has several advantages over the west for growing wheat and barley. These crops grow better in a dry climate, and the rainfall in the east is below 750 mm (see p. 46). Frost breaks up the soil during the colder winters, helping to prepare it for sowing. There is more sunshine in summer for ripening and harvesting the crops.

A second important influence on where crops are grown is soil, but a much larger and more detailed map would be needed to show these variations. Soil is a layer covering the underlying rock. It is made up partly of minerals derived from the rock, and partly of organic matter derived from plants, animals, and microscopic organisms. The fertility of soils depends largely on what minerals they derive from the underlying rock and on what organic matter they contain. Soils also vary in depth and in how much water they are able to hold. On chalk they are shallow, because there is little vegetation to provide organic matter. They are also dry, and rich in lime. On clay, they are wet and sticky. The best soils are mixtures. Loam is a mixture of sand and clay, and marl of lime and clay. Dry soils favour grains: wet soils favour pasture.

A third influence on farming is distance from markets. Farms which are near large towns often specialize in crops for local markets. The influence of the large

56

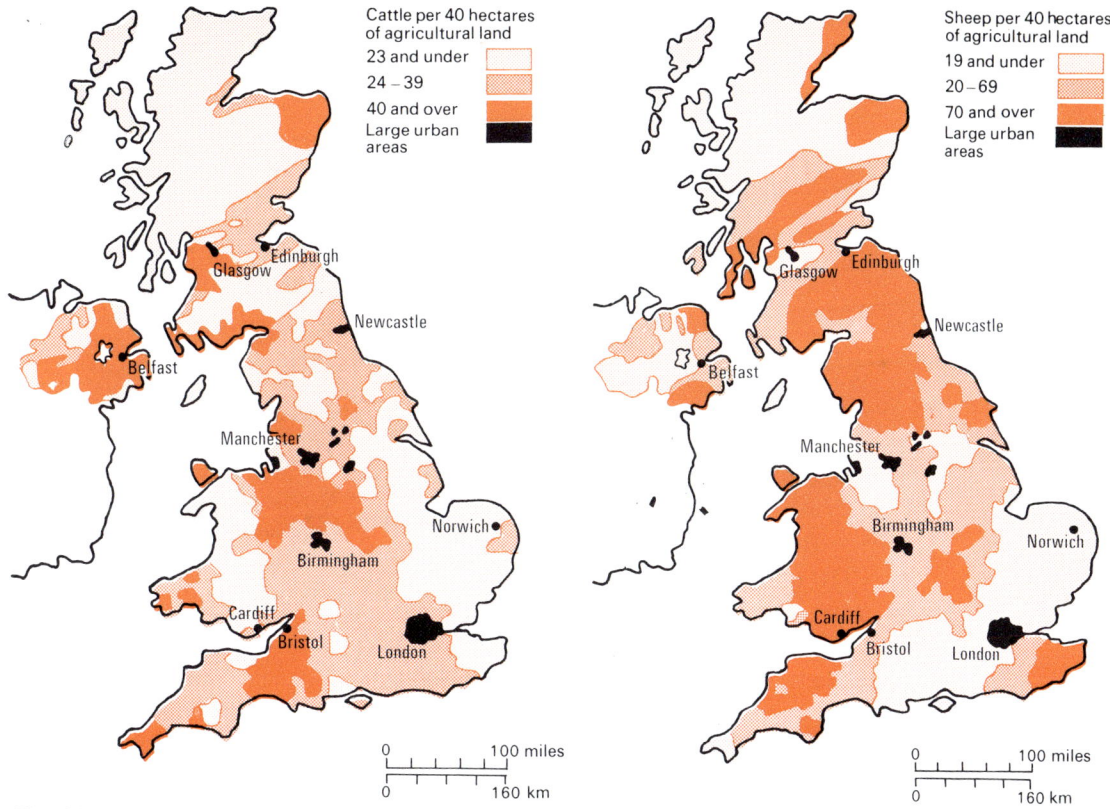

Fig. 61   Distribution of cattle.   Fig. 62   Distribution of sheep.

market of London, and the growing towns around London, is particulary clear in
south-east England and the London Basin.

The type of farming generally practised in the Vale of Oxford has been described
already. By looking at some of the other agricultural regions of Lowland Britain,
we can see how climate, soils, and nearness to markets have influenced the crops
which are grown.

Lincolnshire. Fig. 38 shows that the layers of rock which make up the scarplands
in Lincolnshire are close together, and they divide the country into several strips
running from north to south, each with a different soil.

The limestone lands in the west, which were once poor heathlands, have been
improved by the use of fertilizer into good farmlands, used chiefly for wheat and
barley. On the chalk hills, too, grains are the chief product, and the farms and
fields are large, but the famous local breed of cattle, the Lincoln Red, are also
raised. The clay lands are used for mixed farming, especially dairying, but a lot of
wheat is also grown. Much of the coast plain was formerly marsh, and is fen country
which has been reclaimed to form very rich farm land, intensively farmed in small
holdings (40 hectares or less) which produce wheat, sugar beet and potatoes. Agriculture is highly mechanized and fertilizers are much used. Some industry, notably
the many sugar beet factories and the brewing industry, depends directly on agriculture.

57

4. FARMING

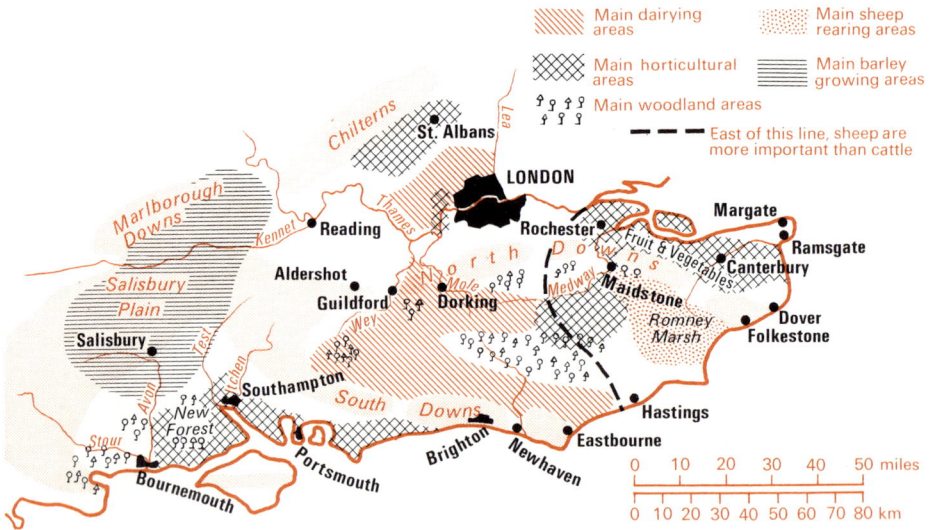

Fig. 63   Soils and farming in south-east England and the Hampshire Basin.

The *Hampshire Basin* is one of the parts of England where there has been most change in agricultural land use. It is surrounded by a rim of chalklands which are used for barley, cattle and sheep. These chalk downs used to be sheep country; cattle were raised only in the water meadows near the streams which cut deeply into the land. Today, however, much of the land on the hills is ploughed to grow temporary grass which is fed to cattle; and much of the soil is artificially fertilized so that it can grow barley.

South of the chalk is a region of marls where there is mixed farming. The sandy soils of the New Forest are too loose and dry to be used for farming. Near the large towns along the south coast there is a great deal of market gardening. Strawberries and watercress are two of Hampshire's specialities.

Kent, Surrey and Sussex. The warm sunny summers with temperatures over 17 °C help to account for the high yields of wheat in Kent and Sussex. Fruit ripens well here, and Kent is famous for its orchards and hop fields. Farming varies also with rock and soil: hops are grown on the mixed soils of the Medway valley, grains and sheep are found on the chalk hills, cattle on the clay vales. On the sands there is still a large amount of woodland.

However, because there is such a large demand for milk in London, much of the western weald, whether chalk, clay or sand, supports dairy cattle. The quality of the soil matters less than nearness to markets, especially as soils can be so easily improved. Nearness to the market also accounts for the intensive market gardening, which is found in north Kent and on the coast between Brighton and Littlehampton.

An area which has kept a strong individual character is Romney Marsh. This is a

58

Fig. 64   Picking hops by machine   Fig. 65   Farming country in Yalding, Kent, near Maidstone.

flat land similar to the fens which has been drained since Roman times. It provides excellent sheep pasture, and up to 35 sheep per hectare are fattened here. The sheep spend the winter on hill farms and are moved to the lowland pastures in summer for fattening. Even in Romney Marsh, however, changes are taking place. Some of the land is now used to grow bulbs and potatoes, and many farmers have moved into the area from Lincolnshire to effect this change.

Most of the farming in the *London Basin* is geared to the large markets provided by London itself and the many outlying towns. In parts of Surrey, land is used for 'hobby farming'. A few businessmen who work in London run farms, usually specializing in high quality dairy cattle.

The lower slopes of the North Downs and Chilterns are used for market gardening, that is, the growing of vegetables, flowers and glasshouse products. Market gardening is an example of extremely intensive farming. A market gardener usually has only a small amount of land, and he must produce far more per hectare than the average farmer of a mixed farm in order to make a living. Even so, the same change is taking place in market gardening as in mixed farming—more is being produced from the land than formerly, by growing new crops and by irrigating, and by applying fertilizers. The following description tells something of the work of a market gardener.

A market garden near St. Albans

This is a small, roughly square holding of 5·9 hectares. The highest land is 90 m, the lowest 80 m. About one-third of the holding on the higher land is level. The rest slopes gently down to a road which forms one boundary of the holding, on the eastern side.

The higher part is poor, stony soil containing many flints, and is not good enough for vegetables, so it is used for grain—usually barley. This is sold to a local miller. About 2·5 hectares is planted in grain. Below this, just over 1 hectare is used for green vegetables, such as spring cabbage, autumn cabbage and Brussels sprouts. Some potatoes are also grown.

Below this, the land is divided into small, narrow strips planted in rows aligned up and down hill. All these rows are near enough to piped water so that they can be irrigated. The soil here is deeper and less stony than that on the higher ground. Crops grown include cut flowers, e.g. dahlias, chrysanthemums; plants for bedding, e.g. lupins, forget-me-nots; seedlings of cabbages; beetroot, carrots. Also in the lower land, in the north-east corner of the holding where it opens on to the road, there are 3 storage sheds, 12 rows of frames and 4 glasshouses. Chrysanthemums are grown in the glasshouses, and lettuces and marrows are grown under frames.

The market gardener must work up to sixteen hours a day most of the year. Weeding is the biggest job, for selective weed killers cannot be used where so many different crops are grown close together. Hand operated cultivators and rotivators are used, but not much tractor work can be done because the rows are planted close together to make full use of the good land on the lower levels. One tractor is kept, and one full time labourer is employed. The market gardener runs a stall in the St. Albans market on a Saturday. The rest of the produce is sold to florists and greengrocers in St. Albans.

---

6. Copy the section of Lincolnshire on p. 35. Leave a large space above the section. Read the description of Lincolnshire p. 57, and write notes above your section about farming in the different regions. (See p. 126 for an example of how to do it.)

7. Draw a section of south-east England (p. 36). Write notes above, as explained in question 6, to describe farming in the different regions.

8. Draw a map of the market garden described above. (A square of side 14 cm gives a scale of approximately 1 cm representing 20 m.)

9. List the differences between the market garden described on p. 59–60 and the mixed farm described on p. 53.

10. Draw a sketch of Fig. 65 to show the proportion of land used for (a) hops (b) orchards (c) pasture. Use a symbol to show oast houses [where hops are prepared for the maltster].

5. Urban Growth in South-east England

London is outstandingly larger than any other town in Britain, and is one of the greatest cities in the world. The map of London below shows the way it has grown through the centuries. The area shaded in the centre shows the original Roman city—Londinium—although its size is exaggerated on the map.

The Romans built Londinium where the Thames was narrow enough to be crossed, but where the open sea could still be reached easily. Londinium was on the main road (Watling Street) from Dover to Chester. There were low gravel hills which gave firm ground for building close to the river bank. Today St. Paul's Cathedral and Leadenhall Market stand on these same hills. Two small rivers, the Fleet and the Walbrook, flowed into the Thames on the north bank, providing sheltered creeks for ships. Highways of land and sea met at London, and it quickly became the largest city of Roman Britain. From this beginning London has spread outwards in all directions.

Fig. 66   The growth of London.

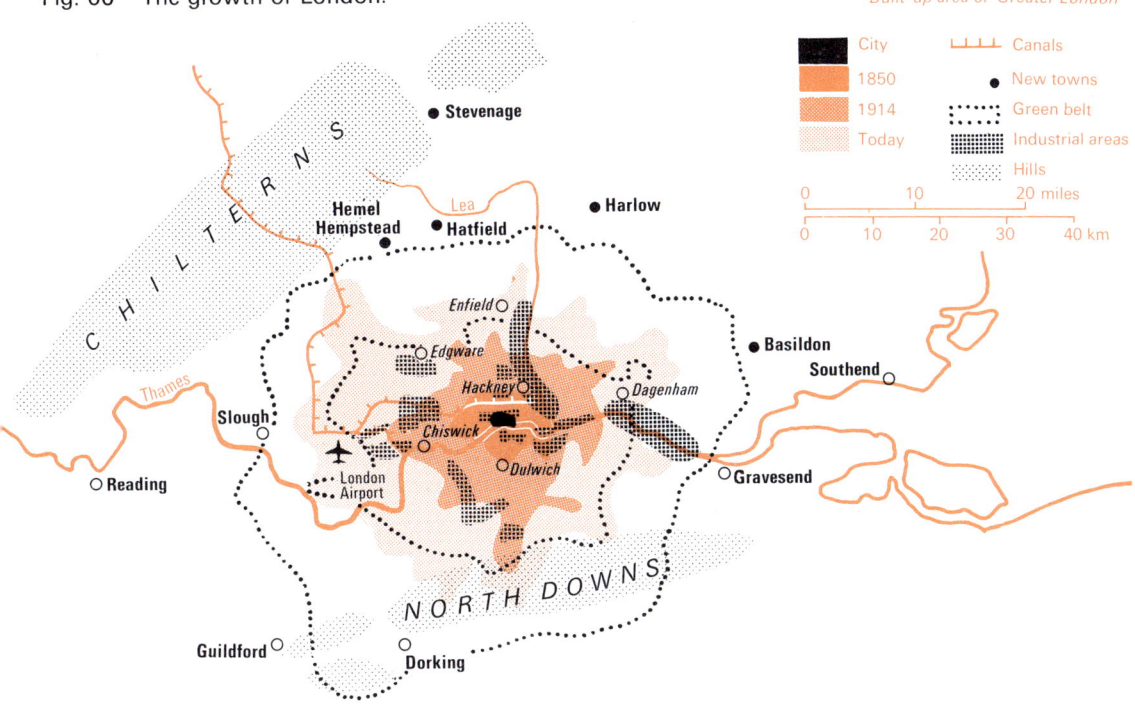

Fig. 67 Housing in London: terraced houses in Camden Town.

Fig. 68 Housing in London: town housing with a rural touch, Hampstead Garden Suburb.

You can recognize some of the different stages of the growth of London by the buildings in the London streets. Tall houses with pillared porticos, elegant squares and crescents, are typical of the eighteenth and early nineteenth centuries. They were constructed by wealthy aristocrats and merchants at a time when it became fashionable for country gentlemen to own a town house, and they give London some of its finest architecture. Victorian terrace rows stretching beyond the central districts show later stages in building, while in the remoter suburbs there are streets of semi-detached houses with gardens. As the houses grew out further from the centre of London, the railways, above ground and underground, kept pace with or sometimes even preceded them.

London's appearance has changed rapidly during the last twenty years. One reason for this is that during World War II large parts of London were damaged or destroyed, so that they had to be rebuilt. Since the war, building techniques using concrete, steel, and glass have made it possible to build high structures more easily. They are still expensive to build and to run, but land in central London is so expensive that it is worth building costly skyscrapers so that as much floor space as possible can be provided. (see Fig. 69).

The skyline of London has changed, as tall hotels and office blocks have been built in the centre, while in many London boroughs large blocks of flats have been built to replace derelict property.

5. URBAN GROWTH IN SOUTH-EAST ENGLAND

Why has London grown so large? There is no one answer to this question, but the following summary shows some of its advantages.

Site

1. Lowest crossing place of Thames.

2. Originally built on low, gravel terrace which formed hills beside river, giving firm well drained building land. The surrounding land was marshy in Roman and mediaeval times.

3. Marshy land made it possible later - from late eighteenth century onwards - to dig out dock basins. There was plenty of empty, easily excavated land downstream of the city centre.

Position

1. Centre of London basin - became a focus of road and rail routes for south-east England and for much of the country - there were no barriers to communication in any direction - even in the low chalk hills routes went through the many gaps.

2. Thames mouth is opposite Rhine mouth and this encouraged trade with the great ports of Europe e.g. Rotterdam, Amsterdam and Antwerp.

Functions

1. Political capital for Britain and the Commonwealth.

2. National and international financial centre.

3. Major port and entrepôt [reshipment of imports].

4. Manufacturing industries employ about 40% of Greater London's working population.

5. Great cultural centre, e.g. universities, museums, theatres, national art galleries.

6. International airways junction.

7. Centre of road and rail systems.

8. Major shopping centre.

9. Tourist centre.

Every town has a use; performs a function. Often the main function of a town was to provide a meeting place for exchanging goods. Then a market town grew up. The list above shows that London is a town of many functions; each one means work for thousands of people.

Although all the functions have helped London to grow, two have helped it in the past more than others: the port and the manufacturing industries.

63

Fig. 69   The City of London, 1966. St. Paul's Cathedral had recently been cleaned, and the dome was being repaired. The buildings around St. Paul's were flattened by bombing during World War II, but the Cathedral itself withstood the attack. Many tall office blocks have been built in the City since the war.

Fig. 70   The south bank of the Thames at low tide. As the barges are flat bottomed they can lie on the mud beside a wharf when the tide goes out. Deptford power station is shown on the left.

5. URBAN GROWTH IN SOUTH-EAST ENGLAND

The Port of London

At the end of the eighteenth century, the port of London was a row of wharves and jetties built along the river. So many ships came to London that they were crowded in the port and could hardly find space to berth. Moreover, they had to wait for high tide before they could reach the wharves. The docks listed below were therefore built. They were dug out from the marshy banks of the Thames downstream. The water in the docks could be kept deep all the time and ships could easily reach them.

Since they were originally built, many improvements and additions have been made to the docks. The newest development is at Tilbury, where there are seven container ship berths.[1] This means that 1 million tonnes of goods can be handled at each berth every year, instead of 100 000 tonnes.

Name of Dock	Date opened	Chief goods handled	Special equipment
London and St. Katherine Docks (closed 1969)	1805 1828	Wine, wool, spirits and a variety of other goods chiefly from Europe, Australia and the far East.	Warehouses and showrooms for special commodities such as tea, oil, dried fruit, iodine. Vaults and cellars for wines and spirits.
West India and Millwall	1802 1868	Grain, sugar and green fruit from the West Indies and North America.	Mechanical handling equipment for sugar and grain and large granaries for storage.
Surrey Commercial	1810	Timber from Scandinavia, Russia and Canada.	Mobile cranes for handling timber and large storage sheds.
Royal Docks: Victoria Albert King George V	1855 1880 1921	Meat, grain, tobacco and bananas from the Americas.	Electronic handling equipment and cold stores for meat. Conveyor belts for handling bananas. Large warehouses.
Tilbury Docks	1886	Passengers and container cargoes.	Berths for 'roll on-roll off' continental ferries. Dry docks for repairs. Seven container berths. Good rail and road connections.

[1]See page 229.

65

Fig. 71   The Royal Docks, looking west. The docks are parallel to the river. The river can be seen in the foreground and in the distance. The King George V Dock is on the left, and the Royal Albert Dock is on the right. The Royal Victoria Dock is beyond the range of the camera. Find the locks and the lock gates, the railways and warehouses, and the various types of craft.

The docks handle most of London's exports, but three-quarters of the imports come to riverside wharves and jetties. The Port of London officially extends along the whole of the tidal river—for 148 kilometres as far as Teddington Lock. There are 600 wharves and jetties along the river, and they are just as important as the docks. Many of the wharves are above London Bridge. No seagoing ships can go beyond London Bridge, except specially designed colliers ('flat irons') with masts and funnels which can be lowered, so nearly all the goods which are

66

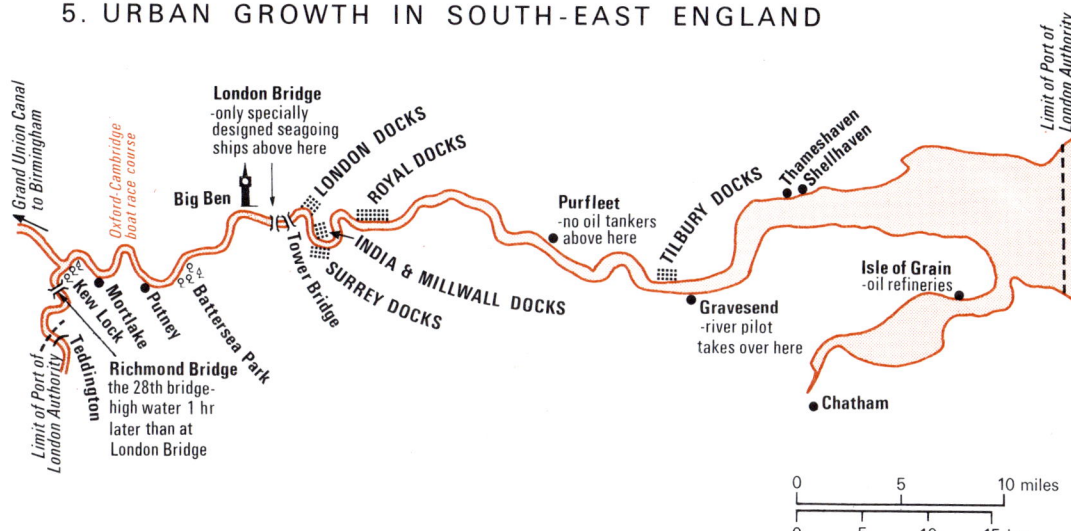

Fig. 72   The extent of the Port of London.

unloaded at the wharves above the bridge have to come by barge or lighter. Goods are unloaded from ships on to barges which are then pulled, often six at a time, by tugs. They can go up the river under all the twenty-eight bridges of the Port of London area. The movement of the tide helps to carry them up or down stream.

The greatest number of wharves are found in the City area of the river, from just above London Bridge, to just below Tower Bridge, the part known as the Pool of London. There are general wharves which import chiefly food, and others which handle specialized cargo. For example Smith's wharf in the city handles 'teas, furs, bristles, mica, shellac, manufactured drugs, exotic goods from the Far East (like lychees, bamboo shoots, lotusnuts, chow chow, and Hoy Sin sauce); and essential oils (rosewood, peppermint, lime, aniseed, and spearmint)'.[1] Some of these goods need special storage in the warehouse, or skill in handling.

Above and below the City, the wharves handle bulky goods, especially coal for the gasworks and power stations, and raw materials for industry or the building trade.

The largest import by weight of the Port of London is oil, and yet no oil tankers go above Purfleet. Below this point, therefore, are the jetties and refineries of Thameshaven, Shellhaven, and the Isle of Grain. Like other ports, London has greatly increased its imports of oil.

The port employs 35 000 people including 25 000 dockworkers. It also supplies a vast number of industries with their raw material, helping London to be a huge manufacturing centre as well.

[1] *Geography of Greater London*, Phillip 1964, p. 59.

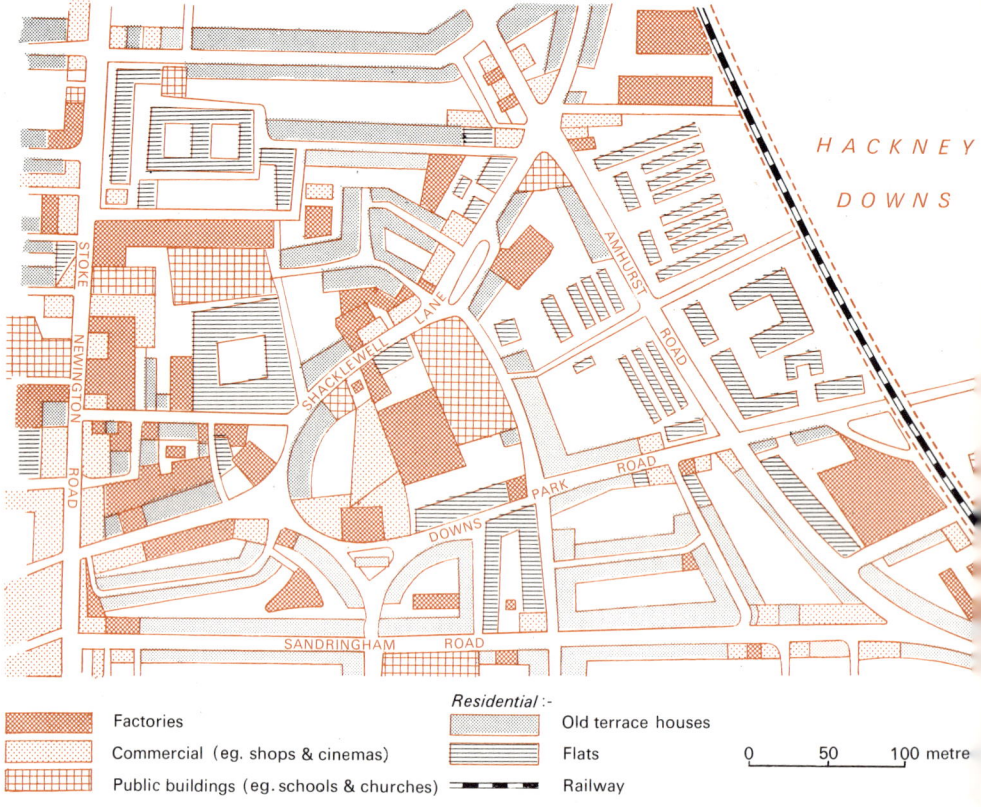

Factories		*Residential* :-	
		Old terrace houses	
Commercial (eg. shops & cinemas)		Flats	
Public buildings (eg. schools & churches)		Railway	

0   50   100 metre

Fig. 73   Part of Hackney, north-east London.

Manufacturing Industry

Many of London's manufacturing industries, especially in the central districts, are old established. In the east and north-east districts they have often grown from the traditional trades of certain areas. For example, the clothing industry is concentrated largely in Whitechapel, where it was practised by Jewish immigrants in the last century, and in Hackney. Furniture is made in Shoreditch, and a variety of engineering industries are found in the area immediately north of the City.

In these parts of London, a casual observer might hardly notice the industries. Some are carried on in converted houses, where only a few people work. Factories and houses are intermingled and much of the work, especially in the clothing industry, is 'outdoor' work—that is, done by people in their own homes. The map above shows an area in Hackney where houses and factories have grown up haphazardly without any kind of plan.

5. URBAN GROWTH IN SOUTH-EAST ENGLAND

The manufacturing area of north-west London shaded on Fig. 66 (page 61) looks quite different. The factories have been built in the twentieth century and are newer and larger. The streets are more open and the houses are mostly semi-detached with gardens.

Many of the factories on the edges of London make 'consumer goods'—that is, goods which are bought directly by ordinary families. Consumer goods include 'durables'—such things as record players or washing machines—and food. Manufacturers of consumer goods often prefer to build their factories where there are large numbers of people—people to work in the factories and people to buy the goods. The nearer the factories are to the market, the better. This is one reason for the snowballing growth of London. The people provide labour and markets, which attract new industry, which in turn attracts more people.

But the expansion of modern industry is not the main reason for London's growth. In fact in the congested centre of London the number of people working in factories has actually gone down, although in the more accessible ring round London it has gone up.

The greatest increase has been in the number of people employed in service industries. People who work in transport, shops, building, gas and electricity are all working in service industries. The large population ensures that there is a big demand for these services. Many people working in London are also employed in the professions, administration and finance. Much of the work of these service industries is done in offices, and the proportion of work done in offices is increasing as Fig. 74 shows. In the centre of London, 15 000 more office jobs have been created every year in the 1960s.

More work is now done in offices than formerly partly because the things we make are more complicated than they used to be. More people must therefore work at research and design. At the same time selling has become more competitive, and so sales and advertising employ more people. Manufacturing, however, is now more mechanized, so fewer people are needed at the manufacturing stage.

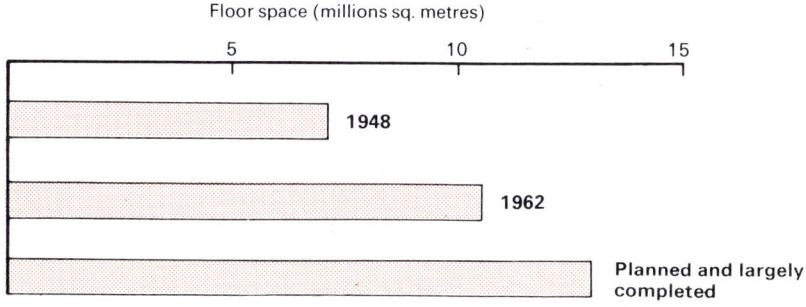

Fig. 74   Growth of offices in Central London.

5. URBAN GROWTH IN SOUTH-EAST ENGLAND

Offices are attracted to London because it is a great commercial and financial centre. Hundreds of firms which operate mainly in other parts of Britain still have an office in London. London is a financial centre not only for Britain but also internationally, and banks and insurance companies have their head offices in London. A walk through the City of London shows a great concentration of financial activities. The Bank of England, Commonwealth and foreign banks, the Stock Exchange, the Mint, are all found within a region known as 'the square mile'.

The growth of offices, therefore, largely accounts for the spread of London. Offices have taken over the central districts and provided a great deal of extra employment. At the same time houses have spread farther and farther out on the edges. Although London's population has declined, many people who live outside London still go there to work. The map on p. 73 shows that the greatest increase in population has been in the ring of land immediately around London.

The size of London has created many problems for town planners. To limit the spread of buildings over the countryside, a 'green belt' was drawn round London. At the same time, new towns were built outside London to house 'overspill' population. There are now restrictions on building offices in central London, to try to stop more people travelling there each day. Transport and traffic problems are enormous.

---

1. Use the description on p. 61 to draw a sketch map of Roman London.
2. Look at the map, Fig. 66. What is the distance from Slough to Gravesend? Hemel Hempstead to Crawley? How many kilometres was London from east to west in 1850? When did London begin to spread over the North Downs?
3. Look at Fig. 73. How much of the area shown is open space? What do you notice about the position of most of the shops? What is the main type of housing in the area? What changes might a town planner make to this area?
4. What arguments can be used for and against the construction of large blocks of flats as normal family housing?
5. What solutions can you suggest to London's traffic problems?
6. Look at Fig. 76, opposite. Make two columns headed Greater London and Metropolitan region. Compare the two areas under the headings (a) percentage employed in manufacturing industry (b) percentage employed in service industries, and give reasons for the differences.

Towns have grown in other parts of the country besides the South-east, and urban growth has presented problems elsewhere. Towns in the South-east have grown especially rapidly partly because more jobs have been provided here than in other parts of the country. Service industries in particular have expanded faster in the South-east than elsewhere, partly because of the influence of London and the focus of routeways on London.

Fig. 75 Hammersmith flyover, London, built to help the long distance traffic enter and leave the centre of London more easily.

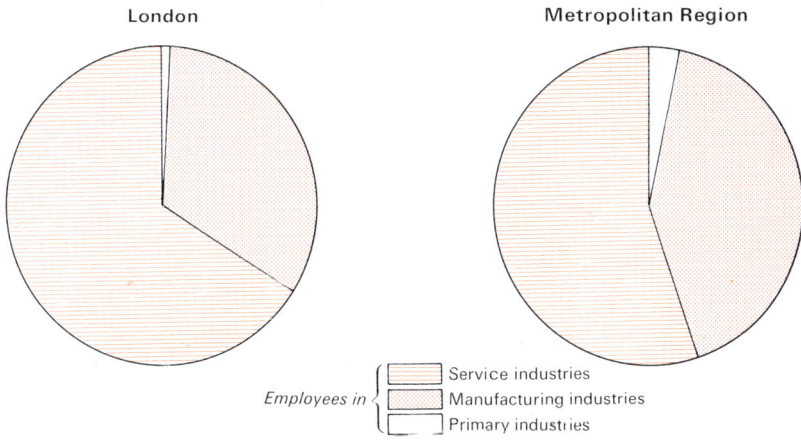

Fig. 76 Employment in London and the Metropolitan Region.

5. URBAN GROWTH IN SOUTH-EAST ENGLAND

Population in some towns of south-east England

	Total population	
	1951	**1966**
Basildon	43 000	111 000
Basingstoke	17 000	35 000
Bournemouth	145 000	151 000
Brighton	158 000	162 000
Crawley	10 000	61 000
Dover	35 000	36 000
Eastbourne	58 000	66 000
Folkestone	45 000	43 000
Havant and Waterlooville	35 000	95 000
London (*Greater London Council area*)	8 201 000	7 896 000
Luton	110 000	153 000
Oxford	99 000	109 000
Portsmouth	234 000	200 000
Reading	114 000	125 000
Reigate	42 000	56 000
Rochester	44 000	54 000
Slough	66 000	85 000
Southampton	190 000	209 000
Southend	152 000	167 000
Stevenage	7000	57 000
Welwyn Garden City	19 000	41 000
Woking	48 000	77 000

7. Study the table and the map opposite. What general comment would you make about population changes in towns in the south-east?

8. Which four towns show the greatest increase in population?

9. Which towns show a decrease in population?

10. List the six largest towns apart from London. Draw a map to show these towns. Beside each town draw a bar to represent its total population in 1966. Let 2·5 cm represent 50 000 people. Shade part of each bar to show the amount of increase (or decrease) since 1951.

5. URBAN GROWTH IN SOUTH-EAST ENGLAND

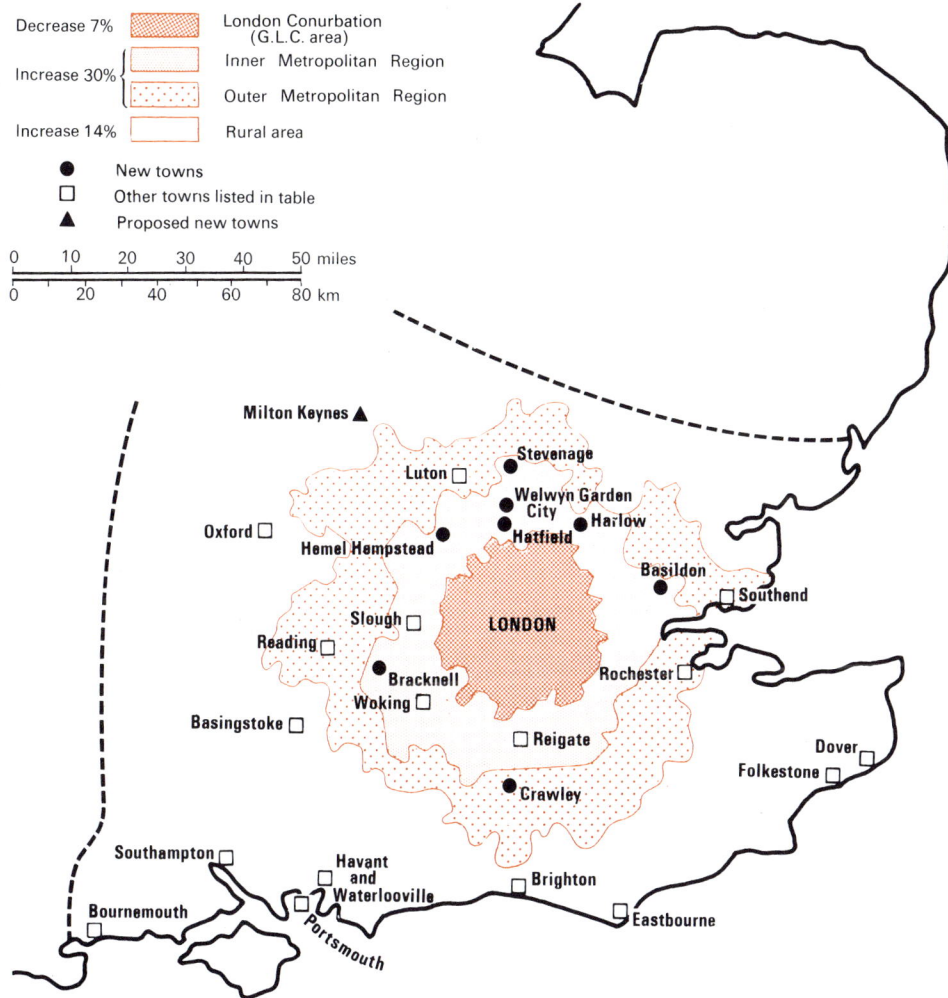

Fig. 77   Population changes, 1951–61.

11. From the map name the area of the South-east which had the greatest increase in population between 1951 and 1961.

12. Use your atlas and Fig. 77 and (a) List the towns from the table which are on the south coast. What other towns are marked on your atlas on the south coast? (b) Find Reigate, which is a gap town in the North Downs. What other gap towns are there in the North Downs and the South Downs? (c) Which towns on the list are in the Thames basin?

5. URBAN GROWTH IN SOUTH-EAST ENGLAND

It is estimated that by 1981 there will be 3 million more people in the South-east than there were in 1961. This is such a large number that it is important to plan where towns will grow to house the people, and where the countryside will be preserved. One of the aims of planning, which is carried out by various government departments and local authorities, is to see that new houses are built in the right place.

Fig. 78 shows the plan published in 1967 for the development of the south-east region. The extra people have moved, and will continue to move, largely into 'new towns', some of which are listed in the table at the beginning of the chapter. Urban growth is to be concentrated in corridors so that the towns can make use of the main routeways, and at the same time leave large stretches of undisturbed country-side.

The idea of planning a town from scratch, and building it in a stretch of open country, is not new. Letchworth was begun before World War I and Welwyn Garden City was built between the wars. Both these garden cities were planned,

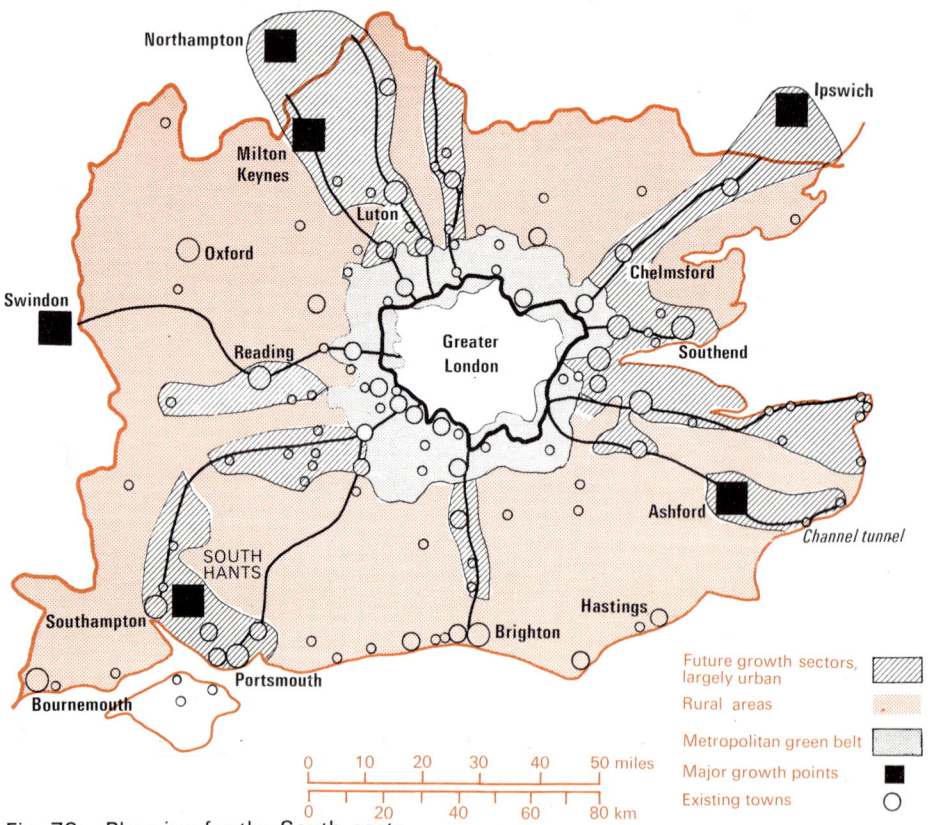

Fig. 78 Planning for the South-east.

5. URBAN GROWTH IN SOUTH-EAST ENGLAND

Fig. 79 East Square, Basildon new town. At Basildon, the factory area is separate from the living area. What other planning ideas have been tried here to make town life pleasanter?

although they were private ventures and not sponsored by the government. The aim was to provide a pleasant place to live in with plenty of gardens and open spaces, and a factory area separate from the houses.

Since World War II, several new towns have been built as a result of government planning, to house people from crowded parts of London and to spread work over a wider area. The new towns have been built beyond the Green Belt. Many of the new towns are experiments in planning and have pedestrian precincts, or different street levels for pedestrians and traffic. Some of the towns which are still relatively small, but which according to the plan will become large in the future, are Basingstoke, Newbury, Ashford and Milton Keynes.

The largest towns of the South-east are still the older towns. Oxford, built at the confluence of the Thames and Cherwell, is the oldest University town in the country, and a focus of routes for the surrounding lowlands. Its recent growth, however, is the result of the motor-car industry. William Morris, later Lord Nuffield, established a works here which grew to be one of the leading motor-car factories in the country and the car factories in the suburb of Cowley are the biggest employers in Oxford. The old city of Oxford is still the main centre for shopping and entertainment, but Cowley, separated from the old city by a single, congested bridge, now has its own shopping precinct, community hall and cinemas.

75

Fig. 80   Adelaide Crescent, built in the famous Regency style of architecture, in Hove, adjoining Brighton. Brighton scenery also includes narrow passages called 'the lanes', broad shopping avenues and seaside promenades.

Reading is situated on the confluence of the rivers Kennet and Thames, south of the gap where the Thames flows through the chalk hills. This position has helped it to be a major corn and cattle market and a focus for the surrounding countryside; the University has a well-known department of Agriculture. Reading is also a locally famous shopping centre. But its position in the London Basin has helped it to grow more recently as a manufacturing town. The largest factory in the town is Huntley and Palmers biscuit works. There are also many engineering products including weighing machines, electrical apparatus and metal boxes.

Along the coast from Bournemouth to Southend are a number of seaside resorts, the most cosmopolitan of which is Brighton. Brighton became a fashionable resort after the Prince of Wales, later George IV, began building his Pavilion there in 1783, and many of the buildings, squares and crescents date from the Regency period. It is known as 'London by the sea' because of its rich variety of entertainment—piers, theatres, cinemas, casinos, a race course and perhaps, in the future, a Marina. The hour-run train service from London makes it easy to reach, while its reputation for sunshine accounts for its nickname 'Dr Brighton'.

5. URBAN GROWTH IN SOUTH-EAST ENGLAND

Southampton is a major port and industrial town, at the head of the large estuary of Southampton water (Fig. 63). Two small rivers flow into the estuary at Southampton, so the town itself has a long waterfront, and is built on a kind of peninsula between the two river mouths. It is most famous as a passenger port, and more ocean-going passengers travel via Southampton than through any other British port. The chief passenger traffic is to North America, but Southampton is also the port for passengers to South Africa, and a ferry service across the channel links it with Cherbourg and Le Havre.

An astonishing change has taken place in the freight traffic of Southampton. Before World War II the goods traffic of Southampton averaged about $2\frac{1}{2}$ million tonnes per year and yet today it is 23 million. The reason for this is that oil imports have increased enormously. Twenty-two million tonnes of the total trade is in oil. The main oil-importing jetties are not at Southampton itself, but further down the estuary at Fawley (Esso) and Hamble (Shell). The Esso refinery at Fawley is the largest in Britain. The waterway has been deepened so that the huge oil tankers can discharge their cargoes at the jetties. 240 000-tonne tankers will be able to discharge part of their load at Milford Haven, then continue to Fawley to unload the rest. Pipelines have been built from Fawley to the Severn Estuary and to London.

Oil is outstandingly the biggest import. Southampton also imports food stuffs, especially fruit from South Africa and exports manufactured goods, some of which come from the Midlands. Although industry is expanding rapidly in Southampton's hinterland, it is still primarily an agricultural region, so Southampton exports only a small proportion of Britain's goods.

Many people working in Southampton are employed in work closely connected with the sea—sea transport and ship repairing are the largest employers. The

Fig. 81   Employment in England and Wales.

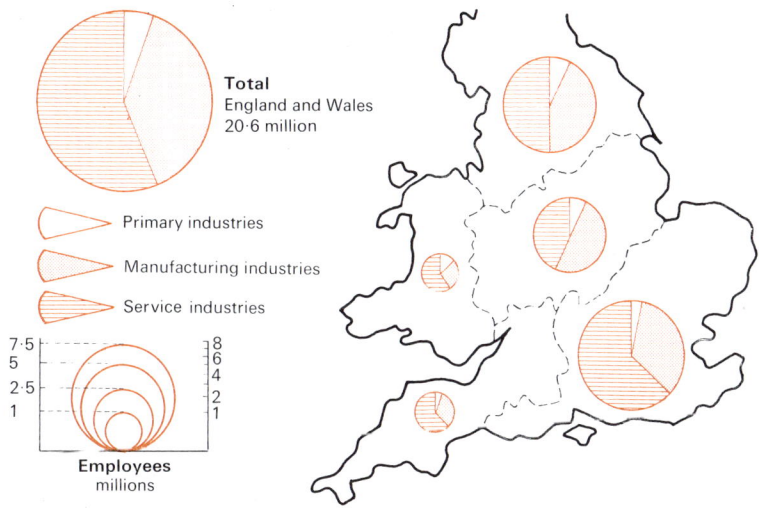

Total
England and Wales
20·6 million

Primary industries

Manufacturing industries

Service industries

Employees
millions

industries which are growing fastest are chemicals—Monsanto works use the oil of Fawley in a large plant producing ethylene, a gas from which polythene is made, and synthetic rubber. Pharmaceuticals and electronics are also growing.

Near Southampton, and guarding the entrance to the port, is Portsmouth. The table at the beginning of this chapter shows that Portsmouth, like London, has actually declined in population. Again like London, neighbouring towns outside the boundaries have grown, e.g. Havant and Waterlooville. Portsmouth was badly damaged during the war and large parts had to be rebuilt. The town is cramped in a small space—Portsea Island—and so has no room to expand. Portsmouth grew, and still largely survives, as a naval dockyard. Ships of the Royal Navy are based here, and refitted and repaired.

Apart from these towns, the towns of south-east England are not large. Their populations number less than 100 000. Any neat classification—for example into ferry ports, seaside resorts, market towns, cathedral towns—is rather blurred today. Most of the towns are manufacturing towns on a small or large scale, and most have a high proportion of their population in service industries. The towns have more than one function and for many the fact that they are less then an hour by train from Central London is the most significant cause of their recent growth.

13. List the new towns shown on Fig. 66. Why are new towns necessary? Write lists also of ferry ports, seaside resorts, market towns, cathedral towns.

14. Look at the diagrams on p. 77. What difference do they show in numbers employed in service industry in different parts of the country? Why are there more service industries in the South-east than elsewhere?

15. What is 'urban landscape'? How does urban landscape differ in the following: Hackney, Letchworth, Brighton?

16. The following are figures for traffic at London Airport. Draw graphs to show the changes which took place.

	Passengers handled	Freight in tonnes
1956	3 060 080	57 014
1960	5 380 937	104 725
1964	9 433 396	195 478
1966	11 455 999	286 241

17. Choosing a site for an airport is a difficult task. Write a list of the problems which must be considered before choosing a site.

18. What arguments can be used for and against (a) siting airports close to large towns (b) expanding the internal airways system of the British Isles?

6. Fenland and East Anglia

A map of Fenland looks very different from that of any other region in Britain. It is criss-crossed by straight lines, and over many square kilometres no contours at all are shown. The land is almost completely flat. The 50 ft. contour roughly marks the edge of Fenland, but most of the land is below 20 ft. The few small patches which rise above the general level are called 'islands'.

Most of the straight lines on the map show artificial drainage—straightened rivers, canals and ditches, all of which help to take water away from the land. Before 1630 most of Fenland was a large marsh. But after that it was completely transformed. Every natural river has been altered, and hundreds of new waterways have been built.

Fig. 82   The 'island' of Ely rising above the fen.

79

Fig. 83 Photocopy of an Ordnance Survey 1 in. map showing part of the Fenland, about 10 miles north-east of Peterborough.

80

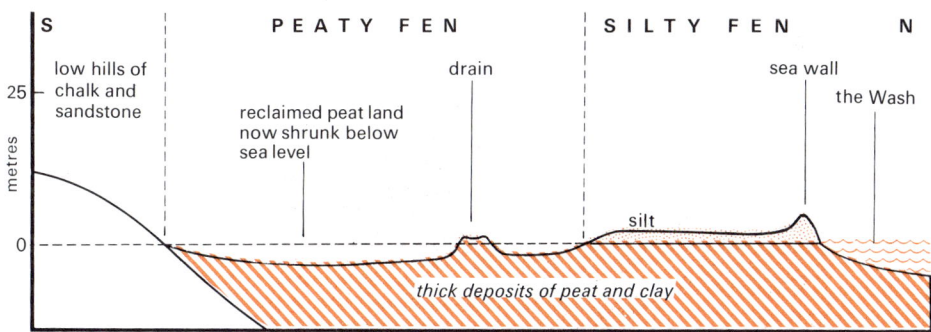

Fig. 84   Section across the Fenland to show the two parts.

This is a description of the land around Crowland as it was before it was drained:

'It was very inaccessible but it was, notwithstanding, full of inhabitants who kept their cattle at a good distance from the town, and went to milk them in little boats called skerries. Their chief profit, however, arose from the catching of fish and wildfowl. No corn grew within 5 miles. The ground about the town "is so rotten and moorish that a man may thrust a pole down thirty foote deepe; and round about it every way is nothing but a plot of reeds".'[1]

There are two parts to Fenland. In the south is the peaty fen, composed of thick layers of peat. Peat is decayed vegetation, and is formed from the marsh plants which grow in Fenland. It is dark brown or almost black in colour and, unlike coal, it has not been greatly compressed, so that it is fairly loose and can be cut or dug easily.

Between the peaty fen and the sea were broad bands of silt. These deposits were carried into the sheltered inlet of the Wash by the sea, forming a barrier of marine silt. The northern part of Fenland today forms the silty fen. Fig. 84 shows the two parts of Fenland.

The draining of the Fens on a large scale was begun in 1630, and the Dutch engineer Vermuyden was employed. It was an immense undertaking. Vermuyden decided that the most practical scheme was to straighten the rivers and thus make the gradient steeper, so that the water would flow away from the land more quickly. In all, five main drains were dug to carry the water away. Besides these, sluice gates to control the flow of water, and many smaller 'cuts' and ditches were built. The flat areas of drained land in the south of Fenland were known as the Bedford levels.

[1] H. C. Darby: *Draining of the Fens*: C.U.P. 1956. p. 26.

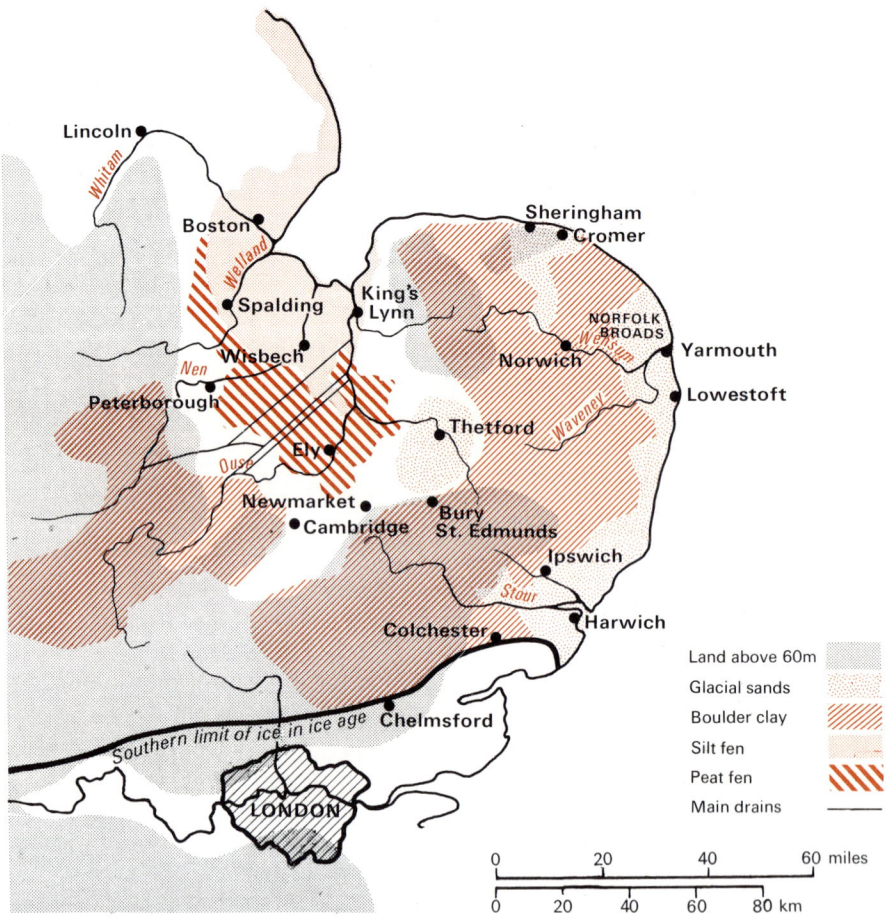

Fig. 85 The Fenland and East Anglia.

One result of draining the peat was that it shrank. Peat shrinks partly because the water is removed. The water helps to preserve the peat, but when the peat is dry and exposed to the air it wastes away through oxidation. Cultivated land in the peaty fen shrinks about 2 cm each year. In 1848 an iron pillar was pushed into the peat in Huntingdonshire so that the top was at ground level. Today it projects over 3·5 m above the ground.

While the peat shrank, the rivers remained at the same height because they flowed through a layer of alluvium which they had deposited in their beds, and this did not shrink. Today the rivers flow about 5 metres above the level of the drained land, and are enclosed between strong embankments. Pumps, now driven by electricity, are used to lift the water to the level of the rivers.

82

6. FENLAND AND EAST ANGLIA

There is a constant danger of flooding. The most recent disastrous floods in Fenland were in 1947. To stop this happening again it was decided to build two new drains to help carry the water from the land. One of the new drains goes round the eastern edge of the Fenland, cutting off the streams before they reach the dangerous area; the other carries extra water to the sea at King's Lynn. It is necessary to keep on improving the drainage of the fens because the peat continues to shrink.

The expense of all the draining has been worthwhile because the Fenland is such a rich agricultural area. The soils are excellent, being deep and stoneless. Peat is a pure form of humus, rich in minerals, and well aerated. 80 per cent of the land is farmed, and one-third of the working population are farmers. Not many cattle are raised, except where the land is still rather marshy, and growing crops for cash is the main enterprise. On the peaty fen, wheat, potatoes and sugar beet are the chief crops, with carrots and celery as subsidiaries.

Within the Fenland there are some areas of slightly sloping land. On the silt, the land is not completely flat, and on the peat, the fen 'islands' of higher land also provide slopes. More fruit is grown on the sloping land, because the cold air which can destroy fruit has a chance to flow away downhill. Vegetables are also grown, and the area around Spalding is famous for peas and beans and bulbs.

There are not many places where towns can be built, and there are few large settlements. Isolated farmhouses a little way back from the main road are more typical than villages. The 'islands' provide sites for some settlements. The most famous of these is Ely, whose splendid cathedral with its octagonal tower forms a landmark for kilometres around. Fig. 85 shows the towns of the Fenland, most of which are market towns with a few modern industries processing agricultural goods. Perhaps the most famous market town is King's Lynn, which has two large market places, one in the south, one in the north of the city. It serves both the Fenland and the north-western corner of Norfolk. It is also a small port, although because of silting it is now some way from the open sea, and the harbour is artificially deepened.

1. Look at Fig. 83, p. 80. Write a list of names from the map which are connected with artificial drainage and protection from flood, or which show that the land was once marshy.

2. Describe the view you would see if you were in an aeroplane above Crowland looking west. Mention relief, roads, waterways, houses, fields.

3. Write a paragraph to explain how the Fenland was drained. Why is it difficult to keep drained?

4. List the differences between the silty fen and the peaty fen under the headings: how they were formed, relief, farming, towns.

5. Draw a sketch of Fig. 82, and label Ely Cathedral on the 'Isle of Ely', flat artificially drained farmland, road raised on embankment above flood level.

Fig. 86   Lavenham, Suffolk. This village retains most of its original mediaeval buildings. The church, like many others in East Anglia, is built of flint which has been quarried from the chalk.

East Anglia

One of the reasons why East Anglia has developed a strongly individual character is historical. For a long time it was remote. It was cut off from other parts of the country by forests and marshes around Fenland and the Thames estuary. It was settled by invaders from the east who came from Europe by sea up the wide estuaries.

Although remote, East Anglia flourished. It probably had the densest population of any part of Britain at the time of the Norman invasion. It became the most prosperous wool producing region, at a time when Britain's most valuable product was wool. It remained pre-eminent in wool production and manufacture right up to the industrial revolution. Its greatest town, Norwich, competed with Bristol and York to be England's second city.

Some of East Anglia's character is the result of glaciation. The region has been as much affected by glaciation as the Lake District[1] but in a different way. During the ice age, several ice sheets advanced one after another across East Anglia. They came from the north, from Scandinavia. Rocks of Scandinavian origin have been found in Norfolk. Ice sheets ground their way slowly across large areas of sands and

[1] See Chapter 14.

84

muds on what is now the bed of the North Sea and crossed the chalky eastern edge of England. Mud, sand and chalk therefore were embedded in the bottom of the ice as it moved. A large quantity of this embedded material was plastered over East Anglia. When the ice melted, it left a deposit over the surface of mud and rock called 'boulder clay'.

Boulder clay is not all the same. It varies in the amount of clay, sand or stones it contains. In East Anglia it contains a great deal of chalk, and is called chalky boulder clay. This makes a soil rich in lime, valuable for farming. At least half of East Anglia is covered with chalky boulder clay. The particles, large and small, which form the boulder clay were churned up by ice, and so the smaller particles were not separated from the larger. Boulder clay is an irregular, unsorted deposit. It differs, therefore, from deposits carried by water, because running water carries away fine particles, and sorts out the particles into different sizes.

But not all glacial deposits are formed under the ice. Another type of deposit was formed at the edge of the ice sheet. Where the ice reached warmer lands it began to melt. Fig. 85 shows the line where melting began at the southern edge of the advancing ice. At the edge of the ice sheet, there was running meltwater. This washed away the finer clay particles, and left the heavier sands and gravels. Several parts of East Anglia are covered with sands which were deposited at the edge of the ice sheet. They are called fluvio-glacial deposits. They are different from boulder clay because they have been affected by running water and have been sorted out into particles of different sizes.

The different kinds of glacial deposits are called collectively 'drift'. Almost all of East Anglia is covered with glacial drift. The underlying rocks are hidden, and do not affect the scenery very obviously. Almost all of East Anglia is below 100 m. The rivers flow in shallow gentle valleys which they have carved out of the drift.

East Anglia is the best farming land in Britain. The gentle undulating slopes are well drained and are easily negotiated by tractors and combine harvesters. The climate is favourable, too, with rather warmer, sunnier summers than are found farther west, useful for harvesting; and frostier winters (frost helps to break up the soil and prepare it for drilling). Above all, the chalky boulder clay provides deep lime-rich soil, which is everywhere intensively farmed. Even the sandy soils nearer the coast can be fertilized and have the advantage of being light and easy to work.

Arable farming is more important than livestock. 95 per cent of the arable land is used for barley, wheat and sugar beet. Grains and roots are traditional crops. It was in Norfolk that rotation of crops was first practised, alternating grain, clover and root crops in successive years. Root crops were fed to animals in the fields, thus adding natural manure to the soil. Today, sugar beet is almost the only root crop grown in East Anglia, and the Government controls the number of hectares sown. Barley is gaining at the expense of wheat here as elsewhere. Other crops grown include potatoes, fruit, mustard, clover seed. More vegetables are being grown for freezing plants, especially peas.

Fig. 87   Arable farmland near Bury St. Edmunds, looking north.

Fig. 88   Part of the Breckland near Thetford. This is a poor heathland with heather, bracken, and pine trees.

A stretch of boulder clay farming country immediately north of Bury St. Edmunds is shown in Fig. 87. Large farms and large fields are typical. The farms are highly mechanized, yields are high, and much fertilizer, weed killers and pesticides are used to maintain them.

Although arable farming is still just as important, East Anglia like everywhere else is a region of mixed farming, and more livestock are now being raised than

86

Fig. 89   Hoveton Great Broad, Norfolk. Draw a sketch of the picture to show water, a lake partly filled in where trees are now growing, and farmland.

formerly. Beef and dairy cattle are reared in central Norfolk, and more pigs and poultry are now being raised. There are, however, fewer sheep than there were and fewer horses. The Suffolk Punch, a strong work-horse used to pull the plough through the heavy soils, is hardly seen today.

Not all of East Anglia is rich farmland. On some of the poorer glacial sands there are stretches of heathland. Breckland (Fig. 88) is the best known.

'Lichen or moss gradually gave way to heath—long stretches of young green bracken, then wide strips of heather, very thick and tall, again more bracken, and so on. Nearby was a solid forest of young fir trees stretching right away over the Suffolk boundary.'[1]

Much of this wild heathland has now been taken over by the Forestry Commission and is planted with conifers.

The Cromer Ridge, also a wooded heathland, is the most obvious line of hills in East Anglia. It is only 90 m high, but its northern slope is steep, and was perhaps once at the edge of one of the ice sheets. In east Norfolk is a famous region known as the Broads. The Broads are shallow lakes (Fig. 89) which were formed by peat-diggers in earlier centuries. The lakes used to be much larger, but have now been partly filled in with mud and growing vegetation.

[1] Julian Tennyson: *Suffolk Scene*. p. 72.

Fig. 90 Norwich, an ancient and great market town, the largest in East Anglia.

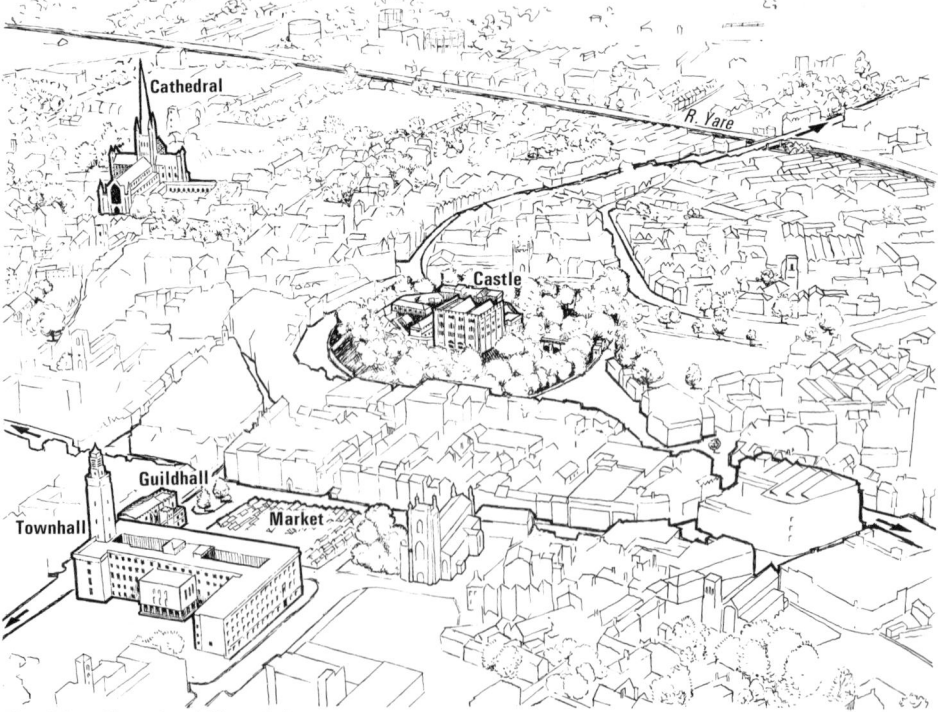

Fig. 91 Sketch of Norwich.

88

Fig. 92 Ipswich, on the estuary of the River Orwell. Look at Fig. 78 to see how near it is to London and how it will be affected by the plans for the South-east Region.

The towns of East Anglia have grown as market centres in an agricultural land. Figs. 90 and 91 show Norwich. Its three outstanding buildings, in a city rich in architecture—there are thirty mediaeval churches—are the Castle, the Cathedral and the Guildhall which overlooks a huge market square. The modern town hall overshadows the smaller Guildhall building. Norwich is the main market centre for miles around. Road and rail maps show that it is a focus of routes. It grew to be one of England's first cities during the centuries when East Anglia produced more wool than any other part of the country, and was also the chief centre of wool manufacture. Wool is unimportant today, but Norwich is the largest industrial town in the region, and gives the lie to the belief that 'there is nothing north of Ipswich but agriculture and ancient monuments'.[1] Its chief industry is food processing (e.g. Colmans Mustard, Robinsons Lemon Barley) but it also has a large shoe manufacturing industry, and manufactures agricultural machinery.

Ipswich is situated at the head of an estuary, like several other towns in the southern part of East Anglia. Ipswich is a market town, and a small port; but today it is also a flourishing manufacturing town. Many of the manufactures are concerned with its agricultural surrounding land: flour mills, breweries, tanning, fertilizers, agricultural engineering. But there are now many new engineering industries in the suburbs which make Ipswich appear to be a north-eastern outpost of the London sprawl.[2] The same change is taking place in Colchester and Chelmsford, which are nearer London.

[1] Eric Fowler in *Norwich and its Region.*

[2] See figure 78, page 74.

6. FENLAND AND EAST ANGLIA

Yarmouth was, with Lowestoft, a fishing port famous for herring. (See p. 171). But few herring are now caught off the East Anglian fishing grounds. Although fishing, chiefly of white fish, is still important in Lowestoft, Yarmouth has turned more to manufacturing and the tourist trade. It is also a small port. Harwich is a ferry port chiefly for passengers to the Hook of Holland. It has some trade with the Netherlands and Belgium, and Scandinavian countries.

6. Describe the differences between boulder clay and fluvio-glacial sands under the headings: how they were formed, what they are made of, present-day land use.

7. Draw a map called 'The poorer regions of East Anglia', and shade and label the areas which are poorer. Write notes beside the map to describe what the land in these parts looks like.

8. Look at Fig. 87. What advantages has this land for arable farming? The rotation of crops used in the field just north of the coniferous plantation on the right-hand edge of the picture was: 1963 ley (temporary grass for sheep or cattle), 1964 wheat, 1965 sugar beet, 1966 barley. Explain the value of each crop. Why is rotation of crops important? In what ways is an aerial photograph (a) more useful and (b) less useful than a map?

9. What differences are there in the relief, soil and land use shown in Fig. 82 and Fig. 87?

10. Use the summaries below to draw annotated sketch maps of Cambridge, Boston, Colchester.

Cambridge	*Boston*	*Colchester*
Built on firm land 15m high at edge of Fenland on bridge point of Cam river. Market town, ancient university town. Modern manufactures include Pye and Ekco electrical engineering and other engineering firms; also food and fertilizers.	Built on land below 15m at northern edge of Fenland. Was once a port at mouth of river Witham, but is now 10 km from sea due to silting. Port has revived in recent years and imports include timber, grain, seed potatoes. Manufactures include canning of fruit and vegetables, fertilizers, sawmills.	Built on low hill beside river Colne, 10 km from head of estuary. Was one of leading towns of Roman Britain. Lies in agricultural country-side and is a market town. Manufactures diesel engines and lathes. Has grown rapidly in 1960's due largely to fast electric train service to London. Essex University also built here in 1960's.

11. Make summaries similar to those above for Norwich, Ipswich, Kings Lynn.

90

7. The Coasts from the Wash to the Severn

A study of coasts is the study of two things: first, the general shape of the coastline, whether it is indented or smooth, which an atlas map shows; second, the features of the coast—the details of beaches, cliffs or sand dunes, for example. The shape and features of a coast depend on the following factors, all of which affect each other:

1. The strength and direction of the waves.
2. The character of the rocks along the coast—whether they are hard or soft, well consolidated or loose.
3. The action of rivers or ice eroding the land at the coast.
4. Changes in sea level.
5. Artificial changes to the coast by man.

Fig. 93 The strength of waves varies with the fetch (see next page). Here the winds blow most often from the south west, so the dominant waves have a long fetch and are strong. [Adapted from: K. E. Sawyer, *Landscape Studies*, Arnold (1970) p. 60.]

91

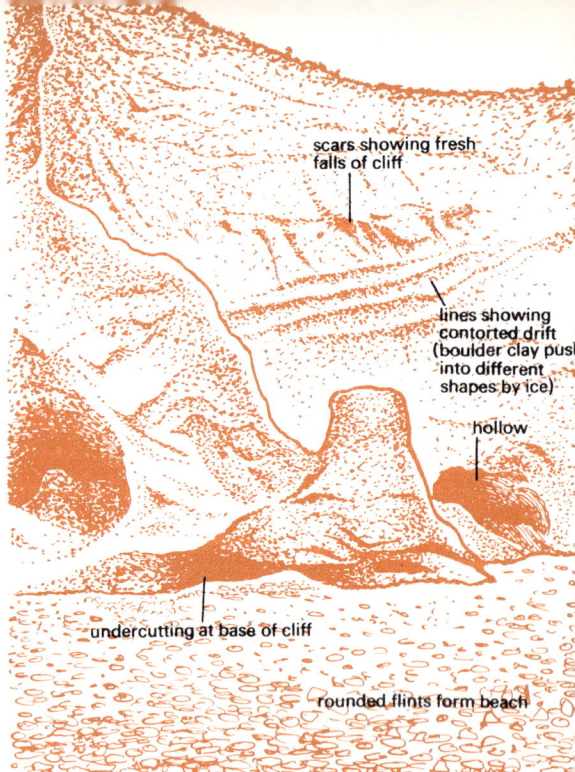

scars showing fresh falls of cliff

lines showing contorted drift (boulder clay pushed into different shapes by ice)

hollow

undercutting at base of cliff

rounded flints form beach

Fig. 94a Part of the cliffs at Sheringham, Norfolk, being eroded in soft, loosely consolidated boulder clay.

Fig. 94b Sketch of Fig. 94a.

Waves erode the coasts as they break on them. The sheer weight of water pounding on the rocks helps to weaken them. Air is trapped in crevices in the rocks. When the waves break a great pressure is exerted on the trapped air, which helps to split the rocks. Waves pick up sand and pebbles as they wash back down the beach, and these batter the rocks when the waves break.

Waves form because of the movement of winds blowing over the sea. If the winds have crossed the sea uninterrupted for a long distance, they are said to have a long 'fetch'. Waves are more powerful agents of erosion when there is a long fetch, and less powerful when there is a short fetch.

The coasts of East Anglia

The waves which break on the East Anglian coast are of medium strength, but they are very destructive because the rocks of the coast are mostly composed of soft, loosely consolidated material which disintegrates easily.

The pictures above show part of the north coast of Norfolk between Cromer and Sheringham. Here the rock which forms the cliff is boulder clay which was deposited during the ice age. Hollows are worn in the base of the cliff, so that the top of the cliff is undermined, and the soft rock is also easily eroded by rainwater. Fresh falls of rock can always be seen along this coast.

7. THE COASTS FROM THE WASH TO THE SEVERN

Old inhabitants of Sheringham can remember playing football in fields beyond the fence which now runs along the cliff edge. Because the rock is soft and crumbly, it is quickly broken down and washed away by the waves. No features last long, and the prominent rock in Fig. 94 which has managed to remain upright is not a permanent feature of the coast.

The beach is covered with rounded pebbles. They are mostly flints which have been ground against each other by the waves until they are smooth. Some of the flints were embedded in the boulder clay, but some are eroded from chalk which lies underneath the clay. When the tide goes out, a platform of chalk worn down by the waves can be seen. It has been cut into deep grooves and hollows, as flints have scoured back and forth across it. This exposed rock worn away at the base of the cliff is called a 'wave cut platform'.

Most of the material which is eroded by waves—boulders, chips of rock, pebbles, sand or mud—becomes part of the beach. The finest particles are carried out to sea. A section drawn along a beach from top to bottom is called a beach profile, and it shows what type of material—coarse or fine—is found at different heights. Gradually the larger pieces are worn down.

An ideal beach profile would show the largest boulders at the top of the beach, then large pebbles, small pebbles, sand grains, muds. Many actual beach profiles are not exactly like this. In the one at Sheringham, for instance, (Fig. 95) the waves have not completely sorted out the smaller pieces from the larger, partly because so much new material is constantly being eroded from the cliff, and partly because new material is also eroded from the wave cut platform lower down the beach.

Beach material is also moved sideways along the beach, because waves usually break at an angle to rather than parallel with the coastline. The movement of

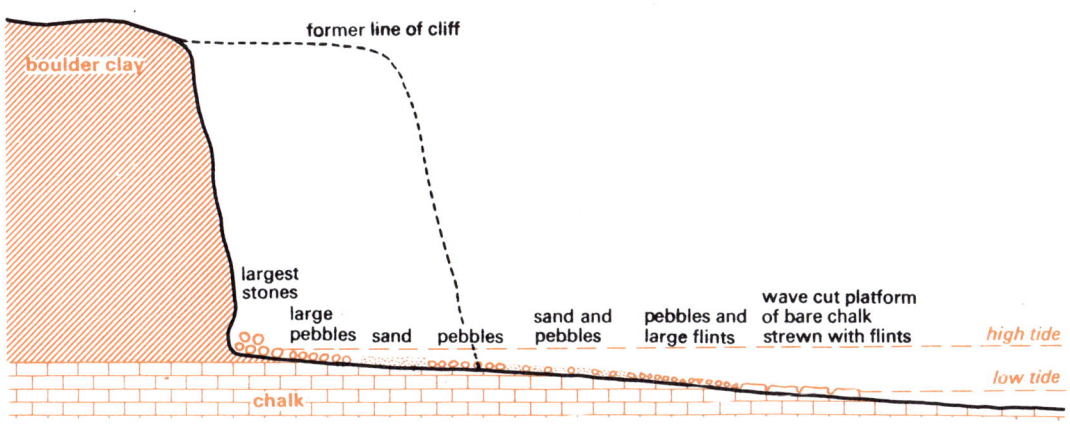

Fig. 95   Beach profile near Sheringham.

beach material sideways is called beach drift, and it is because of this that groynes —walls of stone or wood—are built down the beach to try and stop the material moving.

Beach drift can sometimes carry sand and pebbles straight past a bend in the coastline, building a continuation of the beach called a 'spit'. The map below shows Blakeney Point, which is a sand and shingle spit. Beach material has been carried westwards in a straight line past the bend in the coast. This spit was originally much smaller than it is today, but gradually it grew and it is now about 13 kilometres long.

The seas behind the spit are sheltered. Tides have gradually carried in sand and mud which have been trapped behind the spit and deposited on the bed of the sea. The mud has built up to form, first, mud flats—stretches of oozy mud exposed at low tide, a favourite haunt of birds; then, salt marsh. The salt marsh (Fig. 99) is cut by dozens of small creeks which fill with water at high tide. Some plants are adapted to these wet salty conditions.

Fig. 96 Beach drift, the movement of beach material along a beach from one side to another. Particles move up the beach obliquely as the waves break, but move down straight. Gradually each particle is moved along the beach.

Fig. 97 Blakeney Point, Norfolk.

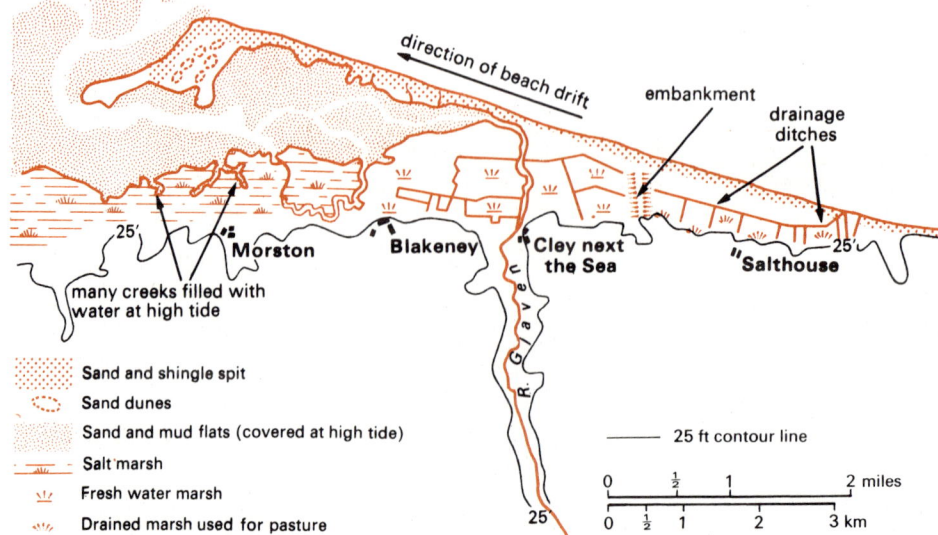

7. THE COASTS FROM THE WASH TO THE SEVERN

Tides and rivers occasionally carry sand and mud over the salt marsh, which builds up to a higher level as the deposits settle around the plants. Parts of the marsh have become so high that they are never covered by salt water. Here, the plants of the salt marsh can no longer survive, and are replaced by freshwater plants. Much of the freshwater marsh has now been drained and is used as pasture for cattle. Four stages—mud flats, salt marsh, freshwater marsh and reclaimed drained marsh, can be seen behind the Blakeney spit, where there was once a shallow arm of the sea. On the spit itself sand has blown to form sand dunes where a coarse grass called marram grows.

Thus, although land is being lost all the time in parts of the coast because of erosion, in other places it is being built up by deposition. Scolt Head Island, west of Blakeney Point, and Orford Ness (Fig. 98), both spits in East Anglia, are similar to Blakeney Point in the way they were formed.

The great building up of spits has made the coast of East Anglia straight, north of Orford Ness. South of Orford Ness the coast is indented. There are many inlets

Fig. 98   Orford Ness, Suffolk, looking south. The River Alde nearly reaches the sea just south of the town of Aldeburgh. Orford Ness is a long spit which has grown southwards past the mouth of the river, so that the river has to make a long diversion before it can reach the sea.

Fig. 99   Salt marsh at Blakeney, Norfolk. The low hills in the distance are the old coastline. Compare the photograph with Fig. 97

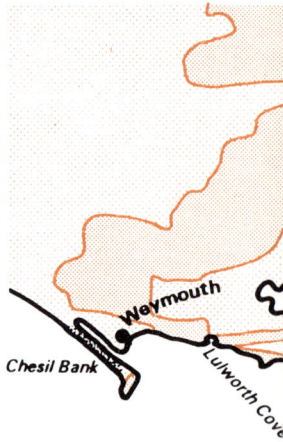

Fig. 100 Part of the chalk cliffs near Dover.

made by the estuaries of quite small rivers (Fig. 102), such as the Blackwater, Stour and Orwell.

The estuaries are large because the sea level has risen to flood the river mouths. Because it is a low coast with shallow tidal water, some of the features of the coast are similar to those at Blakeney. Here again there are mud flats and marshes. In many places spits have begun to grow across the river mouths.

1. Draw a sketch of Fig. 98. Label the North Sea, Aldeburgh, river Alde, point where river was turned back by spit, the deposits of Orford Ness.

2. What is a beach profile? Explain how you would make one.

3. Use Fig. 97. (a) How long is the sand and shingle spit shown? (b) What types of deposit are shown on the map? (c) What types of vegetation are shown? (d) How has the area been influenced by man? (e) Describe the position of the four villages shown. Why are they less important now than they once were?

4. Draw a map of the East Anglian coast from the Wash to the Thames, and label (a) A coast being cut back by erosion (b) Two spits where new land is being formed (c) Estuaries of a drowned coast. Mark five coastal towns. Use Fig. 85 page 82 as a guide.

The south coast

Fig. 101 shows the south coast of England from Dover to Weymouth. The coast juts out in headlands where hard rock meets the sea. This is partly because the hard rock can stand up to the attack of the waves.

Wide crescent-shaped bays have been worn back where soft rock meets the coast, for example between Eastbourne and Hastings, and here there are long beaches. The soft rock cannot withstand the attack of the waves so well, so it has been worn

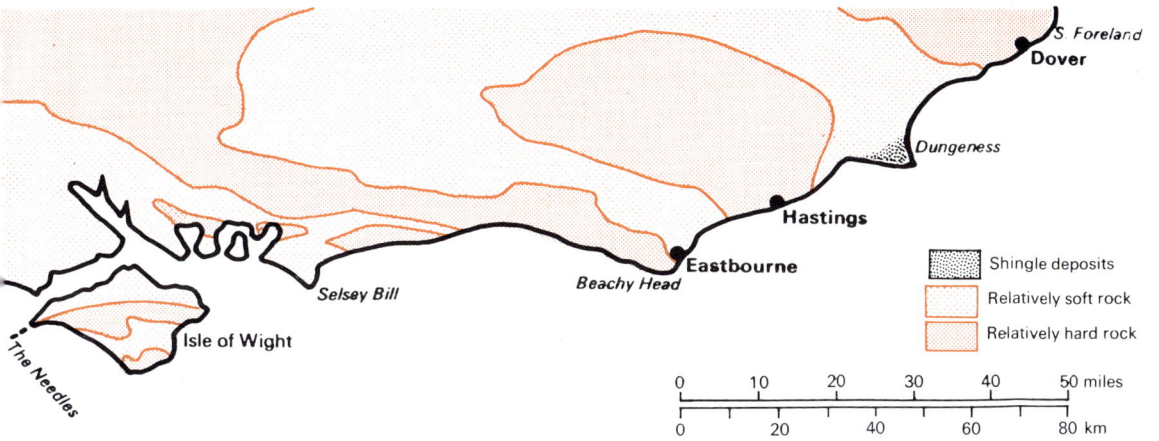

Fig. 101 Bands of hard and soft rock along the south coast.

back to form bays. Some of the points jutting out from the coastline have been formed by beach drift and are types of spit, like Dungeness or Selsey Bill.

The white cliffs of Dover are bold chalk headlands which form a distinctive landmark to travellers returning from France. The picture opposite shows part of these cliffs. Chalk usually forms perpendicular cliffs (see p. 27 for explanation of the characteristics of chalk). The top of the cliff is not easily worn back by rainwater or frost, but the bottom of the cliff is quickly eroded by the waves. The cliff is undercut, and the chalk breaks away vertically. The fallen rock, being chalk, is soon dissolved away by salt water, so the picture shows only a few small rocks at the foot of the cliff, which will soon vanish. The dark lines across the chalk are bands of flints. These are hard nodules embedded in the chalk. Flint is not dissolved by sea water. Because chalk contains flints, most beaches along the south coast are composed of rounded flint pebbles.

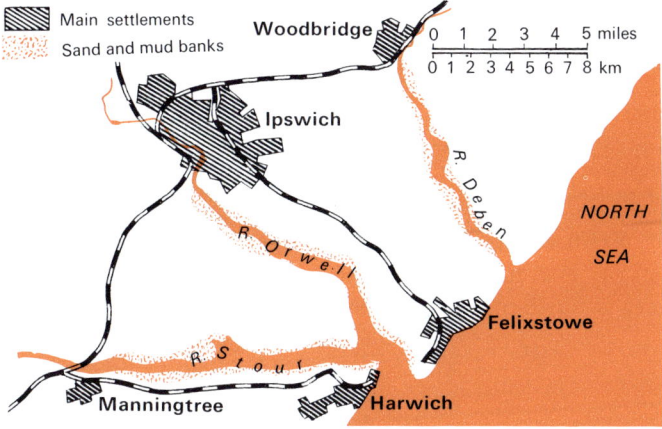

Fig. 102 Estuaries in Essex and Suffolk, a submerged coast. There is no land above 50 m.

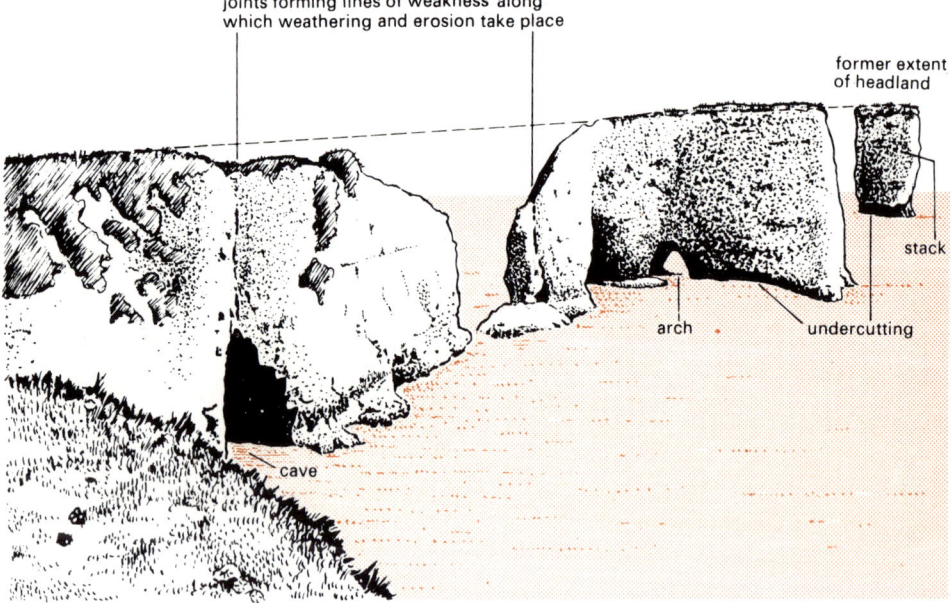

Fig. 103   Old Harry Rocks, near Studland, Dorset.

Although chalk is easily eroded by waves, it is a firm enough rock so that stacks can stand up on their own. Stacks are isolated rocks, often at the end of a headland, which have become separated from the mainland. The drawing above shows a stack and a larger islet. Waves and weathering have worn away the rock, especially along the joints. Eventually they have broken through the headland, forming a passage for the sea. The formation of caves, arches, and stacks are stages in the destruction of the coast.

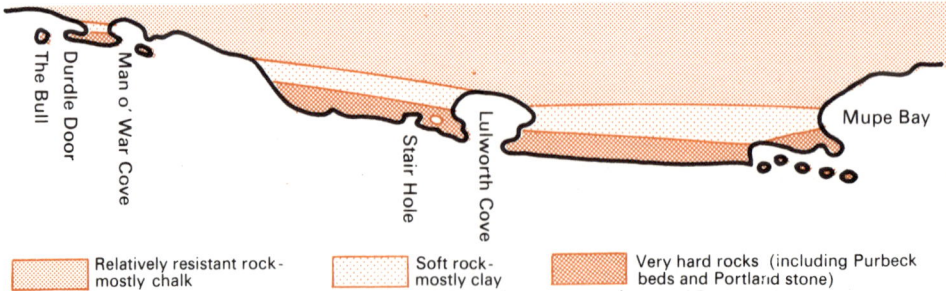

Fig. 104   Part of the Dorset coast. The alignment of rocks here is parallel to the coast.

Farther along the coast, in Dorset, the different layers of rock are parallel to the coast. The diagram above shows part of this coast. The layer of rock closest to the sea is resistant. The sea has found it difficult to erode this rock, and it forms islets

98

Fig. 105   Lands End.

Fig. 106   Durdle Door, a natural arch formed in resistant rock in the Dorset coast. The camera is pointing southwards, looking towards the English channel. Find Durdle Door in Fig. 104.

like the Bull and elongated headlands like Durdle Door. Where the sea has worn through the hard rock, it has been able to erode the soft rock behind fairly easily. It has carved out the perfect half moon of Lulworth Cove in the softer rocks, and farther east, the much larger bay at Mupe Bay.

The South-west

The coast of Cornwall and Devon is very intricate. It is jagged with numerous small headlands and inlets, offshore rocks and islets (Fig. 107). One reason for this is that along this coast there is a great mixture of rocks. Whereas along the coast of Sussex and Kent there are broad bands of rock meeting the coast, in Cornwall the rocks are very varied over a small area. The waves can erode some more easily than others, and so bays and headlands are formed.

On the whole, however, the rocks of the South-west are much harder than any of the rocks of eastern England, and therefore they have been able to resist the tremendous battering from the Atlantic waves which attack this part of the coast. Land's End and the Lizard stand out as two headlands because they are composed of exceptionally resistant rock.

99

Fig. 107 Near Mullion, on the south-west tip of Cornwall.

Fig. 108 The island of Lundy, Devon. The roof of a cave has collapsed, and the sea is wearing a narrow inlet along a joint in a rock.

Fig. 109 Part of the broad ria (or submerged river valley) at Plymouth.

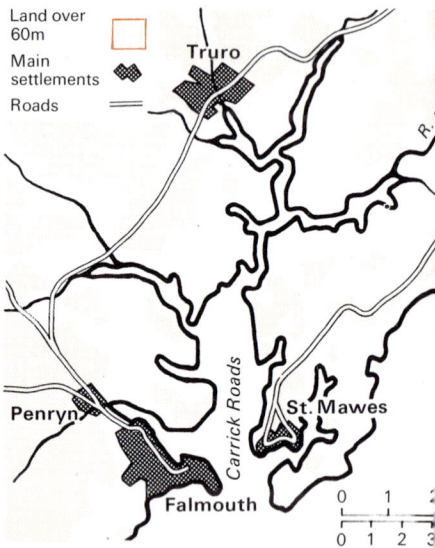

Fig. 110 Falmouth Ria, South Cornwall, a submerged coast.

Fig. 107 shows part of the Cornish coast near Penzance. The rocks are metamorphic (a rock altered by heat or pressure so that it becomes very hard). Erosion by rain has caused the top of the cliff to be sloping. The rock has many joints and openings, and caves have formed along these. Arches have formed, and a separated islet, too large to be called a stack, can be seen. The beach material is large—rocks rather than pebbles—not yet broken down by the waves, but already slightly rounded. A rough beach has collected in a sheltered spot behind the islet. On

100

Fig. 111 The Spit at Westward Ho, Devon. Compare this photograph with Ordnance Survey Map B, facing p. 25.

Fig. 105 many similar features can be seen. Sometimes the joints become so enlarged that narrow inlets are formed. Fig. 108 shows this beginning to happen, as the roof of a cave collapses.

In the sheltered bays of the South-west there are sandy beaches. The rocks of Devon and Cornwall include granites and sandstones. Both these rocks, when broken down into tiny grains, become sand.

The waves attacking this coast have discovered every weakness in the rocks— either bands of softer rocks, or joints—and have broken them down and carried beach material into sheltered bays between the headlands. They have created a magnificent variety of coastal scenery.

The coasts of the South-west have also been affected by changes in sea level. Long branching inlets called 'rias' are typical of the Cornish coast. A ria forms when the lower part of a river valley is drowned by the sea. A ria is therefore a feature of 'submergence'. Most of the rias of the South-west are surrounded by low plateau country about 75 m high. Because a ria is a drowned river valley, a section across it is V-shaped, and the depth increases steadily out to sea.

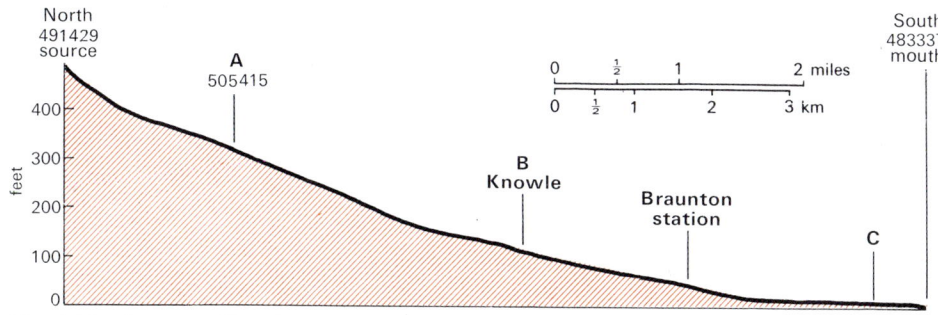

Fig. 112 Long profile of a river flowing through Braunton.

101

Fig. 113 Sand dunes on Braunton Burrows. The prevailing westerly wind has blown the sand a long way inland. Compare this photograph with Ordnance Survey Map B facing p. 25. How wide are the Braunton Burrows? How high above sea level do they reach? Look at Fig. 97 and find a similar area of sand dune.

5. The following is a list of coastal features. Divide them into two groups under the headings (a) Features of Erosion, (b) Features of Deposition: stack, spit, mud flat, cave, cliff, beach, wavecut platform, sand dunes, salt marsh, arch.

6. Rias, fiords and estuaries are formed by submergence. What does this mean? How do the three features differ? [See p. 220 for a description of fiords.] Use an atlas map to make a list of the rias of the south-west peninsula.

7. Draw a sketch of Fig. 105 (Land's End) and label: headland, stack separated from headland, inlet forming along enlarged joint, heavy beach material at base of cliff, sandy beach in sheltered bay, sloping cliff eroded by rain-water.

8. Use the Ordnance Survey Map B, facing p. 25 to answer the following: What do the symbols at the following grid references show? (a) 424340, (b) 457326, (c) 465385, (d) 478382, (e) 434396.

9. Draw a large map of the coast features of the headland which is mostly in sq. 4240. Label the main features shown.

10. Describe the coast from Putsborough Sand to Westward Ho under the headings (a) shape of the coastline, (b) features of erosion, (c) features of deposition.

11. Draw a sketch of Fig. 111 and use the map to label on your sketch pebble ridge, Northam Burrows, marsh, old coastline, Westward Ho.

12. Fig. 112 shows a profile of the river which flows from north to south through Braunton. (a) Describe the shape of the valley at the three points A, B and C. (b) Copy the profile, and add arrows to show entry of left bank tributary, main A road crossing river, entry of right bank tributary, old meander cut off.

8. The South-west

'All who have travelled through the delicious scenery of North Devon must needs know the little white town of Bideford, which slopes upwards from its broad tide-river paved with yellow sands towards the pleasant upland on the west. Above the town the hills close in, cushioned with deep oak woods, through which juts here and there a crag of fern fringed slate; below they lower, and open more and more in softly rounded knolls, and fertile squares of red and green, till they sink into the wide expanse of hazy flats, rich salt marshes, and rolling sand hills, where Torridge joins her sister Taw, and both together flow quietly towards the bar, and the ever-lasting thunder of the long Atlantic swell.

'Pleasantly the old town stands there, beneath its soft Italian sky, fanned day and night by the fresh ocean breeze, which forbids alike the keen winter frosts, and the fierce thunder heats of the midland; and pleasantly it has stood there, for now, perhaps, eight hundred years.

'But at the time whereof I write, Bideford was not merely a pleasant country town, whose quay was haunted by a few coasting craft. It was one of the chief ports of England; it furnished seven ships to fight the Armada, and was the centre of a local civilization and enterprise. And it is to the sea life and labour of Bideford, and Dartmouth, and Topsham, and Plymouth (then a petty place), and many another little western town, that England owes the foundation of her naval and commercial glory.' from *Westward Ho* by Charles Kingsley, 1855.

The coasts and lowlands

Much of the regional character of the South-west—its mild climate, its pleasant green scenery, its close contact with the rough Atlantic—is summed up in this description written a hundred years ago. The South-west is a peninsula, at its widest nearly 130 km, but at its narrowest less than 25 km across. The influence of the seas which nearly surround the peninsula is reflected in its landscape and in the livelihood of the people.

The seas around the peninsula are warm. The ocean currents of the Atlantic travel north-eastwards from tropical seas, and the winds which blow off them are warm. The winters of the peninsula are warmer (8 °C Jan. average at Penzance) than in any other part of the United Kingdom. The winds also bring rain, and the South-west has at least 250 mm more rain each year than East Anglia. Only a few

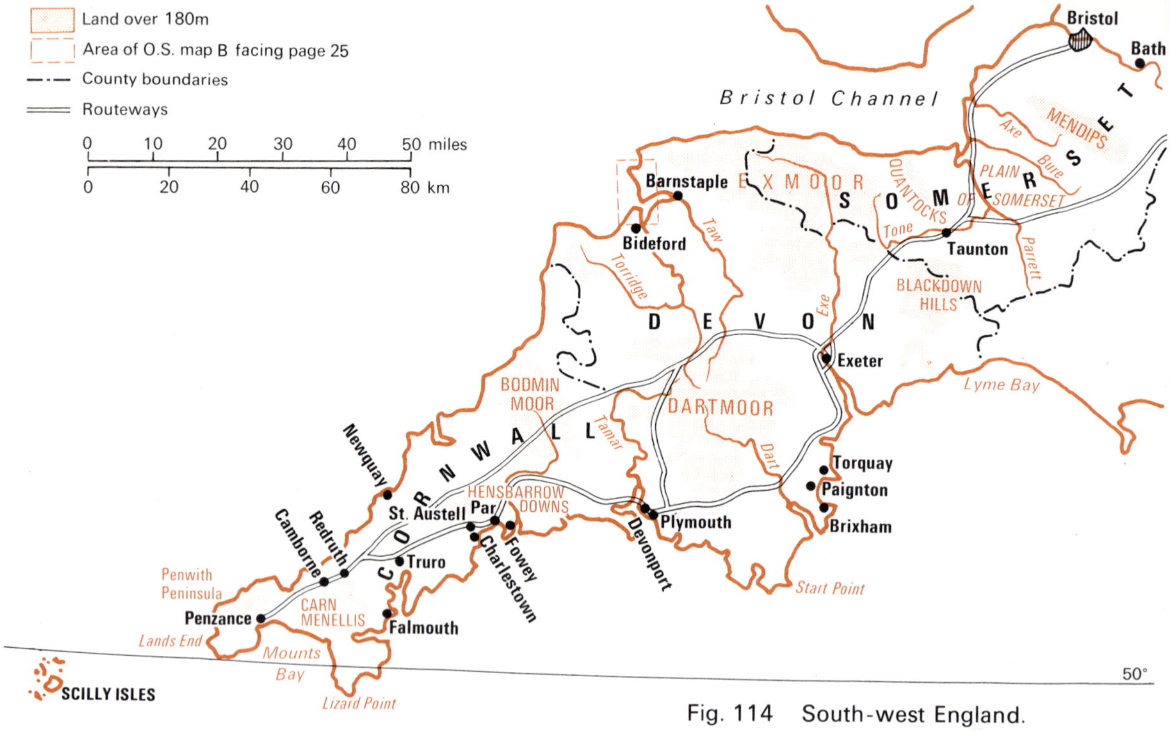

Map (Fig. 114)

Legend:
- Land over 180m
- Area of O.S. map B facing page 25
- County boundaries
- Routeways

Scale:
0　10　20　30　40　50 miles
0　20　40　60　80 km

Bristol

Bath

Bristol Channel

MENDIPS

SOMERSET

Axe

Brue

EXMOOR

QUANTOCKS

PLAIN OF SOMERSET

Barnstaple

Taw

Bideford

Torridge

Tone

Taunton

Parrett

BLACKDOWN HILLS

D E V O N

Exe

Exeter

Lyme Bay

BODMIN MOOR

DARTMOOR

Dart

Newquay

Tamar

C O R N W A L L

Redruth

HENSBARROW DOWNS

St. Austell

Par

Torquay

Paignton

Camborne

Fowey

Charlestown

Truro

Devonport

Plymouth

Brixham

Penwith Peninsula

CARN MENELLIS

Start Point

Penzance

Falmouth

Lands End

Mounts Bay

SCILLY ISLES

Lizard Point

50°

Fig. 114　South-west England.

Fig. 115　The harbour at Mousehole, Cornwall. Like many Cornish coast towns, this is both a fishing village and tourist centre.

sheltered regions on the leeward side of the hills get less than the average of 900 mm to 1000 mm.

Few people today earn their living directly from the sea as sailors or fishermen. There are many old fishing villages—Brixham, Fowey, Falmouth, Newquay, for example—in the sheltered creeks and rias around the coast. Pilchards and mackerel are the main fish caught from these ports, but over the last hundred years the fishing industry has declined. The South-west has suffered from competition with the east coast ports, which are nearer the large markets.

Indirectly, however, many more people depend on the sea. Most of the towns are along the coast. The old fishing ports have become tourist centres and many people are employed in the hotel and catering trades. The beautiful coast and sandy beaches are the main attraction in the summer months. The mild winters of the 'Cornish Riviera' enable some hotels to have a large winter trade as well.

The largest resorts are Torquay (54 000) and its neighbour, Paignton, which are now part of a larger administrative unit called Torbay. But small resorts with a population of about 10 000 are more typical.

Plymouth is becoming a tourist centre; it is the largest town in the peninsula, and the county borough has a population of 250 000. It is the main service centre for Devon and Cornwall. It is built on a magnificent deep water harbour, shown in the photograph on p. 100. A naval dockyard was established at Devonport, and this is still the largest employer. But Plymouth is not an important port. The area which it serves is almost entirely agricultural and there are few manufacturers to produce goods for export, or requiring imported raw materials.

Most of the lowland areas of Devon and Cornwall have been eroded from a rock known as Old Red Sandstone. The lowlands are really a low plateau, averaging about 75 m in height, which breaks off abruptly in cliffs along the coast. The name Devon comes from a Celtic word meaning 'deep valley', for rivers have cut deep, narrow steep-sided valleys through the lowlands.

On the plateau are found most of the farmlands of the South-west. The rocks have weathered to form deep rich red soils. The small fields are divided by embankments and thick hedgerows. Only the valley sides are thickly wooded, for they are too steep to cultivate.

Even the inland areas are not very far from the warming influence of the sea. The mild temperatures and abundant, well distributed rainfall give Devon and Cornwall some of the richest pastures in England. The grass grows for up to ten months in the year. Three-quarters of the farmland in the South-west grows grass.

Every few years the grass is ploughed up and the fields are spread with lime or fertilizer. They may then be re-sown with grass, or another crop may be grown to form part of a rotation. The main crops grown are barley or dredge corn (a mixture of oats and barley), turnips, mangolds, kale, or cabbage.

The crops are grown to provide winter feed for animals. Dairy farming is the chief enterprise on the small farms of the South-west. (More than half are smaller than 20 hectares). The cattle can be kept out of doors nearly all year and less winter feed need be grown than in other parts of the country. Dairy produce needs fast transport to the markets, and fresh milk is sent to London on trains with refrigerated waggons. In the remoter parts it is sent to local creameries, to be made into butter, cheese, or cream, which keep longer. Pigs are also fed on skimmed milk.

On the south side of the peninsula are some low-lying drier areas sheltered from the westerly winds—in Mounts Bay, the Fal Valley, the Tamar Valley, the Exe Valley and the west side of Lyme Bay. These are market gardening regions. The mild winters enable market gardeners to have vegetables, fruit, and flowers ready for the markets earlier than other parts of the country. Green vegetables—especially broccoli, cauliflower, cabbage, and spring greens—potatoes and soft fruits are grown. Cider apples are grown in the Tamar Valley.

The Scilly Isles also specialize in growing spring flowers. The daffodils come out at the end of January and are flown to London and the Midlands. Spring flower and vegetable growers rely on getting their produce to the big cities before any other producers in Britain are ready. They have, however, increasing competition from growers in Mediterranean countries.

The land use of the lowlands of Somerset is similar to that of Devon and Cornwall. They are mostly pastures for dairy cattle and the main products are milk, butter, cheese and cream. Pigs supply bacon curing and sausage making factories and battery hens are kept for eggs.

But the landscape of the Somerset lowlands is very different from the lowlands of Devon and Cornwall. The 'Somerset Levels' along the rivers Bure and Axe are like the Fenlands. They are flat drained marshlands and the soils are silt and peat. The land along the coast is three to six metres higher than it is further inland and drainage is difficult. The Somerset Levels are still liable to flood in winter and spring, and the animals are moved to higher ground in winter.

The towns in agricultural inland areas of the peninsula are marketing, collecting and distributing centres for local farm produce. The largest are Taunton, a major route centre often called the gateway to the west, and Exeter.

Exeter (90 000) has been an important centre since the Romans established it as their westernmost city in England. It became a cathedral city and a centre of the mediaeval wool trade. As it is a focus of routes in east Devon, and the lowest bridging point of the River Exe, it became a market centre. It provides the surrounding farming areas with services such as hospitals, entertainment and shops. It is a university town and a popular holiday and retirement centre.

1. Read the description of the country around Bideford, just south of Westward Ho, and look at Ordnance Survey Map B, facing p. 25. (a) Find examples on the map of 'deep oak woods', 'softly rounded knolls', 'wide expanse of hazy flats', 'rich salt marshes', 'rolling sand hills'. What are 'fertile squares of red and green'? (b) What features mentioned in the first paragraph are not shown on the map? (c) What features marked on the map were not there when this description was

Fig. 116   Near Braunton, North Devon. The land shown on this photograph is also shown on Ordnance Survey Map B, facing p. 25.

written? (d) What evidence is there on the map that there is a tourist industry here? (e) Look at the photograph of the land north of Braunton above. What does the photograph show about farming in the area? How is it typical of Devon and Cornwall? (f) The bottom left-hand corner of the photograph is approximately at grid reference 475370. Identify as many features of the photograph as you can.

2. Look at the climate statistics below, and find the three places on the map,

107

8. THE SOUTH-WEST

p. 104. Which place has (a) The highest winter temperature? (b) The highest range of temperature? Explain the differences in rainfall and temperature between Plymouth and Torquay. Which is the wettest season? [See p. 44–6 ch. 3].

	Plymouth		Torquay		Bath	
	Temperature °C	Rainfall mm	Temperature °C	Rainfall mm	Temperature °C	Rainfall mm
J	7	109	6	104	5	76
F	6	79	6	74	5	58
M	8	69	7	66	7	51
A	9	56	9	58	9	53
M	12	58	12	61	12	58
J	15	46	15	51	16	46
J	17	56	17	66	17	71
A	17	66	17	74	17	71
S	15	66	15	74	14	66
O	12	84	12	97	11	84
N	9	109	9	109	7	81
D	7	104	7	104	5	74
Total		902		938		789

3. List the occupations of the people who live in the lowlands of the South-west. Add a note beside each to describe how it is affected by nearness to the sea.

4. Places which rely strongly on a tourist industry face many problems. Suggest what these problems are.

5. Find the large rias of the South-west. (See p. 101). Why do rias make good harbours? Why are there no very large ports in Devon and Cornwall?

The uplands

Not all the peninsula is a gentle, rolling countryside of green fields. The map shows highlands rising above the low plateau. The geological map shows that several of the highlands are composed of granite.

Granite is a rock that was once molten. It did not pour out over the earth as lava, but cooled beneath the surface and solidified into a hard and resistant rock. It shows at the surface only when the rocks above it have been worn away. Deep cracks, or 'joints', are found in exposed granite. They are seen in the bare rock tors which top the granite uplands. Rocks like granite which cooled from a molten condition are called 'igneous'. Granite can be recognized by its large crystals, formed as the rock cooled slowly beneath the surface.

Molten rock is extremely hot and the heat changes any solid rock it touches. As the neighbouring rocks cool down they acquire a different form. These changed rocks are called 'metamorphic'. Metamorphic rocks are found round the edges of the granites of Devon and Cornwall.

The granite uplands are bleak moorlands rising to over 600 m in Dartmoor.

108

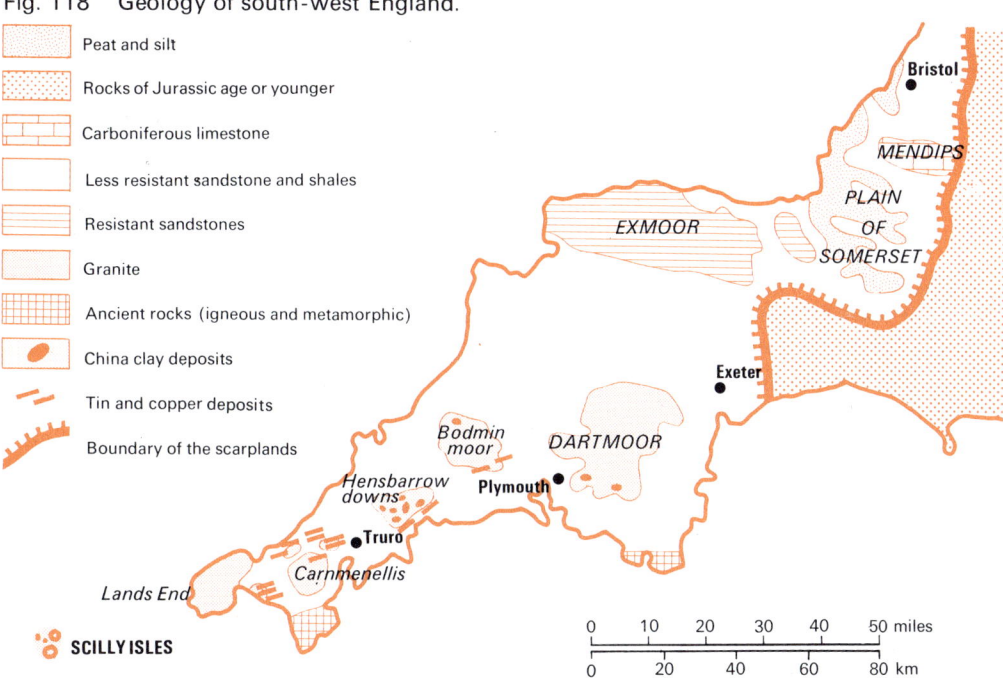

Fig. 117   Saddle Tor, Dartmoor, Devon. Notice the cracks in the granite. How high is the Tor?

Fig. 118   Geology of south-west England.

Peat and silt	
Rocks of Jurassic age or younger	
Carboniferous limestone	
Less resistant sandstone and shales	
Resistant sandstones	
Granite	
Ancient rocks (igneous and metamorphic)	
China clay deposits	
Tin and copper deposits	
Boundary of the scarplands	

Bristol

MENDIPS

PLAIN
OF
SOMERSET

EXMOOR

Exeter

Bodmin
moor

DARTMOOR

Hensbarrow
downs

Plymouth

Truro

Carnmenellis

Lands End

SCILLY ISLES

0   10   20   30   40   50 miles

0   20   40   60   80 km

Fig. 119 The Dart Valley, near Hannaford, Dartmoor. The River Dart here leaves the moorland and enters the lowlands. Notice where the woodlands, moorlands and fields are.

Westwards they become smaller and lower through Bodmin, St Austell, Carnmenellis and Land's End to the Isles of Scilly. The moors are windswept and treeless, outcrops of bare rock scar the hillside, and there are many boggy hollows where water collects. The granite produces thin, sandy, infertile soils and the moors are used for grazing sheep and some beef cattle.

The few farms are found in the shelter of the valleys round the edges of the moor. The only town on Dartmoor itself is Princetown, which houses the famous prison. Where granite forms the coast it rises from the sea in bold cliffs and headlands. (See Fig. 105).

On the granite uplands too the quarrying of china clay flourishes, mainly in the St. Austell district. Granite contains felspar, quartz and mica. It is the felspar crystals, forming only 10 per cent of granite, which decompose to form kaolin, or china clay, so there is a great deal of waste. Being soft, the mixture is quarried by jets of water from high pressure hoses which loosen it and wash it down into the bottom of the pit. The waste material, mainly white glistening quartz grains, settles out and is dumped in tips round the pit, forming conical hills. The china clay is taken by rail to the small ports of Fowey, Par and Charlestown, and three quarters is exported. Some of the china clay is sent by sea to Liverpool, and then to the North Staffordshire potteries, where it is made into porcelain. But its main use today is as a 'filler' in paper making. It is also used as a base for cosmetics and sweets, and in the production of oilcloth, linoleum, rubber and paint.

On the edges of the moors, in the metamorphic rocks, many minerals are found. Tin has probably been worked in Cornwall since the late Bronze Age, about 1000 B.C., and there are records of Phoenician and Greek traders obtaining Cornish tin.

110

Fig. 120   An old tin mine, Cornwall.

Tin was first found in the gravels of the river beds, and was obtained by washing the gravel. The tin had been eroded by rivers from the mineral veins in the metamorphic rocks. By the late fifteenth century the tin veins were being worked directly by shaft mining. Copper began to be worked at this time too. The main mining areas lay in west Cornwall, the Penwith peninsula and the Camborne-Redruth area, but St. Austell and the southern edge of Bodmin Moor were also productive.

The peak of production came in the eighteenth and nineteenth centuries when tin and copper were exported to South Wales for smelting. As new and cheaper sources of tin and copper were found in Malaya and the U.S.A., Cornish mines began to close. A few tin mines still remain and at times when world prices are high others reopen, but at present Cornwall provides less than 5 per cent of the tin used in Britain. The evidence of mining is still to be seen in the landscape, 'areas of derelict land, of gorse and briar, with crumbling engine-houses and stamping mills: all now roofless, with vacant spaces for windows through which the wind blows mournfully throughout the winter months'.[1]

Two other hill ranges are not made of granite. Exmoor is composed mostly of resistant sandstone. In appearance it is similar to Dartmoor, for it is exposed and treeless, but there are no tors on the summits of Exmoor. Neither Exmoor nor Dartmoor were covered by ice during the ice age, for the ice advances stopped short of the south-west peninsula. The shapes of the hills and valleys and the coverings of soils are the result of river erosion and weathering and this makes them different from the other main highland areas of Britain.

[1] W. G. V. Balchin: *Cornwall. The History of the Landscape*, Hodder and Stoughton 1954. p. 102.

111

Fig. 121   China clay quarries, St. Austell, Cornwall.

The Mendips, further north, are composed of Carboniferous limestone and many of the features which are found on a grander scale in the limestone parts of the Pennines are reproduced in this small hill range. Cheddar Gorge is the best known limestone feature in the country.

6. What is (a) an igneous rock, (b) a metamorphic rock? How are they different from sedimentary rocks? (See also p. 35).

7. What rock are the following highlands made of: (a) Dartmoor, (b) Exmoor, (c) Mendips? Are these igneous, metamorphic or sedimentary?

8. Sketch the photograph Fig. 121. Label: (a) waste heaps (b) pool at bottom of pit (c) section of pit which has not been used for a long time (d) route to top of pit (e) train carrying china clay.

9. Look at the divided circle showing land use in the South-west. (a) Where is most of the rough grazing? (b) What proportion of the land is used for permanent grass? (c) What other type of grass is grown?

10. Compare the two graphs for the South-west and East Anglia. (a) Why is there less rough grazing in East Anglia? (b) What advantages has East Anglia over the South-west for arable farming? (c) What 'other uses' of the land are there, which are not listed?

Fig. 123   Land use in the South-west.   Fig. 122   Land use in East Anglia.

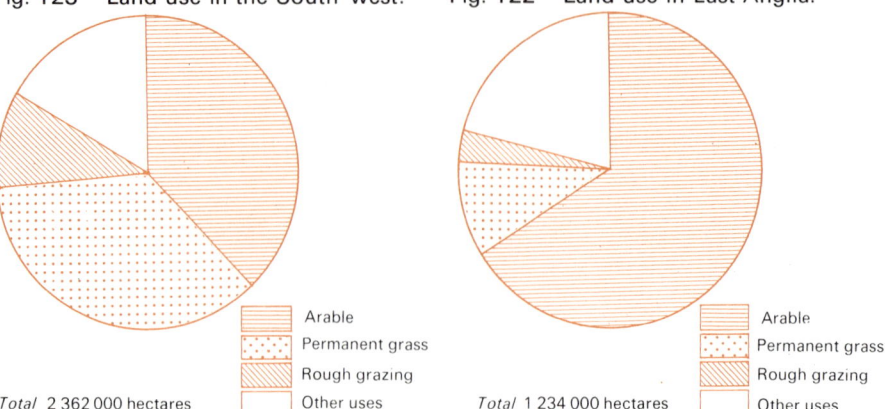

Arable
Permanent grass
Rough grazing
Other uses

Total 2 362 000 hectares

Arable
Permanent grass
Rough grazing
Other uses

Total 1 234 000 hectares

11. Draw a map called 'Land Use in the South-west'. Shade in different colours (appropriate ones) (a) Farmlands of the low plateau (b) Market gardening regions in the south (c) Moorlands above 180 m (d) Plain of Somerset. Add notes to your key to describe the farming of each region. Mark also two mining areas, and eight towns including seaside resorts, fishing ports, and large service centres.

12. Look at the map showing routeways (Fig. 114). How have they been affected by (a) the shape and (b) the relief of the peninsula?

13. Draw a sketch map, called 'Taunton, Gateway to the West'.

Bristol

North of the Mendips, outside the peninsula, but still in the region officially defined as the South-west, is the city of Bristol, with a population of nearly half a million.

Bristol has been an important seaport for many centuries. By 1400 it was the second seaport of England, trading with Ireland, the west coast of France, Spain and Portugal. Ships came up the 13 kilometres of river from the sea on the tide and were left on the mud to be unloaded as the tide ebbed. The main export was wool cloth from the thriving Cotswold wool textile industry.

With the discovery of America Bristol's position on the west side of the country, facing the Atlantic, was advantageous. It was the base chosen by a number of voyagers in the age of discovery, notably John Cabot, the discoverer of Newfoundland, who set sail from Bristol in 1497.

The seventeenth and eighteenth centuries were Bristol's time of greatest prosperity. Plantations in the West Indies and the colonies in Virginia sent sugar, rum and tobacco into the port of Bristol and tobacco processing and sugar refining were established in the city. In the nineteenth century cocoa was imported from West Africa and chocolate making began.

Bristol, like Liverpool, was involved in the three-cornered trade between Britain, West Africa and America. Slaves were carried across the Atlantic to the West Indies and to America; the ships returned to Bristol loaded with sugar, rum and tobacco, and left again for Africa with small cargoes of cloth, firearms and metal goods.

In 1807 slave trading was prohibited. The decline of the Cotswold wool industry reduced Bristol's exports and her trade began to decline. There was no large coalfield near Bristol to provide power for manufacturing industries and the port was too far away from the developing industrial areas in the north and midlands to serve them. Bristol lost ground to other, better situated ports, particularly to Liverpool.

Ships were larger and they found the 13 kilometres journey up river to Bristol difficult and the city docks inadequate. To remedy this the course of the Avon through Bristol was diverted and the old course made into a huge dock. This was an ambitious scheme but also an expensive one. To retrieve the money the city

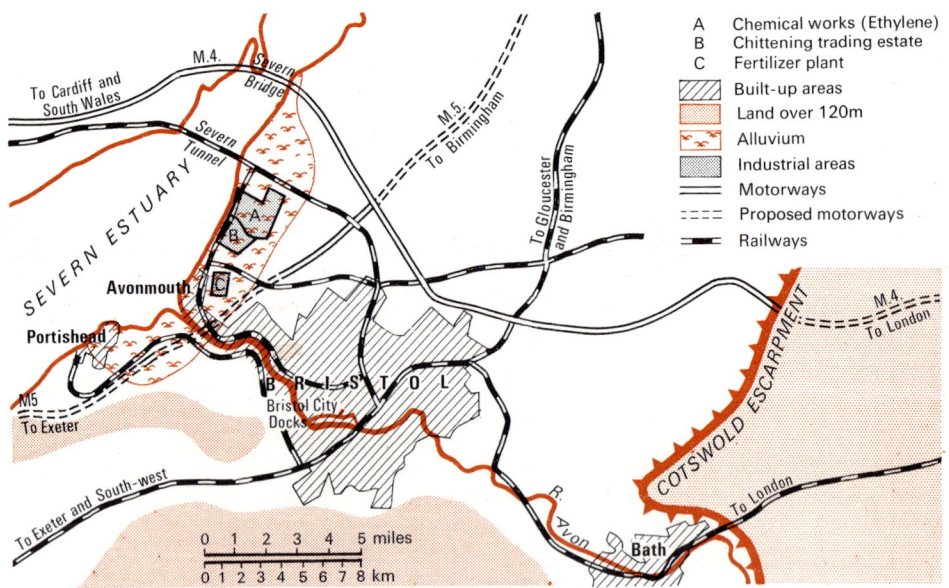

Fig. 124   Bristol and Severnside.

placed high dues on goods coming into the port, which only resulted in further losses of trade to other ports, where the goods were handled more cheaply.

In 1877 an outport was opened at Avonmouth, followed in 1879 by one at Portishead. The largest dock at Avonmouth was completed in 1908, and only small vessels travel up river to the city docks. As a port Bristol now ranks eleventh in Britain for total trade.[1]

As Bristol was not well situated for industrial development in the nineteenth century its old established industries of tobacco and chocolate making remain important. The aircraft industry and its associated engineering industries came to Bristol between the wars.

Bristol's position as a port and industrial city is likely to change considerably during the next decades. The Severn estuary, with its new road bridge, excellent motorway communications with London, South Wales and the Midlands and expanding port facilities, is likely to become an increasingly important industrial area. Along the banks of the Severn estuary are extensive areas of alluvium which have been avoided by settlement in the past because of their dampness. This provides building land close to the city of Bristol and the ports and is the site of new factories and industrial estates.

The biggest developments are two new I.C.I. chemical works. One plant imports its raw material through Avonmouth and manufactures fertilizers from it. The other plant is linked to the oil refinery at Fawley (Southampton) over 100 kilometres away by pipeline, through which ethylene, a by-product of oil-refining, is pumped. From ethylene this plant makes polythene and terylene. A plant for synthetic fibres

[1] See page 158.

114

has also been established at Brockworth, near Gloucester. There are large new nuclear power plants along the estuary. The Chittening trading estate has also been established in Avonmouth which will bring a greater diversity of industry to the area and trade to the port.

14. Why was the site for the Severn Bridge chosen? What advantage does it bring to the South-west? What other regions benefit? (Refer also to p. 183).

15. What advantages have the estuaries of Britain got for modern industrial developments?

16. Look at the table, p. 158, showing the trade of our leading ports. Why is Bristol at the bottom of the list?

Fig. 125 Bristol city docks. Find the location of the photograph on Fig. 124. Make a sketch of the photograph to show the old course of the Avon, now converted into a dock, and the new course of the Avon. Shade in the area mostly covered by warehouses and marshalling yards. Mark the lock gates at the main entrance to the dock, the swing bridge, and the main routeways.

9. The Pennines and the Surrounding Lowlands

The high hills of the Pennines are called the backbone of England, for they extend down the middle of the country from the northern borders to the Midlands. Some of the highest points are Cross Fell (893 m) Pen-y-Ghent (693 m) Ingleborough (723 m) and the Peak (636 m). Between the plateaux of the uplands there are long valleys called dales.

Use Figs. 127 and 142 and your atlas to answer the following:

1. How long is the hill range from the Scottish border to the Midlands?
2. What are the three main passes through the hills? Which of these is the highest?
3. Name the rivers which drain the hills (a) westwards (b) eastwards.
4. Draw a map to show that the Pennines are a watershed.
5. What types of rock are found at the sources of the rivers Coquet, Ure, Calder, Trent?
6. Name the types of rock you would cross on a straight route from (a) Lancaster to Newcastle (b) Preston to Sheffield.
7. The Eden valley is a fault line valley. What does this mean?
8. The south Pennines are an eroded anticline. What does this mean? Where in south England is there an eroded anticline? (Refer to p. 36).
9. State two differences between the rock which forms the Vale of York and the rock which forms the Pennines.
10. In what counties are Weardale, Wharfedale, Dovedale, the Peak District, the Lake District, the Cheviots?

Fig. 126   Geological sections through the Pennines: North Pennines, faulting.

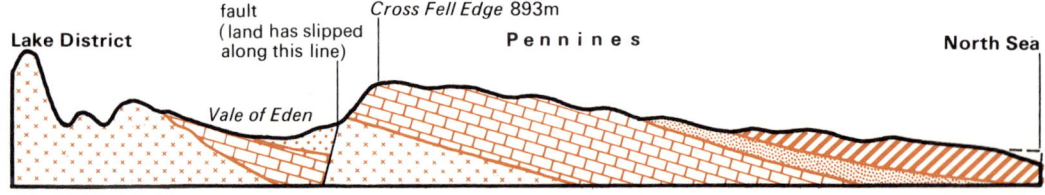

A fault is a deep crack in the rocks which form the earth's surface, along which the land has slipped. Like most mountain districts, the Pennines have been affected by faulting. The steep edge of Cross Fell, shown on the diagram, was formed when the land to the west slipped downwards. (see also ch. 15 page 237)

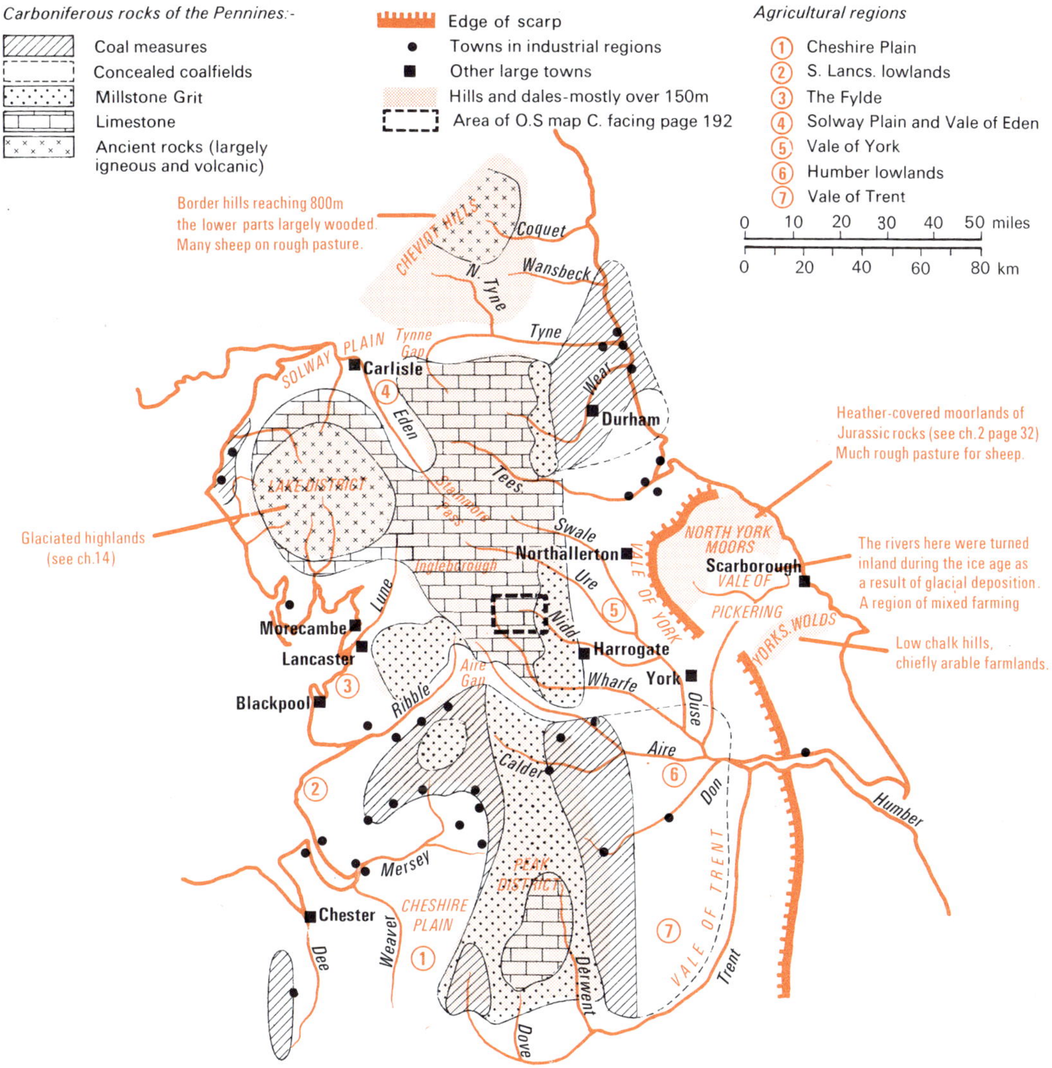

Carboniferous rocks of the Pennines:-

	Coal measures
	Concealed coalfields
	Millstone Grit
	Limestone
	Ancient rocks (largely igneous and volcanic)

Edge of scarp
● Towns in industrial regions
■ Other large towns
Hills and dales-mostly over 150m
Area of O.S map C. facing page 192

Agricultural regions

① Cheshire Plain
② S. Lancs. lowlands
③ The Fylde
④ Solway Plain and Vale of Eden
⑤ Vale of York
⑥ Humber lowlands
⑦ Vale of Trent

Border hills reaching 800m the lower parts largely wooded. Many sheep on rough pasture.

CHEVIOT HILLS
Coquet
Wansbeck
N. Tyne
Tyne
Tynne Gap
SOLWAY PLAIN
Carlisle
④
Eden
Durham
Wear
Tees

Heather-covered moorlands of Jurassic rocks (see ch.2 page 32) Much rough pasture for sheep.

LAKE DISTRICT
Glaciated highlands (see ch.14)
Ingleborough
Lune
Swale
Ure
Northallerton
NORTH YORK MOORS
Scarborough
VALE OF YORK
VALE OF PICKERING
YORKS. WOLDS

The rivers here were turned inland during the ice age as a result of glacial deposition. A region of mixed farming

Low chalk hills, chiefly arable farmlands.

Morecambe
Lancaster
Aire Gap
Ribble
Nidd
Harrogate
⑤
Wharfe
York
Ouse
③
Blackpool
Calder
②
Aire
⑥
Don
Mersey
PEAK DISTRICT
Chester
CHESHIRE PLAIN
①
Weaver
Derwent
Trent
Dee
Dove
⑦
VALE OF TRENT
Humber

Fig. 127   The Pennines and the surrounding lowlands.

Fig. 128   South Pennines, folding

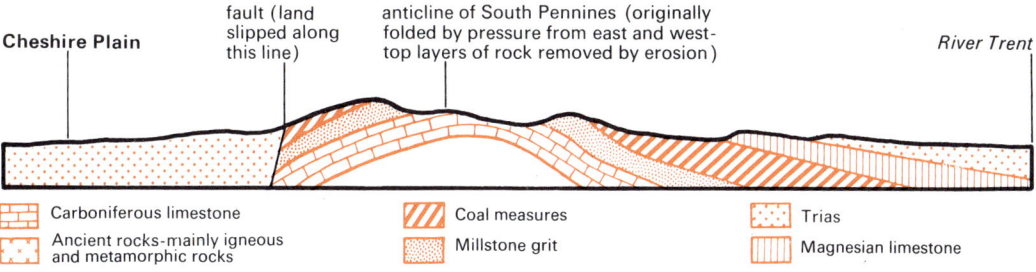

Cheshire Plain
fault (land slipped along this line)
anticline of South Pennines (originally folded by pressure from east and west-top layers of rock removed by erosion)
River Trent

Carboniferous limestone
Ancient rocks-mainly igneous and metamorphic rocks
Coal measures
Millstone grit
Trias
Magnesian limestone

The Pennines are composed of Carboniferous rocks. The name 'Carboniferous' is given to the age in geological history when these sedimentary rocks were being formed. It does not imply that all of them contain carbon or coal deposits. Carboniferous rocks are older than any of the rocks of the scarplands. The Coal Measures are found on the edges of the Pennines. Most of the higher ground is composed of either Carboniferous limestone or Millstone Grit. These two rocks give rise to very different scenery.

Scenery of the limestone

Fig. 127 shows that the limestone is found throughout most of the north Pennines and in part of the south Pennines. The scenery of limestone is distinctive and easy to recognize, and it has developed because of two special properties of limestone:
1. Limestone is soluble in rain-water.
2. There are many cracks in the rock called 'joints'.

When rain-water falls on to limestone, it flows over the surface until it finds its way down the joints. Because of the numerous joints, limestone is highly permeable, and the water flows away underground through a complex system of channels and passages. The water swirling away underground hollows out the rock along its route by dissolving it, so that many of the most striking features of limestone are never seen except by pot-holers exploring the intricate passageways with torches.

Fig. 129 shows some of the underground features of limestone. The pot-holes or swallow holes lead to the underground drainage system. They are deep pits in the surface, often big enough for a man to climb down. Gaping Ghyll hole, near Ingleborough, is 110 m deep. The pot-holes are formed from joints which grow wider as rain-water and streams continuously flow down them.

Underground, the water channels become larger until they form caves. Some of the caves are high, but others are low tunnels running more or less at a level along the layers of rock. Pot-holers often have to squeeze their way along the tunnels on their stomachs before reaching the next high roofed cavern. Caves are believed to form along the water table (see p. 27). The fact that caves are found at different

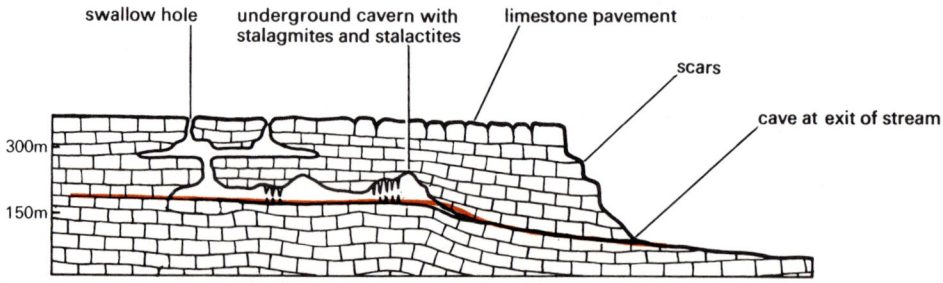

Fig. 129 Underground features of carboniferous limestone scenery.

Fig. 130   Limestone pavement, Ingleborough.

Fig. 131   A pothole near Ingleborough.

levels suggests that at other times the level of the water table has been different. In the caves there are often pinnacles of hardened lime (stalagmites and stalactites) growing from the floor and roof where water has dripped through. When the underground water reaches the water table it cannot sink any lower. It emerges from the rock on the valley side. Sometimes a river pours out from a cave.

Because the water flows away underground, the surface of the limestone is dry. Most of the limestone is covered with shallow soil, but in places the surface is formed of bare rock which is pitted with hollows and grooves making it difficult to walk over. The picture above shows this 'limestone pavement'. The hollows have been formed by solution of limestone along the joints.

119

Fig. 132   The Dib, Conistone, a dry valley south of Kettlewell. Find the valley on Ordnance Survey Map C, facing p. 192. (G.R. 9867.) Draw a sketch of the photograph and label precipitous slopes, scree, scree fixed by grass.

Fig. 133   Deepdale in Derbyshire, a famous valley formed in limestone. How is this valley different from the one shown in Fig. 132? How are the two valleys alike? Compare this picture with Fig. 137.

120

Fig. 134   The Westmorland borders between Brough and Bowes. This is part of the limestone plateau where there is little bare rock and less obvious limestone features, although the dry valleys, stepped surfaces, stone walls, isolated stone farmhouses and rough grazing all suggest limestone country.

Where the valleys are deep enough to reach the water table, there are streams; the Pennines are famous for their beautiful dales and rivers—Dovedale, Wharfedale, Wensleydale. But many of the valleys, especially on the plateau, are dry. The picture opposite shows a dry valley in the Kettlewell district. It is very different from a dry valley in chalk country. The bare white rock stands out precipitously on the valley sides. The rock is loosened by frost, and loose scree tumbles down. Grass eventually grows on the scree slopes. A profile across the valley shows steps on the valley sides. Along the sides of the main valleys, too, edges of harder rock form long ledges called 'scars'.

It is not completely understood how the dry valleys were formed, but probably continued solution along joints and the collapse of cave roofs both helped to make these gorge-like valleys.

The features of limestone country—swallow holes, caves, gorges, limestone pavements, precipitous slopes of bare white rocks—are better developed and more obvious in some places than in others. The country around Ingleborough is a splendid example of limestone scenery. In other places, the limestone is part of a large plateau where grass grows and sheep graze and where the fields are divided by rough stone walls.

Apart from its use as grazing ground, the limestone is also used as a building and road stone; and for the manufacture of lime and cement. In the past the veins of lead and other minerals which occurred in it were mined. Deep man-made ditches where the lead was dug out of the ground sometimes extend for half a mile over the surface. They are called lead rakes. Explorers of minerals discovered many of the best known caverns in the limestone country, and man-made tunnels in places lead to the natural underground caves.

Scenery of the Millstone Grit

The largest areas of Millstone Grit are found in the south Pennines. The grit differs in many ways from limestone. Carboniferous limestone is more or less the same in composition throughout hundreds of feet of thickness; but Millstone Grit is a general and rather misleading name given to layers of different kinds of rock. Some of the layers are a hard, dark, gritty sandstone which made an excellent grindstone—hence the name 'millstone grit'; others, are finer sandstones or flagstones. But some of the layers are a much softer rock called shale (formed of compressed muds).

In the Millstone Grit country the high plateaux are formed of grit, but underneath there are layers of shale. One of the best known grit-stone plateaux is Kinderscout—'The Peak' of the Derbyshire Peak District (Fig. 137).

Kinderscout is 610 m high, and 3 to 8 kilometres across. The top is completely flat except for a few isolated jutting out rocks, rather like the tors of Dartmoor,

Fig. 135 Mam Tor, the shivering mountain, is immediately south of Edale Valley, and is composed of shale and grit. Compare the photograph with Fig. 136. The long ridge stretching away from the bare rock face is the same as the ridge on the south of the diagram. Write a description of the differences between the valley and the hill slopes in this photograph.

which have managed to resist erosion. On this flat land the water does not drain away easily, so that the whole surface is covered with peat bog. The peat bog, about 2 m in depth, is black and hummocky, pitted with pools and hollows. It is easy to get lost on this wild featureless plateau.

At the edges of the plateau, streams cut deep gullies. They are constantly cutting their headwaters back into the grit, which breaks off in blocks and falls into the stream beds. The stream beds are strewn with rocks. Between the plateaux of grit there are valleys eroded in the weaker shales, like the one shown in the picture.

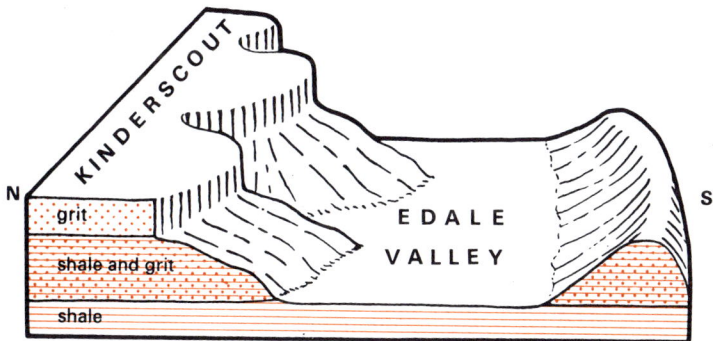

Fig. 136   Diagrammatic sketch to show rocks and scenery in the Peak District, Kinderscout and Edale valley, north of Castleton in Derbyshire.

Fig. 137   Grinds Brook valley at the edge of Kinderscout. There are heavy boulders in the stream bed. The stream has cut a deep valley in the edge of the plateau. In the background, the level summit of Kinderscout can be seen.

Farming is almost impossible on the high peat moors of the Millstone Grit. The lower moors are covered with heather and on these moors sheep graze. But the only use of much of the high moorland is for grouse shooting. In the Millstone Grit country, also, many reservoirs have been built. The water is soft, for it collects no lime on the sandstone, and it supplies the cities on the edges of the hills. The demand for water is growing continuously, as more is used in homes and in industries. There are schemes to flood more of the Millstone Grit valleys in the future.

Over most of the Pennines the landscape is one of limestone or grit moorlands. The type of rock has been important in deciding what the scenery looks like. The work of running water has also influenced the scenery here as everywhere else, both by creating the peculiarities of the limestone country, and by carving the broad green dales so characteristic of the northern hills.

Some of the valleys had glaciers moving down them during the Ice Age. The glaciers helped to straighten the valleys, and make them lower than they would otherwise have been. Boulder clay covers much of the lowlands, sometimes moulded into groups of low hillocks called drumlins. There are many drumlins in the vale of Eden and in the Ribble valley.

One striking feature of the landscape which crosses much of the Pennines is the Whin Sill. A thick layer of igneous rock, called a sill, has been pushed between layers of sedimentary rock over a very large area. Whin Sill can be picked out as a ridge running over the plateau for kilometres, and it continues to the Farne Islands off the Northumberland coast. The hard upstanding rock was excellent for defence, and Hadrian's Wall and Bamburgh Castle both made use of it.

The Kettlewell District

Ordnance Survey Map C, facing p. 192 shows part of Wharfedale in the Yorkshire Dales. Fig. 139 is a simplified geological map of the district. Both Carboniferous limestone and Millstone Grit scenery are shown on the map.

Some special features of the map need explaining: 'moss' means peat bog; 'featherbed moss' refers to cotton grass; 'allotments' refer to nineteenth century enclosures of fields. The course of streams, little lakes, and dams in the south-east corner show that the drainage has been altered by man. This happened when lead was mined in the district. Rushes of water were used to wash away surface covering and expose lead veins.

The little black squares dotted throughout Wharfedale mark stone barns, formerly used for storing hay and for winter feeding of cattle. Many of these have now fallen into disuse; others have been converted into modern cowsheds.

Use Ordnance Survey Map C, facing p. 192 to answer the following:

11. Compare Fig. 139 with the map. (a) Describe the relief and drainage of the Millstone Grit country (b) Name four uses, past or present, to which this country is put. Give evidence from the map.

124

Fig. 138   The village of Kettlewell, in Wharfedale, about 50 km north-west of Leeds.

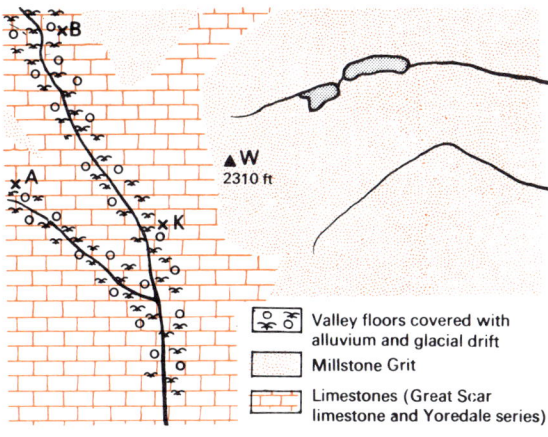

Fig. 139   Geology of the Kettlewell district on a third of the scale of Ordnance Survey Map C, facing p. 192.

▲W
2310 ft

Valley floors covered with alluvium and glacial drift

Millstone Grit

Limestones (Great Scar limestone and Yoredale series)

12. What evidence is there on the map that most of the western part is limestone country? List as many features as you can, giving either names or grid references from the map.

13. Compare Fig. 138 with the map. Find on the map the two valleys in the background of the picture, the plain of the river Wharfe, the limestone scar in the right of the picture. Give a six-figure grid reference for the point the picture was taken from.

125

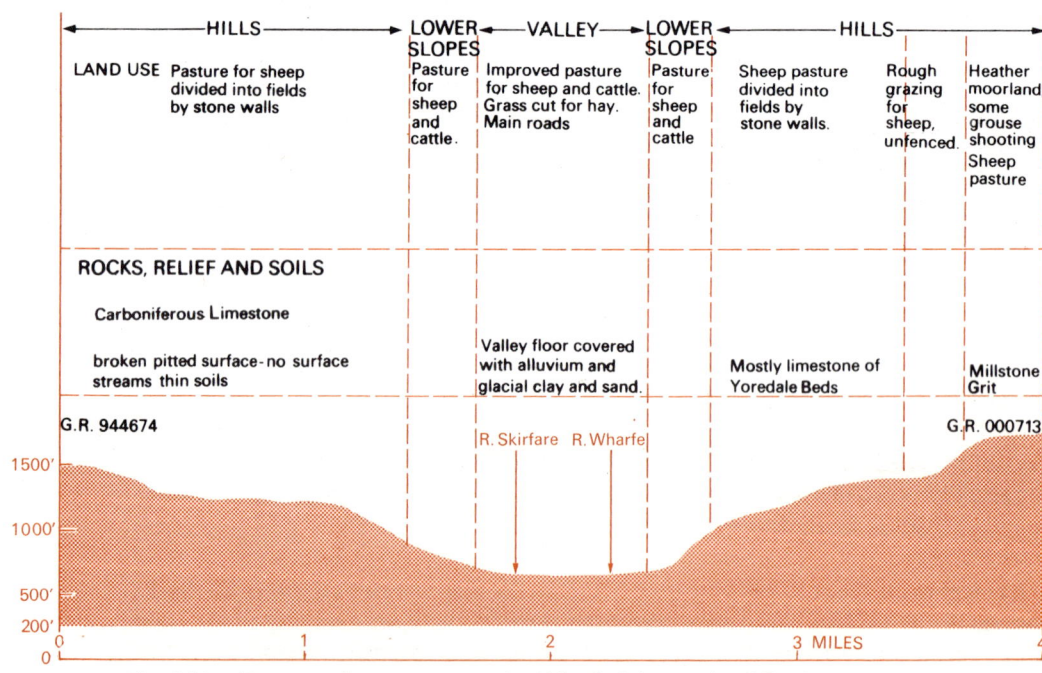

Fig. 140 Wharfedale, south of Kettlewell.

←————HILLS————→	LOWER SLOPES	←—VALLEY—→	LOWER SLOPES	←————HILLS————→		
LAND USE Pasture for sheep divided into fields by stone walls	Pasture for sheep and cattle.	Improved pasture for sheep and cattle. Grass cut for hay. Main roads	Pasture for sheep and cattle	Sheep pasture divided into fields by stone walls.	Rough grazing for sheep, unfenced.	Heather moorland, some grouse shooting Sheep pasture

ROCKS, RELIEF AND SOILS

Carboniferous Limestone

broken pitted surface- no surface streams thin soils

Valley floor covered with alluvium and glacial clay and sand.

Mostly limestone of Yoredale Beds

Millstone Grit

G.R. 944674

G.R. 000713

R. Skirfare   R. Wharfe

1500'

1000'

500'

200'
0

0   1   2   3 MILES   4

Fig. 141 Transect diagram across the Wharfedale, north of Conistone.

126

14. Compare Fig. 140 with the map. This view was taken south of Kettlewell. Which way was the camera pointing? Name the large wood on the opposite side of the valley. How high is the level summit in the background? How high is the lowest land shown?

15. All the farms are built in the villages, rather than scattered over the country. Suggest reasons for this distribution.

16. Describe the distribution of woodland.

17. Where do parish boundaries follow the tops of hills or watersheds?

Nearly all of the Pennine hills and valleys are used for farming, chiefly for rearing sheep and cattle. Fig. 141 shows the use of land at different levels in Wharfedale. Each farmer usually owns a variety of land at different levels.

The heather pastures on the high moors are used for sheep. They can feed here when the grass is covered with snow. Sheep and cattle are raised on the lower slopes of the hills, and in the valleys. Cattle are raised both for beef and dairying. With improved roads and lorry transport it is now possible to market milk fairly easily. The climate on the hills is cool and wet. Over 1000 mm of rain falls everywhere, and in many places the figure is over 1500 mm. It is difficult to grow crops. There is hardly any arable farming, although grass is cut for hay.

In parts of the Pennines, and particularly in the hills north of the Tyne Gap, plantations of coniferous trees cover the slopes between about 200 and 360 m. The largest area of continuous woodland in Britain is found here. These slopes were originally wooded with deciduous trees like birch and ash. But over the centuries the forests were felled by man, and sheep pastures took their place. The new trees, replacing the sheep pastures, are mostly spruce and pine, and most of the planting has been done by the Forestry Commission since World War I. New villages have been built in some of the plantations for forestry workers.

On either side of the Pennines are areas of lowland which are marked on Fig. 127 They form the best farmlands of northern England.

18. Find the lowlands numbered on Fig. 127. Which lowlands are separated (a) by hills (b) by long estuaries? How long is the lowland which stretches from the Tees to Nottingham?

19. Draw a map to show northern England, the 150 m contour, six rivers and the lowland areas numbered on Fig. 127. Read the following description of farming in these lowlands, and add notes beside your map about each region.

The western lowlands are wetter than the eastern, and dairying is the main type of farming in the Vale of Eden and in the lowlands around Morecambe Bay. Wheat does not grow well here, and oats and potatoes are the chief arable crops.

In spite of the large built-up areas and the network of roads and railways, the plains of south Lancashire (Region 2 on Fig. 127) form one of the richest and most

127

intensively farmed regions of Britain. There is much dairying, although it is not so dominant as in the Cumberland lowlands and north Lancashire. Poultry and pigs are also kept. But most of the available land is used for crops. Enormous quantities of vegetables and potatoes are grown to supply the towns within this countryside.

East of the Pennines, there is a large lowland which extends from the Tees to Nottingham. The climate here is much drier than it is west of the Pennines, with less than 750 mm of rain in most parts. There is therefore much more arable farming in the east than there is in the west.

However, this is really a region of mixed farming, for the soils vary a great deal locally. Some are heavy boulder clay; some are wet alluvial soils; some are poor glacial sands which have been artificially improved. Nearly all the land can be farmed. Cattle are raised on the wetter soils; wheat and barley are grown on the better drained soils; sugar beet and potatoes are grown on the improved sands.

On a generalized farming map, the Vale of York looks like an extension of East Anglia and Lincolnshire: the land is intensively used; there is both livestock and arable farming, but of the two, arable farming is generally more important.

At the head of the Humber estuary is a region where farming is almost as intensive and as concentrated as it is in south Lancashire. This region is also close to industrial towns, and vegetables are grown to supply the markets of the Yorkshire West Riding towns.

The Vale of Trent is part of the East Midlands. The raising of beef cattle, particularly the fattening of cattle for the market, and arable farming are the main farming activities.

There are enormous areas of land in northern England which are rural—rich farmlands throughout the Vale of York, empty hills which provide beautiful scenery for visitors from the northern cities, including Britain's first National Park—the Derbyshire Peak District. In the rural districts there are few large towns—the county towns of York and Lancaster are small compared with, say, Manchester or Leeds; there are many market towns or seaside resorts. But most of the people of northern England live in the industrial districts which are described in the next chapter. The rural north is the background against which the industrial north has grown.

20. Read the account of Carlisle below, then draw a map to show its position as a border town.

Carlisle (72 000) is the largest town of the lowlands around the Solway Firth. It grew up on the border between Scotland and England. A Roman fort was built here on Hadrian's wall. Later a mediaeval castle was built to guard the route between England and Scotland.

Carlisle lies at the lowest crossing point of the river Eden and at the head of Solway Firth. Routes from both south and north focus on the city—from the south, via the Eden and Petterill river valleys and along the west coast; and from the north, along the rivers Nith and Annan, from Glasgow, and along the river Liddell, from Edinburgh. There is also a coastal route from Stranraer. East of Carlisle is the Tyne Gap, which forms the only break in the northern part of the Pennines, and which gives an easy east-west route to Newcastle.

Because of this position Carlisle became a railway junction in the mid-nineteenth century, and is still a major rail centre with fully automated goods yards. It is also a manufacturing town, and has engineering (vehicles, cranes, metal boxes) and biscuit making industries. Its main function, however, is as a service centre for the surrounding region.

21. Use the information given below and the maps in this book to draw a sketch map of either York or Lancaster.

York	Lancaster
In centre of broad vale between Yorkshire Wolds and Pennines. On crossing point of river Ouse where a low ridge of moraine lies across the vale, so there are low hills beside the river. Was England's second city in mediaeval times, and a great wool market, and is still the seat of the Archbishop of the northern ecclesiastical province. In nineteenth century it became a major railway junction, and is today a focus of road and rail routes and a market town. University is now established. York is the headquarters of Eastern Region British railways. Manufactures include railway carriages and chocolate (Rowntrees and Terrys).	Near mouth of river Lune where it is still tidal, and where a hill is close to the river. Was a small port, flourished in eighteenth century with West Indian trade, and was county town of Lancashire. Today is market town serving the rural lowlands of north Lancashire, and a manufacturing town. University is now established. Industries include the making of linoleum and plastic floor coverings, and synthetic fibres. Also brewing, animal feed-stuffs, and engineering.

10. Industries of the North

On either side of the Pennines are found the industrial towns where most of the people of northern England live. Most of these towns grew enormously during the nineteenth century, and a number of them eventually formed huge conurbations. A conurbation is a large built-up area formed when several towns spread and join together, or when one large town absorbs all the neighbouring smaller ones. The conurbations of the North are shown on Fig. 142. They have grown around Liverpool, Manchester, Newcastle, Middlesbrough and in the Yorkshire West Riding between Leeds and Huddersfield.

The predominant industries of the North in the nineteenth century were coal-mining, iron and steel, railway and ship building, textiles and engineering. As these industries grew, they provided work for thousands of people, so that the towns

Fig. 142   Industrial towns of the North.

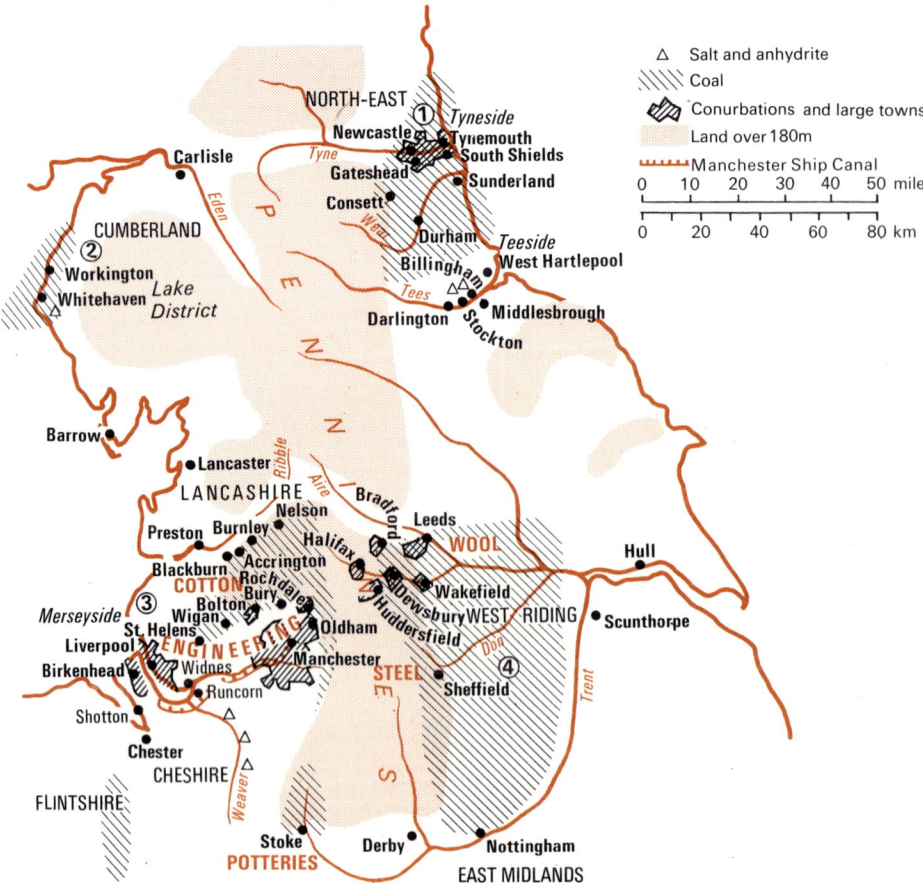

grew too. Manufacturing industry and trade increased all through the nineteenth century and the industrial North became even more productive. It was the part of the country which produced the largest share of the manufactured goods needed at home; these goods were also sold abroad to pay for growing imports of food and raw materials. This growth and prosperity reached a peak in the early years of the twentieth century.

However these basic industries suffered severely between the two world wars, when there was a long-drawn-out economic depression. Thousands of people became unemployed, and the worst hit regions, Merseyside, the North-east and West Cumberland became known as 'depressed areas'.

In the last century manufacturers built their factories where there were natural advantages such as water supply, a coal-field, or easy transport. Today there is another major influence on the location of new factories; the growth of new industry is largely controlled by various government departments. The change towards planned development has been gradual, starting in the mid-1930s. The government gained more control over industrial development during World War II. The depressed areas have been renamed 'development areas', and in 1964 the country was divided into a number of economic planning regions shown on the map below. One of the aims of economic planning is to see that the development areas have

Fig. 143 Economic planning regions.

131

their share of new factories, especially in growing industries such as electrical engineering and vehicles.

It is largely as a result of official encouragement, by government departments and local authorities, that new factories have been built in the North, especially in areas where there has been much unemployment. The new manufacturing industries have given the whole region much more variety than it had before, and the development areas are now again more prosperous. But many problems still remain. Nearly every northern town has gone a long way with rebuilding and slum clearance, and their appearance is changing rapidly as new blocks of flats and shops are put up and open spaces made, but the story of their industrial past can still be read in old factories, poor housing, abandoned mines and overgrown canals and railway tracks.

Coal Mining

It was wealth in coal which made it possible for the North to develop so vigorously during the industrial revolution. The most important coalfields are the North-east (Northumberland and Durham) and the Yorkshire-Derby-Nottingham (Yorks-Derby-Notts.). Some coal is also worked in south Lancashire and a little in Cumberland, at Whitehaven and near Workington.

The rocks known as Coal Measures are not composed entirely of coal. The Coal Measures near Sheffield, for example, are over 1500 m thick; but the coal itself is found in forty separate seams, the thickest of which are only about 2 m. The coal seams originated early in geological times (Carboniferous) when the land was covered with dense forest. From time to time the forests were submerged by the sea, and were buried under layers of mud and sand. This compressed the vegetation which gradually became coal. During the time Coal Measures were being formed, this process occurred many times.

The layers of coal are not horizontal, for they have been tilted by later movements of the earth's crust. The North-east and Yorks-Derby-Notts. coalfields dip gently down towards the east so that in the east other rocks lie on top of the Coal Measures. See Fig. 128 p. 117. This eastern part is called the concealed coalfield. The western part, where the Coal Measures reach the surface, is called the exposed coalfield. When mining began it was easier to mine the exposed coalfield, where the coal is nearer the surface, and can even be quarried. But most of the best coal has now been worked out, so it is no longer profitable to mine coal over much of the exposed coalfield. In some places, such as west Durham, the mining villages are decaying; the pits are closed.

The concealed coalfields, however, now produce a great deal of coal. The Yorks-Derby-Notts. coalfield is the one which has most increased its output during this century. This coalfield has large reserves because it extends so far eastwards under other rocks. Many of the seams are thick, and are unbroken by faults, so they can be worked easily. Their main disadvantage is that they are deep,

Fig. 144   Kellingley, Yorkshire, a few miles east of Leeds. This is a new mine, built on the flat land east of the Pennines. Find the railway.

often more than 900 m below ground level, which makes mining more dangerous. The chief hazards are collapsed roofs, gas and fire.

Many changes are taking place in the mining industry today. The move from the exposed to the concealed coalfields is one of them. Efficiency of the mines is being increased: pits which no longer produce enough coal to make them pay are being closed down; and machinery is being installed so that each miner can produce more coal. The mines are now highly mechanised. In 1947, less than 3 per cent of the coal was mechanically cut, but today the figure is over 80 per cent. At the pit head, there are coal washing plants because mechanically cut coal tends to contain a great deal of waste; and so does coal cut from the thinner seams. There are fewer miners today, but the output of coal per man is greater.

There is also a change in the look of the mining town. The winding shaft, the spoil heaps, the closely packed cottages at the pit head can still be seen. But new mining towns built on the concealed coalfields are different. An example is Kellingley in Yorkshire. Here is a large mine where 3000 men work. The village is built away from the mine. The waste from the mine is being dumped in an old quarry nearby. When this is full, it may be possible to stack the waste back in the spaces left by the coal, although this still costs too much. At the pit head there is a coal washing plant and a plant for the manufacture of tar and coke.

133

Some of the mining is opencast. The coal is cut from the surface, so no shafts are dug. About 7 million tonnes a year come from opencast mines. They became a major source of coal during World War II, because coal could be mined quickly and cheaply with mechanised diggers, although the seams are quickly worked out.

Fig. 147 shows that Britain produces much less coal today than in 1913. One of the main reasons for the decline is that coal exports have dwindled. In 1923 97 million tonnes of coal were exported; in 1966 the figure was less than 3 million. The countries to which we used to export, such as Sweden or Argentina, have now developed their own supplies of coal, oil, or hydro-electricity and no longer need our coal. Moreover, ships and railways no longer need coal as they are nearly all driven by oil or electricity.

A great deal of coal, however, is still needed in Britain. The total amount consumed in the country is almost as great as it was in 1923. The population has grown, and more power is used in homes and factories than ever before. There has been a striking change in the way the coal is used, for a large amount is now converted into gas and electricity. More than 90 per cent of the electricity generated is thermal electricity, and is produced in stations powered by coal. Electricity is then sent as power to homes and factories through the grid system.

Fig. 145 Opencast coal mining at Wid-drington, Northumberland. Find the coal seam at the bottom right. Why is opencast mining often cheaper? What great disadvantage is there in opencast mining?

Fig. 146 Calder Hall nuclear power station, Cumberland. Find Calder Hall on Fig. 148. This was the first nuclear power station in the world to produce electricity on a full commercial scale. It was opened in October 1956, and supplies electricity to the national grid. Large quantities of water and a fairly remote position are the main needs for a nuclear power station.

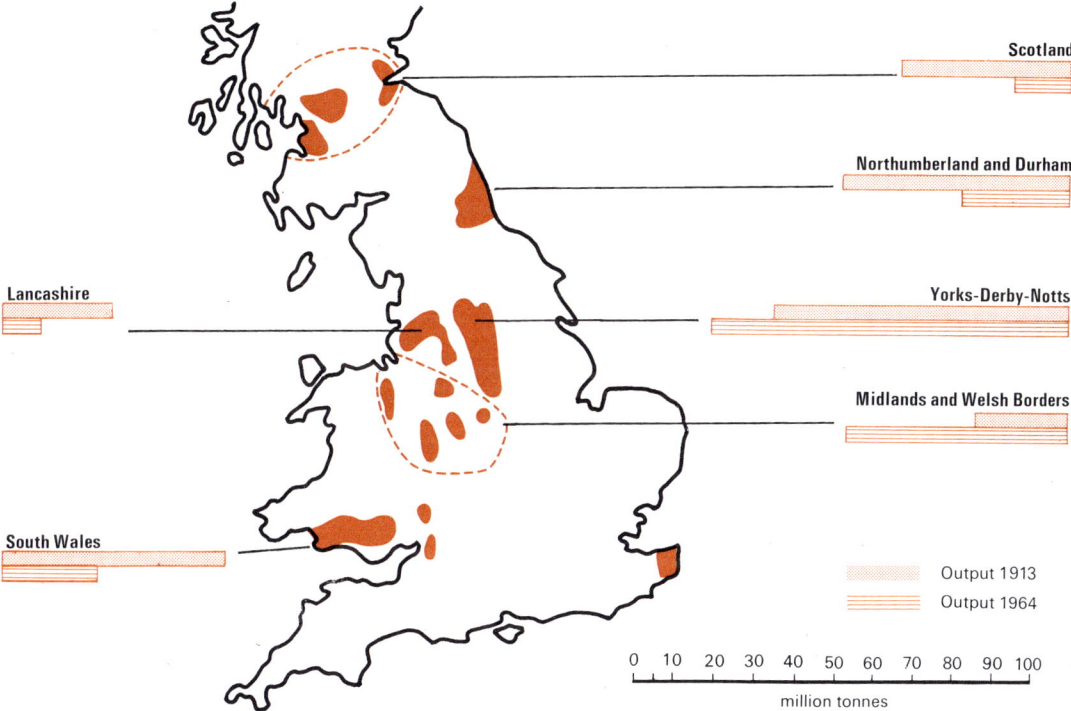

Fig. 147   Output of major coalfields in 1913 and 1964.

During the industrial revolution, coal was used to make steam power, and this was the main form of power used to drive the machinery. In the nineteenth century, industries gradually moved away from sources of water power such as the Pennine streams, and were built on the coalfields. Because the North was so rich in coal, industry flourished and the towns grew rapidly. But power can now be carried cheaply over long distances through the electric grid, and during the twentieth century industries have grown away from the coalfields. The most prosperous industrial regions in this century are now the South-east and the Midlands, and not the northern coalfields.

Coal is still one of Britain's most valuable resources, but it is not so important as it was. Hydro-electricity is confined to a few highland areas, but oil, natural gas, and nuclear reactors supply an increasingly important share of the power used.

1. Use Fig. 142 to draw a map of the North of England to show the coalfields. Shade the coalfields. Add a bar beside each to show how much coal it produces. Use Fig. 147 to get the correct length of the bar.

2. Using Fig. 147, describe the change which took place (a) in the total amount of coal produced in 1913–1964 (b) in the output of the three northern coalfields 1913–1964. List the main reasons for the change.

135

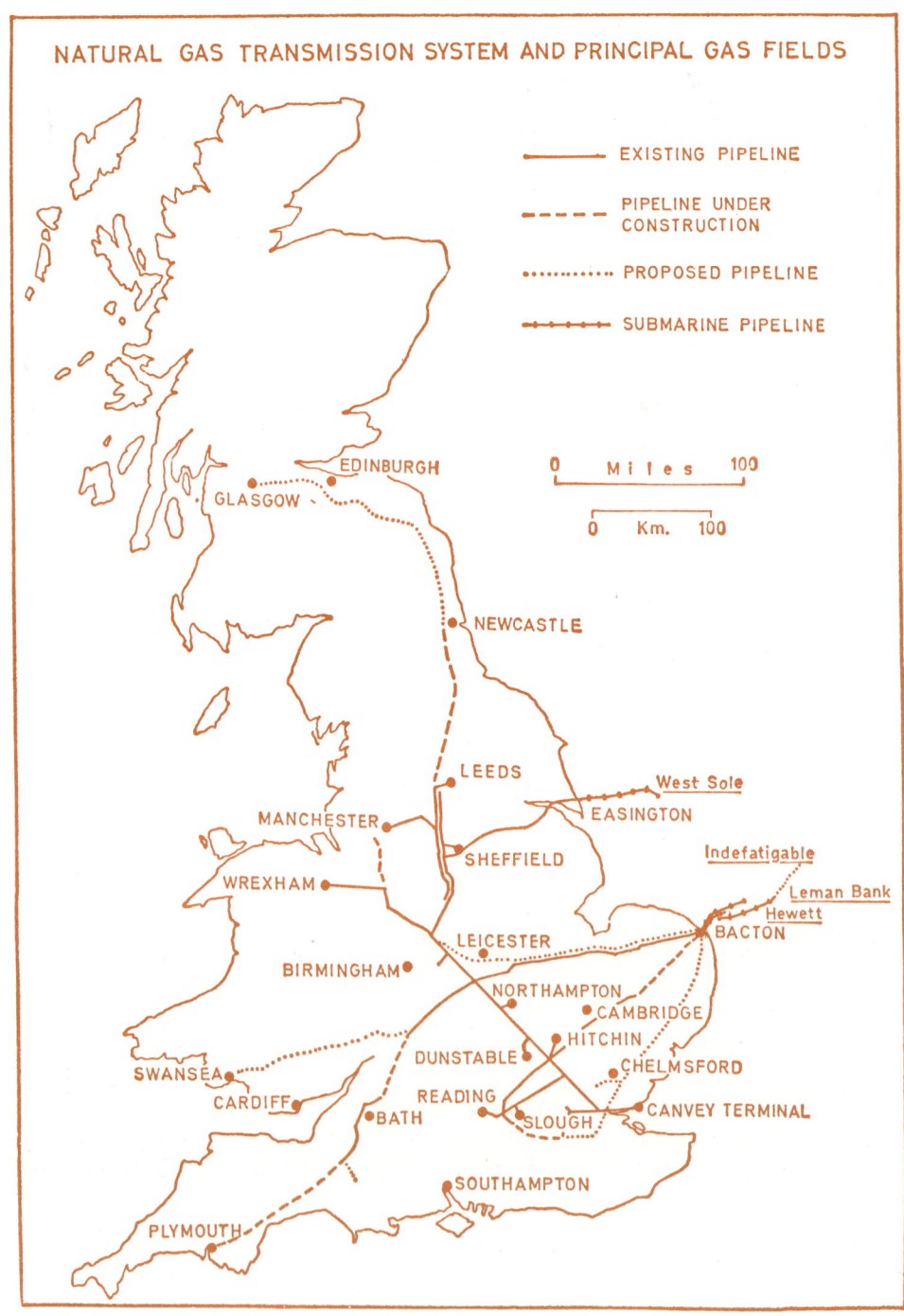

NATURAL GAS TRANSMISSION SYSTEM AND PRINCIPAL GAS FIELDS

EXISTING PIPELINE

PIPELINE UNDER CONSTRUCTION

PROPOSED PIPELINE

SUBMARINE PIPELINE

0   Miles   100

0   Km.   100

EDINBURGH
GLASGOW
NEWCASTLE
LEEDS
West Sole
MANCHESTER
EASINGTON
SHEFFIELD
Indefatigable
WREXHAM
Leman Bank
Hewett
BACTON
LEICESTER
BIRMINGHAM
NORTHAMPTON
CAMBRIDGE
HITCHIN
DUNSTABLE
CHELMSFORD
SWANSEA
READING
CANVEY TERMINAL
CARDIFF
BATH
SLOUGH
SOUTHAMPTON
PLYMOUTH

10. INDUSTRIES OF THE NORTH

3. Using Fig. 149, describe the main changes which took place in the use of fuel and power between 1923 and 1966.

4. Study the table below. What does it show about post-war changes in the coal mining industry?

	Numbers employed in mining		Output per man shift in thousand tonnes	
	1954	1966	1954	1966
North-east	143 000	81 000	1·11	1·58
Yorkshire	139 000	99 000	1·39	1·94
East Midlands	100 000	77 000	1·88	2·58
North-west	64 000	32 000	1·11	1·49

5. Write paragraphs under the headings: Formation of coal; Exposed and concealed coalfields.

6. What arguments can be used for and against (a) cutting down on coal and increasing the use of other sources of power (b) building more nuclear power stations.

Heavy iron and steel industry

Coal mining and the iron and steel industry were the two basic industries of nineteenth century Britain. Coal provided power, and iron and steel provided the raw materials from which machinery was made. Today, South Wales produces more steel than any other region, so the iron and steel industry is described in more detail in Chapter 12, pp. 177 to 181.

But there are several major centres of the iron and steel industry in northern England, as the map on page 180 shows. Some of the works, like those at Shotton in Cheshire and Consett in Durham, are vast, solitary integrated iron and steel works. In Sheffield and Teesside, there are several iron and steel works, large and small, among a variety of other industries.

The iron making industry is an ancient one. With the growth of steel making, the industry grew enormously during the nineteenth century. Its development is illustrated by two very different cities—Sheffield and Middlesbrough.

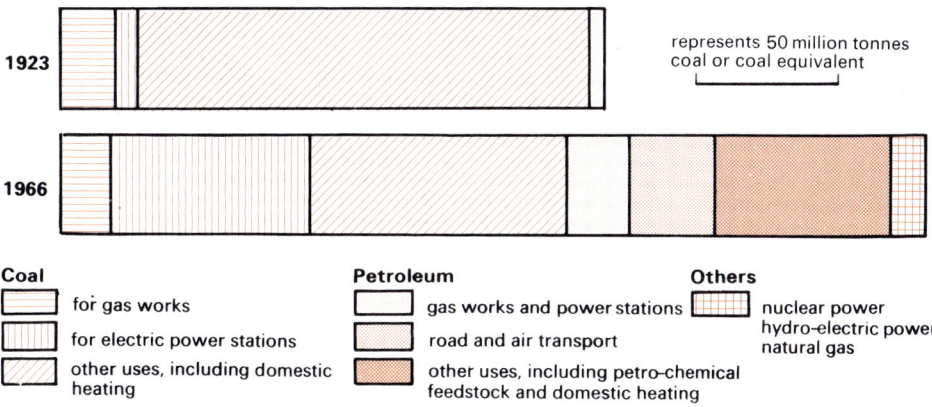

Fig. 149   The sources of fuel and power used in the United Kingdom.

Sheffield

Sheffield has been associated with iron for centuries. Cutlery was made there in the twelfth century, and Sheffield knives were famous in Chaucer's time. Originally iron was smelted with charcoal. Where there were woodlands and ore-bearing rocks, there were charcoal burners and iron smelters. The main iron producing regions up to the eighteenth century were the Weald, the Forest of Dean, and Charnwood Forest as well as Sheffield. Early in the eighteenth century coal began to replace charcoal. Coke was first used to smelt iron at Coalbrookdale in Shropshire early in the eighteenth century. After this, iron works which were not near a coalfield were at a great disadvantage, and gradually closed down.

Sheffield had several early advantages for an iron industry but the two most important were: 1. water power from the Pennine streams, which worked the bellows for forges; and 2. the supplies of qood quality iron ore in bands of the Coal Measures.

Today, Sheffield is famous for steel rather than iron. It was in Sheffield that the first good quality steel was made. Steel is tougher and more malleable than iron. In 1740, Joseph Huntsman, a Sheffield clock maker, invented a method of making steel in a clay container which could withstand the very high temperatures reached as the impurities were driven out of the iron. Huntsman wanted the steel for clock springs, but it could also be used to make a fine cutting edge.

Huntsman's steel was expensive. In 1856 a much cheaper method of making steel was invented by Bessemer, who built his first furnace in Sheffield. It became possible to produce steel cheaply and in large quantities. Steel, rather than iron,

Fig. 150 Sheffield, once known as a dark city in a golden frame. Even in this picture the edge of the Pennines can be seen. There is still red smoke from the smelting works in the valley, but bold new planning is altering the appearance of the city.

could then be used to make railway locomotives and lines, ships and machinery, and was therefore in great demand. The growth of the steel industry made fortunes for many men of Sheffield.

At the turn of the nineteenth century, alloy steels were first made, and it is for

Fig. 151 Steel making in the 1860s by the Bessemer process, invented in Sheffield. In the centre molten iron is being poured into a converter on the left, where it is made into steel. The molten iron is heated to very high temperatures and the impurities are driven out. The converter on the right is 'blowing', flames from the molten iron inside are shooting out. When ready, this is poured out into the ingots arranged in the centre.

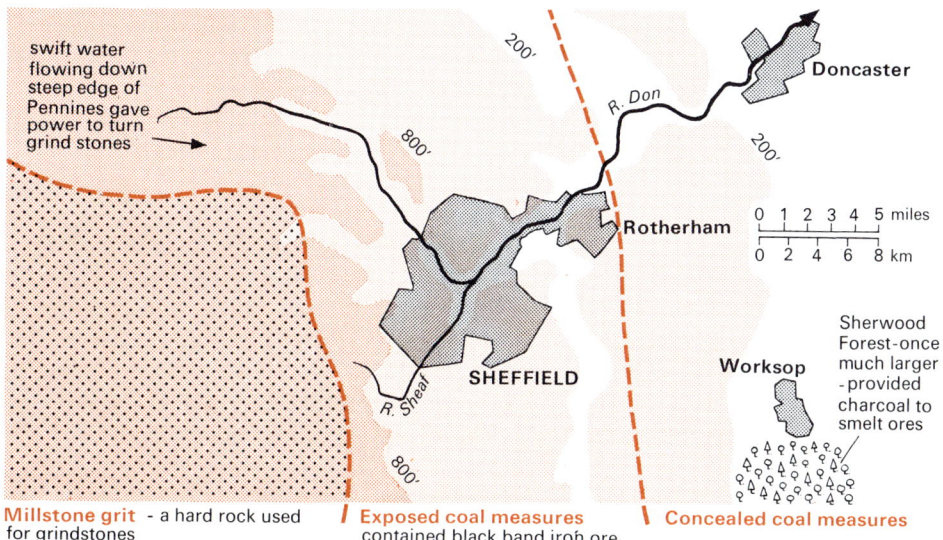

Fig. 152 Sheffield—the extent of the town today. Industrial areas are shown by darker shading.

these that Sheffield is especially famous today. Small quantities of other metals, such as manganese or tungsten, are added to the steel to give it a special quality. Some of the steels now made in Sheffield are so valuable that they are sold by the kilogramme rather than by the tonne.

By concentrating on quality rather than quantity, Sheffield has managed to remain a 'city of steel'. Its advantages of position, however, have disappeared. No ore is mined locally; the city is cramped in narrow valleys with little room to expand, and communications are difficult. Sheffield has survived through industrial momentum: the skill of the people, the money available, the tradition of the area have made it possible for steel manufacture to keep going although there are few raw materials left locally.

Although Sheffield is not the largest producer of steel, there are more steel furnaces in Sheffield than in any other British city. Sheffield does not produce enough iron in its own blast furnaces to supply the steel furnaces. Pig iron is brought in from Middlesbrough and Scunthorpe, as well as iron ore and scrap. Some of Sheffield's steel furnaces are fired by electricity (electric arc furnaces). They are expensive to run, but the expense is justified because of the quality of the product.

Sheffield has often led the way in experimenting with new methods. Stainless steel, alloy steels and Sheffield plate originated here. The British Iron and Steel Research Association has its headquarters in Sheffield, and the University has important metallurgy and engineering departments. Apart from steel the industries of Sheffield include toolmaking, engineering, cutlery and silverware.

Middlesbrough

The development of Middlesbrough has been very different from that of Sheffield. Sheffield was well-known in mediaeval times, but building in Middlesbrough was not started until 1830. Today it is the largest town on the Tees, with a population of 150 000. Middlesbrough was designed as a coal port, and is an early example of a planned town. It was meant to house 5000 people, and a handsome market square, churches, banks and symmetrical blocks of terraced houses were built.

The town began to grow rapidly in 1850 when a thick band of iron ore was discovered in the Cleveland Hills nearby. The Cleveland ore was of poor quality and contained phosphorous. It could not be used to make steel. Middlesbrough, therefore, unlike Sheffield, became essentially a producer of iron. Towards the end of the century, another new process (Thomas and Gilchrist) made it possible to make steel from local ores. At the same time, Middlesbrough began to import good quality ores from Spain. The Tees estuary was deepened and dredged, and there are now good docks along the Tees. The Tees is by tonnage of goods traded one of Britain's major ports, as the Table on page 158 shows.

In the 1960s the Middlesbrough area was second only to South Wales in the production of iron and steel. A high proportion of pig iron is still produced, but

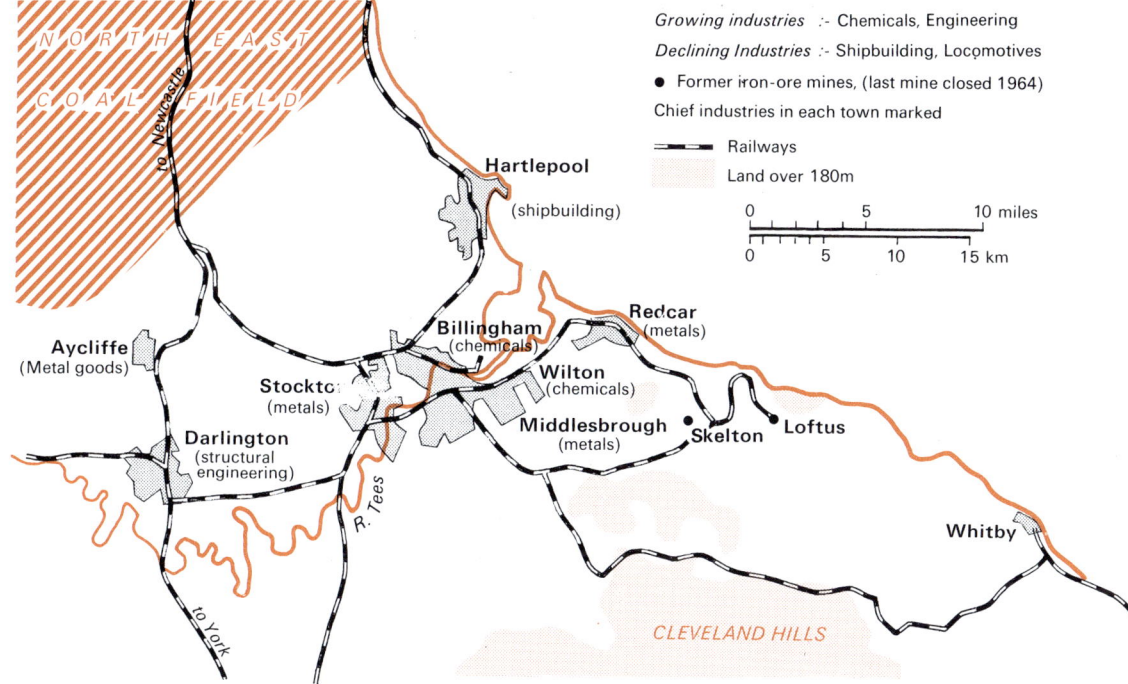

Fig. 153   Teesside.

much steel is also made. No ore is now mined in the Cleveland Hills. Most is imported, although a small amount comes from home ores in Northamptonshire.

The original town square has now been pulled down to make way for new houses, but there are still many streets of nineteenth century terrace houses to remind one that Middlesbrough was a creation of the Victorian iron age.

Chemicals

The chemical industry is extremely complex and difficult to define, because it overlaps so many other industries. Almost every industry needs chemicals in some form. Metal industries and textiles are two examples, and agriculture today needs a huge supply of chemical fertilizer. The chemical industry is one of the most rapidly expanding industries. Britain is one of the world's leading producers of chemicals and chemical products.

In the north of England there are three main areas of chemical production: in south Lancashire and Cheshire, where there are large deposits of salt; on Teesside, where imported petroleum is now the main raw material; and on Tyneside, which has many varied, old established industries.

141

Fig. 154 Northwich, Cheshire, a view looking north. What time of day was the photograph taken? The river in the foreground is called the Weaver. What other word could be used to describe its course? The edges of the river terraces can just be seen at the bottom of the photograph. North of the town can be seen the lakes (flashes) caused partly by subsidence over the salt mines.

In Cheshire there are large deposits of rock salt. There used to be many rock salt mines, but salt mining often causes subsidence, and during the nineteenth century several towns, particularly Northwich, were partly destroyed by the ground collapsing over the salt deposits. Most salt is obtained by pumping water into the deposits which then partly dissolve, and the water is pumped back as brine. It is probably this method of washing out the salt which has caused the subsidence, and hence the trough–shaped pits in the Cheshire landscape which are filled with water, or with waste from the chemical factories. These hollows are called 'flashes'. Today, salt is mined chiefly at Winsford.

The salt deposits have provided a raw material for the chemical industry in Cheshire and south Lancashire (and extending westwards into Flintshire) where general chemicals are produced. The main product from the salt is industrial alkali. The two chief alkalis are sodium carbonate (soda ash), which is used in soap and glass manufacture; and sodium hydroxide (caustic soda) which is strongly alkaline and dissolves easily in water. It is used in rayon, soap and dye production, petroleum refining, textiles and paper manufacture. Another basic chemical used in large quantities is sulphuric acid. The chemical industry is its own best market, and both alkalis and acids are essential to other chemical industries: they are the working chemicals, which are necessary to cause the chemical reactions which bring about a change in composition.

142

The Chemical Industry

	Raw Materials	Intermediate Products	End Products
Organic:	Coal	Coal tar	Synthetic fibres e.g. nylon Plastics e.g. polythene
	Petroleum		Synthetic rubber, dyestuffs, detergents, pharmaceuticals
	Wood Vegetable oils	Cellulose	Rayon and other fibres Soap, fats
Inorganic:	Salt (sodium chloride)	Sodium carbonate sodium hydroxide chlorine	Industrial acids and alkalis (general chemicals)
	Anhydrite (calcium sulphate) Sulphur	Sulphuric acid	
	Nitrogen (from air)	Ammonia	Artificial fertilizers
	Limestone (calcium carbonate)	Calcium hydroxide (+sodium carbonate)	
	Potassium chloride Calcium phosphate		

Widnes and Runcorn are the main chemical manufacturing towns in this area. They used to be easily recognized by the foul fumes and the waste of sludge which surrounded them. But an Act of Parliament made it illegal for factories to emit such waste, and ways were soon found of making good use of it. Chlorine manufacture, for example, became a co-product of the soda factories. In fact, there is little waste in the chemical industry. Most of the escaping gases and liquids can be trapped to make other products. At Stanlow on Merseyside there is now also a petro-chemical works based on imported petroleum.

The largest chemical works in Britain are at Billingham and Wilton on Teesside. The industry here began during World War I. As in Cheshire, there are deposits of salt and anhydrite, which are used to make general chemicals. Anhydrite is one of the raw materials from which sulphuric acid may be made. A characteristic of Billingham is the variety of its chemical produce. For example petrol was made here from coal for twenty-three years, but production stopped in 1958, as so many

Fig. 155   I.C.I. Terylene works at Wilton.

supplies of natural petroleum had been found, it was no longer worthwhile to produce it artificially. More important today are the vast amounts of chemical fertilizer produced. Apart from nitrogen in the air, from which ammonia is made, and limestone, which provides slaked lime, the minerals used in fertilizers are imported, especially sulphur and potassium chloride.

The largest petro-chemical works in the world is the I.C.I. plant at Wilton. It uses petroleum which comes through a pipe under the Tees from Billingham. Petroleum can be distilled to produce a number of hydrocarbons, which range from gases such as ethylene, to petrol and lubricating oils. Half the total output at Wilton is ethylene, the gas from which polythene is made. The works is a mass of storage tanks, heating towers and pipes which carry the liquid and gaseous products of the oil, as well as water for cooling.

The petro-chemical branch of the industry is growing very rapidly, for a variety of new products can now be made from petroleum, including plastics, dyestuffs, synthetic fibres, drugs and detergents. Fig. 149 shows that much more petroleum is now used than formerly. As nearly all petroleum is imported, the oil refineries and petro-chemical works are located by the sea, especially around the estuaries of Britain. Natural gas (methane) from the North Sea may in future be used as a raw material, and more chemical works may be built along the east coast.

The third main area in the North where chemicals are made is Tyneside. General chemicals are less important than they are on Teesside. Chemical industries are traditional and firms are small. There are no giants employing over 5000 people as at Wilton and Billingham. Salt deposits near the mouth of the Tyne were mined in the seventeenth century, and the chemical industry dates from this time. The salt works went out of business when the Cheshire region became a competitor, but the chemical industry survives. The branch which is most obviously linked to other industries is that of paint making, which is traditionally associated with shipbuilding. There are explosives works and coke ovens. Two well-known names are Fablon and Formica, and these plastic sheeting industries have grown rapidly since World War II.

The chemical industry is vast and includes thousands of products. The main chemical works in Britain are shown below.

Fig. 156   The chemical industry.

7. Look at Fig. 142 p. 130. Make a list of the places in northern England where iron and steel are manufactured. Underline in different colours (a) places which are on coalfields (b) places which are by the sea. Why is a position by the sea a great advantage today?

8. Using Fig. 152 list the advantages of Sheffield for the early development of the iron and steel industry. What disadvantages has it today as an industrial town?

9. Read the description of Scunthorpe on p. 31. What advantage has Scunthorpe over Sheffield for an iron and steel industry? How does Sheffield depend on Scunthorpe? How has Sheffield managed to keep its leading position?

10. List as many everyday objects as you can think of which are products of the chemical industry. If possible name the raw material from which each was made.

11. Draw a map of the north of England and on it shade the regions where chemical manufacture is important. Mark and name at least one town in each region. Add notes to explain why the chemical industry is growing so fast.

12. Using Fig. 153, the Table on p. 170 and pp. 140, 143–5, write an account of Teesside under the headings: natural resources, the port, industries and towns.

Textiles

The West Riding of Yorkshire and Lancashire are traditionally regions for manufacturing wool and cotton textiles. Although other industries are also important in these areas, the towns grew during the industrial revolution because of the textile industry.

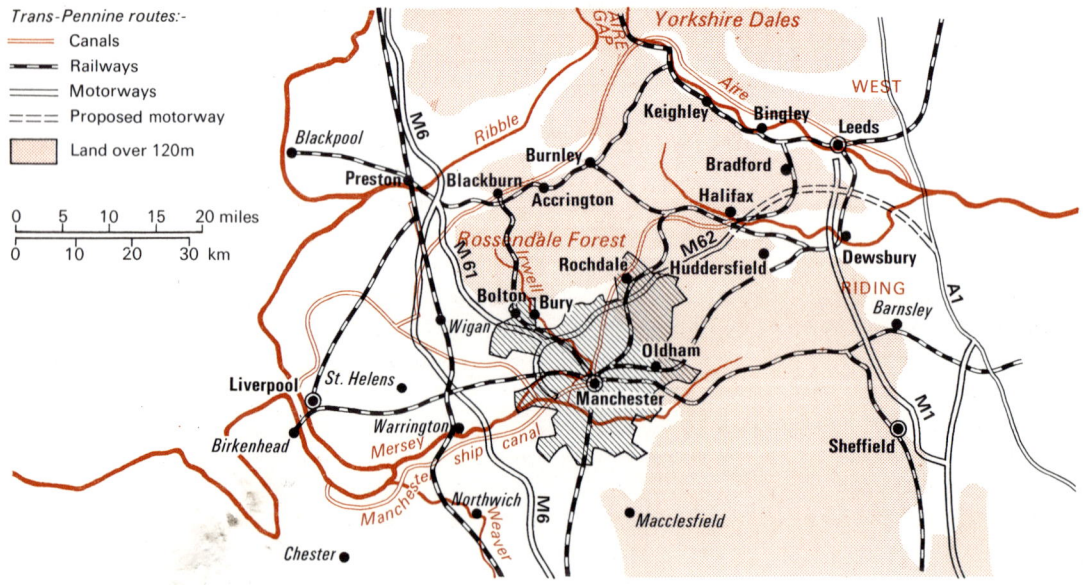

Fig. 157 Lancashire and Yorkshire.

Fig. 158 Leeds is at the eastern edge of the gap made by the River Aire through the Pennines. Road, rail and canal all use this routeway. The river flows through the centre of the city. Beside the waterways are old mills and heavy industrial plants such as the power stations and gas works.

Wool textiles

Over 85 per cent of the wool textiles made in Britain are produced in the area of the Yorkshire West Riding shown on Fig. 157. 'Large towns, small towns, and swollen industrial villages are all bound together by strings of houses and factories, and by a tangle of roads, railways and canals.'[1] Buildings do not cover the whole area continuously, as in the conurbations of Manchester or London, and the main towns are still distinct from each other. The wool towns are built right in the Pennines, and the suburbs of Halifax reach 300 m. Next door to the towns are open moorlands which are used mainly for sheep grazing.

The largest, the busiest, and the most cosmopolitan of the towns is Leeds. It is not only a wool town; its closest link with wool textiles is through the clothing industry and engineering is also important.

In Leeds, as in all the wool towns, large areas of the city were built in the nineteenth century with back to back houses. These are houses which back on to each other with no space between. The average width of a double row is 10 to 12 m. As a result there is a great deal of overcrowding, and a lot of the old property is being cleared to make room for the new blocks of flats. The skyline is rapidly changing.

Bradford is the commercial centre of the wool trade. Wool textiles and some engineering products are made, but it is chiefly important as a business centre. The buying and selling transactions go on at the wool exchange. The city hall like many of the West Riding buildings is built of local stone, which has been cleaned of a century's industrial soot to make a splendid centrepiece.

Besides the large towns marked on Fig. 157 are many smaller towns which extend to the moors. The blackened solid stone houses and the mills beside the streams have hardly changed in appearance since they were built in the nineteenth century. On the western edge of the group of towns is Haworth where the Brontë sisters lived, and the wild country of *Wuthering Heights*. This description of the change

[1] Freeman—*Conurbations.*

147

Fig. 159   Cornholme, an old textile town on the
Lancashire–Yorkshire borders.

Fig. 160   Back to back houses in Cornholme.

Fig. 161   The mills of Reuben Gaunt and
Sons at Farsley, between Bradford and
Leeds. The firm was founded by a local
weaver called John Gaunt, in the
seventeenth century, and the business has
been in the family ever since. About 200
people are employed at Springfield mills,
mostly women.

which the wool industry brought to a Pennine valley comes from *Shirley* by
Charlotte Brontë.

'The other day I passed up the Hollow, which tradition says was once green
and lone and wild; and there I saw the manufacturer's day-dreams embodied in
substantial stone and brick and ashes—the cinder-black highway, the cottages,
and the cottage gardens; there I saw a mighty mill, and a chimney, ambitious
as the tower of Babel.'

There are two types of wool textiles. Worsted goods are made from long fibres
which are combed out parallel to each other to make a sleek, strong yarn. This
yarn is woven to have a smooth finish and is used largely in men's suitings. Woollen
goods are made from shorter fibres which are spun into a fuzzy yarn and make a
cloth of looser weave. Man-made fibres may be blended with both woollen and

148

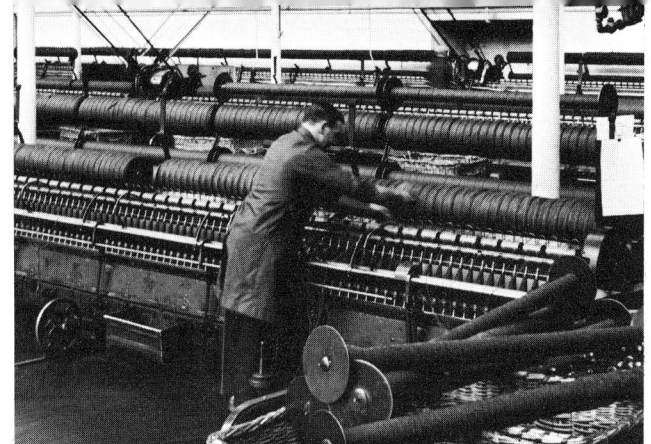

Fig. 162 *above* Broom mills, part of the same firm, showing woollen yarn being spun. The yarn here is made from 'shoddy', which consists of used wool garments and the poorer ends of wool tops torn up into fibres. The yarn here is used to make a mixed cloth of woollen and worsted thread.

Fig. 163 *above right* An automatic loom at Broom mills. The warp yarn is threaded on to the loom, and a shuttle passes back and forth threading in the weft. Each weaver controls six machines. A blend of terylene is often added to the worsted yarn, which makes it stronger and more crease resistant.

Fig. 164 *right* About thirty-five menders are employed at Broom mills to mend by hand any threads which have broken. The cloth manufactured here is in plain colours, for much of it is made under government contract for uniforms. The cloth undergoes several finishing processes which reduce it and bash it into shape to give it a close weave.

worsted yarn. Some of the processes of wool textile manufacture are illustrated in Figs. 162–4. In worsted manufacture, spinning and weaving are usually carried out by the same firm; in woollen manufacture, the different processes are more subdivided and carried out by different firms. Hundreds of chimneys mark the mills where the wool textiles are manufactured.

Most of the wool firms like the one illustrated are relatively small, employing perhaps 200 people, and many are family businesses which have been going for several generations. Some of the smaller firms are now joining together, or being taken over by larger firms; the smaller firms often cannot afford to buy new machinery which is necessary both to replace old machinery, and to increase the amount each worker can produce.

Before the industrial revolution, wool was made into yarn and cloth in many

Fig. 165 Halifax. All the wool manufacturing towns are built on the steep slopes of the Pennines, so it is easy to get a view across the industrial landscape of chimneys, water cooling towers, and the old five-storeyed mills.

parts of the country. The name worsted, for instance, comes from a village in Norfolk where Flemish weavers settled. Spinning and weaving were domestic occupations, carried out on the farms. During the industrial revolution, the West Riding became the leading wool textile manufacturing region.

Yorkshire had two great natural advantages. The first was water. On the edge of the Pennines, hundreds of streams provided plenty of water for all the processes of wool manufacture. Moreover, the streams flowed swiftly, and could be used to provide power to turn the mill wheels. The water was soft, for as it flowed over Millstone Grit in this part of the Pennines, it collected no lime to make it hard. The softness helped in washing, bleaching, and dyeing.

The second advantage was coal. When steam began to be used for power in manufacturing in the nineteenth century, the coal could be mined easily. Railways and canals were built to carry coal to the towns in the Millstone Grit country, while textile manufacture spread eastwards into the coalfields.

Originally, all the wool used was British, but today nearly all of it is imported. Most of it comes from Australia, South Africa and Argentina. It arrives closely pressed in bales covered with sacking and wound round with steel tapes, via London, Liverpool and Hull. The name 'wool' is given to anything which comes from the back of an animal, and includes mohair, camel hair and alpaca, which are often blended with sheep wool fibres.

Wool is one of Britain's oldest industries and wool manufacture is still a major

150

industry. It has not suffered the violent ups and downs of the cotton industry. The quality of the cloth remains excellent, and Britain still exports more than any other country, although today there is much competition from other wool manufacturing countries.

However, new engineering industries have come to the West Riding as to most other regions, and as many people prefer work in engineering factories, wool is beginning to find it difficult to compete with these for labour.

Cotton textiles

It is a short journey from Leeds to Manchester. The Pennines today hardly form a barrier, except in winter when roads may be blocked by snow and ice. Two rivers—the Aire and Calder—cut deep valleys which are used by rail, road and canal. Another rail route tunnels through the hills. The ports of Manchester and Liverpool can be reached easily from west Yorkshire, and the Lancashire ports handle more Yorkshire trade than Hull does.

Although separated from the Yorkshire towns by only a few kilometres of hills, Lancashire is famous for cotton rather than wool. Cotton manufacture does not have the ancient traditions of wool, because the fibre comes from a sub-tropical plant and was not imported in large quantities until the eighteenth century. However, cotton overtook wool textiles in Lancashire, and cotton textiles remained the leading industry of the region until World War II.

West of the Pennines, an area of highland, called the Rossendale Forest, juts out into the Lancashire Plain. Most of the cotton towns are north and south of this highland. The spinning and weaving processes of the cotton industry have been separated more than those of wool textiles. North of the Rossendale Forest are the weaving towns: Blackburn, Accrington, Burnley, Nelson, Colne. South of the Rossendale Forest are the cotton spinning towns: Bolton, Bury, Rochdale, Oldham. Now that large firms have taken over small ones and many mills have closed, there has been reorganization and this specialization is not as clear as it was. Manchester is both the commercial centre of the cotton trade, and a great clothing manufacturing town. The many routeways converging on Manchester help it to fulfil both these functions.

The processes of cotton manufacture are similar to those of wool. Although the threads are finer, cotton was adapted more easily to machinery, and production of cotton grew at the beginning of the industrial revolution more quickly than that of wool.

Lancashire had the same natural advantages as Yorkshire for a successful textile industry during the industrial revolution: plenty of soft water and coal helped the rapid growth of cotton textiles. But a third advantage was the connection with the port of Liverpool. The thrusting enterprise of the merchants of Liverpool led to the growth of the cotton trade, which encouraged the spinners and weavers of Lancashire to change to cotton manufacture. Another advantage was the nearby

151

chemical industry of Cheshire, as many chemicals were needed in bleaching, dyeing and finishing the cotton textiles.

In 1912, the cotton industry employed 622 000 people; in 1966, 100 000. This is one of the changes which has taken place in the cotton industry. Compared with even 20 years ago, it has declined enormously. The main reasons for the decline are: (1) Competition from other countries—much of the cotton cloth made in Lancashire used to be cheap and was designed for countries in Africa, South America and the Far East. These places now make, and even export, their own cotton cloth. They have become industrialized too, usually using textile machinery

Fig. 166   An old cotton mill now used by an engineering firm in Bolton, Lancashire. The mill once employed 350, but today more than 700 people are employed making filters for aircraft, motor vehicles, and general industrial uses.

made in Lancashire. European countries also export cotton and mixed fibre cloth. Britain imports much cloth from Portugal, for example. In fact, since 1958, Britain has imported more cloth than she has exported. (2) Man-made fibres: before World War II these were unimportant, but today not only is much cloth made entirely from man-made fibres, but man-made fibres are often blended with cotton yarn, or woven into a cloth of mixed yarns. It is not surprising that many of the old Lancashire mills now spin and weave man-made fibres as well as cotton.

Because of the steady decline of the cotton industry, the Government took action in 1959 and passed a Cotton Industry Act and radical changes were made. Many of the smaller firms closed down, and grants of money were paid to compensate them. Grants of money were also paid to firms to install new machinery. In this way the industry was modernized so that each person could produce more. The cotton industry is now dominated by a few very large firms, and it is significant that some of them, like Courtaulds, have large interests in man-made fibres.

Cotton is still important in Lancashire but there is now a great variety of industry in the area and a wider choice of jobs in factories making chemicals, vehicles, heavy iron and steel products and many kinds of machines. Machines used to be made locally for the textile mills so engineering is by no means new to Lancashire, but engineering has now overtaken textiles in importance and provides the most exports as well as the most jobs.

Man-made fibres

The production of man-made fibres is closely connected with the chemical industry. The raw materials are either cellulose from wood, or by-products from coal or petroleum. A thick sticky liquid is made, which is pushed through very fine holes in a nozzle to form threads. Man-made fibres can be made so that the yarn is unbroken, when it is called 'filament yarn'; or they can be cut up into shorter lengths called 'staple fibre' so that they are like natural fibres, ready to be combed out and spun.

The greatest advantage of man-made fibres is that they are strong. They are often added to wool or cotton to give greater strength, and they have valuable industrial uses, such as in tyre cords or conveyor belting. Other properties are especially helpful to the clothing manufacturer—for instance some are shrink resistant, or can be permanently pleated. The names of the man-made fibres— rayon, tricel, nylon, terylene—stand for specific properties. They are not all the same. The manufacturer chooses the material he wants according to the properties of the material, and what it can be used for.

Filament yarn and staple fibre are made in many parts of the country, as Fig. 167 shows, often associated with other chemical industries. The Midlands are the main region for their production. But the greatest number of factories weaving cloth made entirely of man-made fibres, or containing man-made fibres, are in the traditional textile counties of Lancashire and Yorkshire.

153

Where the cloth contains both man-made and natural fibres, there are two distinct ways of making it. Man-made fibre may be blended with the natural fibre and spun together to make a single thread which can then be woven; or threads of natural fibre and threads of man-made fibre are woven into a cloth of mixed fibre.

Engineering

Some industries like wool textiles or pottery are found in only a few towns and can be pinned down exactly. But the engineering industry is so widespread that it is difficult to get a clear picture of where it is located. It is safe to say that every

■ Man-made Fibre Plants

Fig. 167   Location of man-made fibre plants.

154

large town in Britain has engineering industries, and so have a great many of the smaller ones. Engineering manufacturers employ more people than any other—about 2½ million in Great Britain, or nearly 12 per cent of the labour force.

One of the reasons for this is that engineering is a very broad term. An engineer may be a mechanical or electrical engineer; a civil, marine, or chemical engineer. Engineers are essential to every manufacturing industry, but industries labelled 'engineering' usually make either metal goods or electrical goods. Metal goods vary from bridges to paper clips: electrical goods vary from computers to light switches.

Metal engineering manufacturers make structural steelwork or machinery and tools.

(1) Structural steelwork

Formerly steel girders were bolted and riveted together chiefly to make bridges. The famous bridges of the railway age, such as those crossing the Tyne or the Menai Straits, were nearly all made out of steel. Today, most factories are built round a steel framework. Steel is used for example to make oil storage tanks, pipes used especially in chemical works, or electricity pylons. The separate pieces of steel are now often welded together. The most famous region for structural steelwork was at Stockton and Darlington on the Tees. The industry has expanded into other regions today, but a large number of structural steel engineering firms are still centred in these two Durham towns.

(2) Machinery and tools

The manufacture of machinery is also an engineering industry. Some of the earliest inventions of textile machinery were made in Lancashire and Yorkshire. Textile machinery is manufactured in many Lancashire towns, and in the West Riding of Yorkshire; mining machinery in Yorkshire and the North-east; and tools of many kinds in Sheffield.

The main expanding industries are those of electrical engineering. Far more electricity is now generated than 20 years ago, and much more electrical equipment is used. Electronics, including various types of computer, are now essential to every large industry. Although this branch of engineering has increased more in the south of England than in the north, it is nevertheless important in the north as well. The following are a few of the products manufactured in the North:

insulated cable and wire	radio valves
generating plant	telephones
turbines	record players
switchgear	television
transformers	domestic appliances.

Most of the products on the first list can be called heavy. They are not everyday objects. Generating plant, for nuclear, oil and coal fired power stations, is never seen by most of us. Other products are in common everyday use.

10. INDUSTRIES OF THE NORTH

Engineering is now a major industry in the Lancashire region. Many new industries have taken over the old disused cotton mills, or have spread in the industrial estates. Engineering is also important in the woollen towns of Yorkshire, especially in Leeds and the Sheffield area, although these places have little electrical engineering.

In the North-east, heavy engineering is a traditional industry dating from the beginning of the industrial revolution, and heavy electrical equipment has been made on Tyneside since World War I. There is no tradition for light electrical engineering, yet far more of these goods are now made here than formerly. Most of them are made on the industrial estates or in the new towns. Many of them are branches of firms which have their headquarters in the South.

The engineering industries have benefited more than any other from government policy to aid the development areas. These are growing industries, and they have changed the industrial basis of the North. The greatest change has been made in Lancashire, where several industrial estates were built by the local councils; many new engineering industries have also been established where there was already a fairly strong engineering tradition, for example in Bolton and Trafford Park. Light engineering industries do not need special advantages except sites for factories, power supply from the electric grid system, and roads and railways to take the goods away. However, they do need people to work in them, preferably people with experience of manufacturing, so the new engineering industries can easily be located in the development areas of the North.

13. What differences between Leeds and Huddersfield are shown by the table below?

1965	Numbers of people employed	
	Leeds	Huddersfield
Engineering and electric goods	23 000	13 250
Textiles	4700	29 500
Clothing and footwear	35 000	657
Distributive trades	39 000	8200
Total labour force	270 993	96 821
Total population	504 000	130 000

14. Look at the table below. What changes have taken place in Blackburn and Burnley? What are the reasons for these changes?

Employment figures	Blackburn		Burnley	
	1952	1965	1952	1965
Population	60 983	55 026	46 008	40 726
Engineering	12 952	14 646	3971	5795
Textiles	16 114	7495	15 572	1900

15. In 1966 a booklet called *Challenge of the Changing North* was published. Why does the North present a challenge? How is the North changing? Which other regions in Britain present a challenge?

157

11. The Northern Ports

The leading ports of Britain

1965	Total trade	Thousand tonnes Coastwise and foreign trade excluding fuels	Fuels
1. **London**	58 059	20 265	37 795
2. **Liverpool**	32 167	15 514	16 651
3. **Milford Haven**	24 837	38	24 800
4. **Southampton**	23 813	1304	22 509
5. **Medway**	22 278	1374	20 932
6. **Manchester**	15 351	5832	9519
7. **Clyde**	12 382	6104	6278
8. **Tees**	9657	6427	3228
9. **Hull**	9439	4620	4818
10. **Tyne**	8820	2402	6418
11. **Bristol**	8345	3805	4539

Liverpool and Merseyside

It is clear from the table above that Liverpool is second only to London as a port. It has become such a thriving port chiefly because it serves such a large hinterland. The immediate hinterland of Liverpool is the industrial area of Lancashire and Cheshire, but goods reach the port from further away, especially from Yorkshire and the Midlands, and even from London. It is a great national port, serving a much wider area than just the region behind it.

Liverpool's growth has been helped by the good communications between the port and its hinterland. In the eighteenth century rivers were deepened and canals built and the network of waterways so made linked Liverpool with towns beyond the Pennines and in the Midlands. In 1830 the first successful railway in Britain was built between Liverpool and Manchester, in spite of great difficulties. The sandstone hills outside Liverpool needed a deep cutting, and a foundation for the line had to be laid over the large marshland outside Manchester called Chat Moss. The railway made another link between the port and its hinterland.

The merchants of Liverpool were enterprising men who had been quick to take advantage of growing trans-Atlantic trade in the eighteenth century. They were also concerned in the slave trade. Ships from Liverpool called in at West Africa and took slaves across the Atlantic to the West Indies and North America, where the plantations were beginning to yield rich crops. The empty slave ships picked up their cargo of sugar or cotton, and returned to Liverpool across the north Atlantic. The cotton was then sent inland to the manufacturing towns on the edge of the Pennines. If Liverpool depended on its rich hinterland, it is equally true that the hinterland depended on Liverpool, and they prospered together.

After 1867 when the Suez Canal was opened, Liverpool established trade with the Far East and Australasia.

Liverpool still imports much tropical and subtropical produce, including tobacco, cocoa, palm oil, ground nuts and rubber. One product, however, easily led the list of exports throughout the nineteenth century. This was cheap cotton cloth which provided as much as 48 per cent of Britain's manufactured exports in the middle of the nineteenth century.

Fig. 168   The pierhead, Liverpool. The city and its docks are built beside the wide estuary of the Mersey.

11. THE NORTHERN PORTS

The estuary of the Mersey is not an ideal harbour, but it is much better than its neighbour, the Dee. The estuary of the Dee is wide and shallow. Charles Kingsley, in his poem 'The Sands of Dee' describes how

'The western tide crept up along the sand,
And o'er and o'er the sand,
As far as eye could see.'

Deposits of mud and sand have steadily accumulated and blocked the estuary, and have cut off the old port of Chester, once a much larger city than Liverpool, from the sea.

The Mersey estuary, however, gets narrower near the sea, so the tide is forced twice each day through a narrow channel, and this helps to keep the channel fairly free of silt. Tidal action is not enough, and a great deal of dredging must still be done.

In its early days entrance to the harbour was hazardous. Today when a ship approaches the port, a pilot is taken on board from Anglesey or the Isle of Man to guide it through the shallows. There is a high range of tide (9 m) so that docks where the water can be kept deep are necessary. The first dock was built as early as 1715. There are now thirty docks on the Liverpool side of the Mersey estuary. The port includes also several docks on the south side of the estuary in Wallasey and Birkenhead.

The equipment at the docks has been improved to help the port handle the enormous amount of cargo which arrives there. Special equipment for bulk unloading of, for example, sugar and ores is used, and the new oil terminal at Tranmere has a floating jetty so that tankers can unload at any stage of the tide. New container berths have been built (see p. 229).

At the same time land communications have been improved. The first Mersey tunnel was built before World War II. More recently, the M.6 and the trans-Pennine motorway (under construction 1969) and a new tunnel help Liverpool's connections with its hinterland. Rail freight liners also deliver directly to Liverpool.

Liverpool and Birkenhead have grown so that they are now part of a large conurbation known as Merseyside, depending not only on the port but also on manufacturing industries. Until recently the main manufactures of the region have been 'port industries': that is, processing imports. The large quantities of food and tropical produce which are imported mean that there are flour mills, sugar refineries, confectionery, soap works, rubber manufactures. Most of these industries are close to the port. Lever Brothers, the soap manufacturers, built Port Sunlight on the south side of the estuary as a garden city (see p. 74). Another important industry was shipbuilding, and 15 000 people are still employed in shipbuilding and repairing. The largest firm is Cammell Laird's at Birkenhead.

However, there is much more variety in the industry than there was. More manufacturers have built works in Merseyside, especially in the new industrial estates on the edges of the built-up area where there are many new electrical and

160

consumer industries. Engineering is the chief employer and growing fastest—37 000 in 1953; 48 000 in 1963.

But the industry which has provided most new jobs is the motor car industry. Three firms built new works on Merseyside in the early 1960s: Vauxhall at Ellesmere Port, Ford at Halewood; and Standard Triumph cars are manufactured at Speke. Here again, one of the reasons the firms chose the Merseyside site was that government restrictions stopped them from expanding in the Midlands. A new growing, expanding industry was wanted in Merseyside, to create jobs for the large number of unemployed.

Merseyside has the highest birthrate in the country, and a large number of immigrants, especially from Ireland. This is one of the reasons why there are still more people than there are jobs.

Manchester

If one had looked at a map of Lancashire in the nineteenth century and noted the position of Manchester 58 kilometres from the estuary of the river Mersey, it would have seemed unlikely that it could ever become a great port. Yet Manchester is today one of the leading ports of Britain.

Manchester grew rapidly with the development of the cotton manufacturing industry in Lancashire. Not far away, where the streams flow swiftly over the edge of the Pennines to meet the plain and the Lancashire coalfields, lay the cotton spinning and weaving towns. Manchester was in a central position where the goods from the cotton towns could easily be collected, packed and stored. It developed as a commercial town serving the cotton industry.

However by 1881 Manchester had suffered a marked decline. There were 18 000 empty houses in the city, and whole streets were deserted. This was partly due to a slump in the cotton industry which followed the American Civil War, but also to the high charges made by the canal and railway companies and especially by the port of Liverpool on goods from Manchester. It cost $61\frac{1}{2}$p a tonne for goods to get to Liverpool and on board ship: it cost only another $33\frac{1}{2}$p to send them to Calcutta.

Persistent men in Manchester made the building of the Ship Canal possible. They prodded Parliament into passing the necessary acts and raised the capital. The canal was completed in six years making Manchester a sea port; the first ship sailed up it in 1894.

Part of the canal was built along the existing waterway, the river Irwell, which was made deeper and wider, and part of it was built by excavating a channel through open country. When it was completed, it was wider than the Suez Canal then was, and just as deep. It has since been enlarged, but surprisingly little enlargement has been necessary.

There are five locks in the canal. The lowest is Eastham lock, which is built where the river Mersey swings to the south side of the estuary. This lock is left

Fig. 169 Runcorn is the main town shown in this picture. In the distance is the bridge over the Mersey, with Widnes on the other side. The photograph was taken at low tide. Find the Manchester Ship Canal going round the edge of the estuary, and the sluice gates leading from the canal which are also at the entrance to the Weaver.

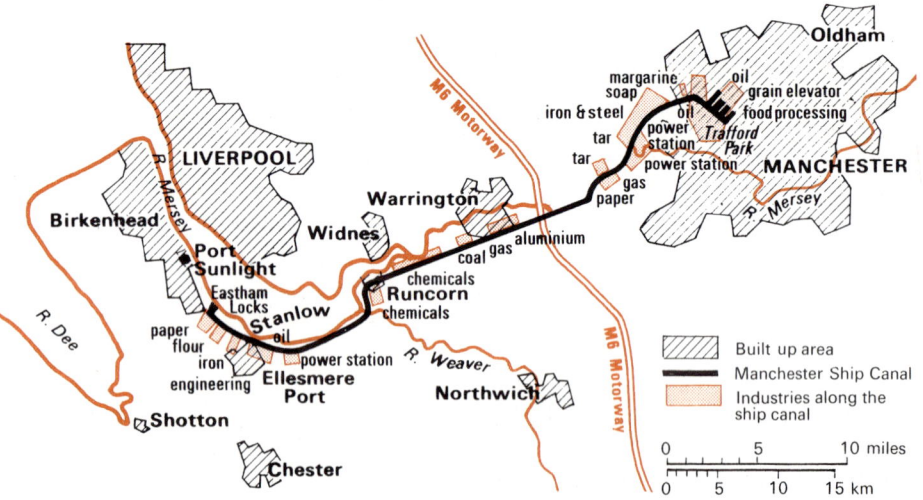

Fig. 170 Manchester Ship Canal.

open for a few hours before and after high tide, making the canal tidal as far as the next locks, at Latchford. Many bridges cross the canal. Some of them are high level bridges, leaving a clearance underneath of 22 metres. Others are swing bridges, and there is also the Barton swing aqueduct, which carries the water of the Bridgewater Canal over the Ship Canal.

162

Fig. 171 Manchester airport at Ringway, 16 kilometres south of the city. The airport was rebuilt between 1957 and 1962. In 1956 Manchester airport handled 8834 tonnes of freight including mail and 391 406 passengers. In 1966 the figures were 37 641 and 1 469 311. Compare these figures with those given for London Airport on page 78.

The port of Manchester therefore extends for 58 kilometres from the new Queen Elizabeth docks on the Mersey estuary by Eastham locks, to the nine terminal docks in Salford at the other end.

The canal has made a great difference to the region. Not only has it made Manchester a major port; it has also brought a great variety of industry to the area. Some of the industrial works lining the canal are shown on Fig. 170. The first development was at Trafford Park, where a large country property was converted into the first planned industrial estate. At Trafford Park today there are over 200 factories employing more than 18 000 people. Many of the works along the canal rely directly on Manchester's imports, for example the oil refinery at Stanlow, which is the second largest in the country, the steel works at Irlam and paper and flour mills.

If any city deserves to be called the capital of the North it is Manchester. The conurbation which spreads out from Manchester to Salford is huge, and houses over two million people. Piccadilly, Manchester, is the busy centre overlooked by tall hotels and office blocks. Streets of gaunt towering commercial houses, each with its gold plaque, are a reminder of Manchester's world-wide connections. As in London, the central districts are largely filled with offices or warehouses, and are empty at nights: but the houses spread out from the centre, both Victorian terraces and newer suburbs. Engineering and clothing are the two main industries, but Manchester has kept its importance as first and foremost a city of commerce.

163

1. Draw a map to show how Liverpool was linked to its hinterland by the following waterways at the end of the eighteenth century: (1) Sankey canal linking it with the coalfield at St. Helens; (2) Mersey-Irwell navigation, linking it with the Manchester and the cotton towns; (3) Weaver navigation, linking it with the salt deposits of Cheshire; (4) The Leeds-Liverpool canal, linking it across the Pennines with the wool and textile towns; (5) Trent-Mersey, linking it to the Potteries.

2. In 1964 Liverpool's chief exports by value in £ million were: machinery and transport equipment £428; other manufactured goods £332, chemicals £124. What great change has taken place since the mid-nineteenth century? The chief import by value was food, drink and tobacco—£287.

3. Compare the figures given in question 2 with those on page 170. Imports are much heavier than exports, but exports are almost as valuable as imports. How do you account for this?

4. Port industries, textiles, chemicals, and engineering are all major industries in the hinterland of Liverpool. Write a paragraph on each, describing (a) what and where it is, (b) any natural advantages which have helped it to become important, (c) any changes which have taken place recently (see also pp. 147–57).

5. Draw a sketch of Fig. 169 p. 162 and label the Mersey estuary at low tide; Widnes, Runcorn and the bridge between them; the Manchester Ship Canal; sluice gates.

6. Look at Fig. 170. Which of the industries lining the ship canal rely on imports? What other raw materials are carried on the canal?

7. How are Manchester and Leeds (a) alike and (b) different? Why has Manchester become the larger town? (See also p. 147).

8. Look at the table of ports at the beginning of the chapter. (a) List the six leading ports in order of coastwise and foreign trade handled excluding fuels. Suggest reasons why three of the top five are missing from your list. (b) Draw a map to show the ports listed in the table. Draw bars beside each port to represent (i) Coastwise and foreign trade, (ii) Trade in fuels. [Look at Fig. 147 p. 135 for an example of how to do it].

Tyneside

Tyneside is the name given to the group of towns which line the estuary of the Tyne from Newcastle and Gateshead in the west to Tynemouth and South Shields in the east. The most famous city of Tyneside, and of the whole North-east, is Newcastle.

Newcastle began as a border town in Roman times. Hadrian's Wall ran just to the north and ended at Wallsend, east of Newcastle. It had an excellent defensive site. A steep bluff of sandstone rose abruptly beside the river. It was here that the Normans built the new castle from which the city gets its name. Newcastle was also at the head of the navigable estuary of the Tyne, and became a great sea port.

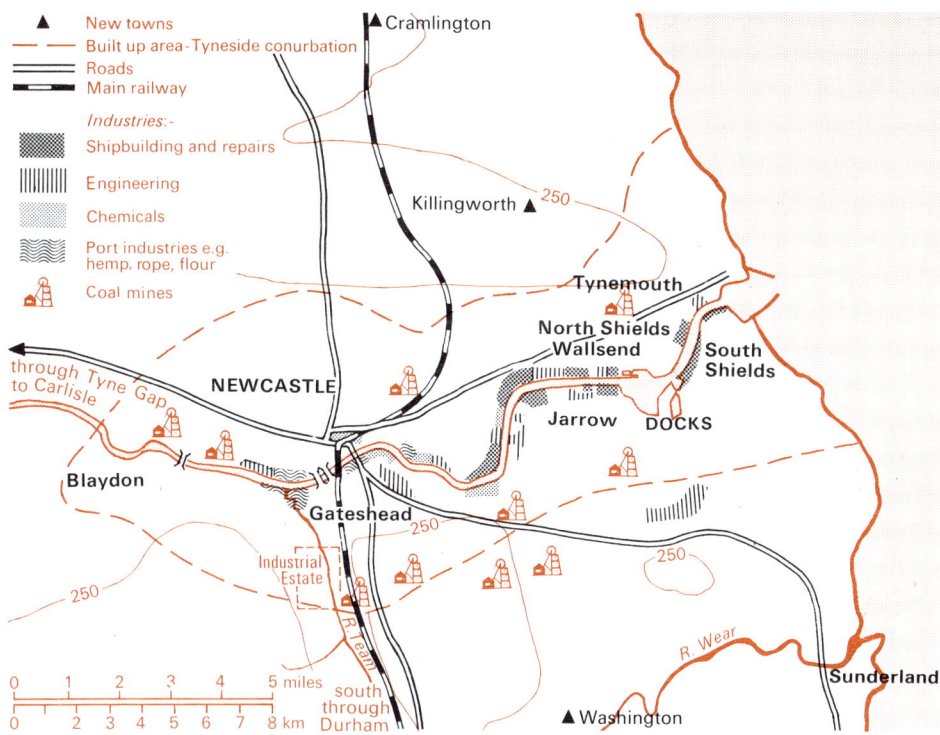

Legend:
- ▲ New towns
- — — Built up area - Tyneside conurbation
- ═══ Roads
- ▅▅▅ Main railway

Industries:-
- ▨ Shipbuilding and repairs
- ‖‖‖ Engineering
- ⋮⋮⋮ Chemicals
- 〰 Port industries e.g. hemp, rope, flour
- ⚒ Coal mines

▲Cramlington

Killingworth ▲ 250

Tynemouth
North Shields
Wallsend   South Shields

through Tyne Gap to Carlisle

NEWCASTLE

Jarrow   DOCKS

Blaydon

Gateshead   250

Industrial Estate

250

R. Team

250

250

R. Wear

Sunderland

0   1   2   3   4   5 miles
0   2   3   4   5   6   7   8 km

south through Durham

▲ Washington

Fig. 172   Tyneside: Blaydon, Newcastle, Gateshead, Wallsend, Jarrow, North Shields, South Shields, Tynemouth.

It is built where the river can be bridged, and is a focus of land routes which lead westwards through the Tyne Gap to Carlisle, and northwards to Scotland.

As the saying tells us, there is no point in carrying coals to Newcastle. Coal was shipped from the Tyne as early as the thirteenth century. At Newcastle, the river cuts a deep valley into the Coal Measures, and it was easy to mine coal from the seams beside the river. Most of it went to London. The coal trade grew steadily over the centuries and reached its peak in the 1920s when over 20 million tonnes were shipped in a year. (See p. 134–5.) Today almost none is exported to other countries, but about 5 million tonnes are sent by sea to London to supply the power stations along the Thames.

This trade in coal was the basis of other industries of Tyneside. The coal trade needed ships. Building of wooden ships started in South Shields, and timber was imported from Scandinavia. But the shipbuilding industry only became important after the invention of steam power, and after iron hulls began to be built. In 1842 the first iron ship was launched. The shipbuilding industry grew phenomenally, using iron, and later steel, from local furnaces and from Teesside. Today, more

165

ships are launched from Tyneside than from any other British estuary except Clydeside (see p. 227). There are also many dry docks along Tyneside where ship repairs are carried out.

The colliers which sailed regularly from Tyneside came back with loads of sand which was needed as ballast to stabilize the ships. This sand formed the basis of a glass industry. The heavy raw material could be imported cheaply, and bottles and glass panes could easily be sent on outgoing colliers without fear of breaking. Other bulky products were also imported as raw materials for making general chemicals, although salt and coal were found locally. The Tyneside chemical industry declined because of competition from Cheshire. The site of the old chemical works on the south bank was for long a derelict wasteland.

The Tyne estuary was constantly busy with traffic although the river was not ideal for ships. There was a shallow bar across the mouth. Ships of only 1 m draught were often stuck for hours on the sands; colliers crowded beyond the sand bar waiting for favourable winds and high tides. However, the Tyne had a great advantage over its neighbours and rivals, the Wear and the Tees. The bed of the river was composed of glacial sands and muds, and these soft rocks could be dredged easily. In 1859, a tremendous scheme was launched to improve the whole waterway. The river was straightened, made to flow through a narrower channel, and dredged. Today, there is a channel 9 m deep for 6 km inland, and at least 8 m deep as far as Newcastle. The improved waterway and the continued trade in coal helped Tyneside to flourish until the beginning of this century.

Tyneside is a good example of changing prosperity over the years. It was one of the worst hit areas during the depression of the 1930s. Shipbuilding almost stopped, as the trade suffered from competition from other countries. The iron and steel industry, heavy engineering and coal mining, all of which were big employers, declined.

One of the attempts to stop the decline of Tyneside was the building of the Team Valley Industrial Estate. Land in the Team Valley west of Gateshead was bought by the government. The land was let, or factories were built and then let, and gradually the estate has filled up. It is entirely industrial—there are no houses. People travel from the Tyneside towns to work on the estate. Industry ranges from the printing of foreign bank notes to the manufacture of television valves. There is variety, but only one heavy industry, the coal mine and coking plant at the northern end of the valley.

In spite of the fact that there is now more variety in Tyneside, the traditional industries are still strong. Fig. 173 shows the location of works lining the river Tyne. Along the river, one can see Stella electricity power station, the Team valley mine and coke ovens, Vickers small arms works, and shipyards lining the banks, and the waste tips which are a reminder of the industrial past.

The five great bridges crossing the Tyne, where the gorge made by the river is very deep, are the most striking features of Newcastle. They are called high

Fig. 173   Newcastle-on-Tyne. The middle bridge is a low-level swing bridge. The view is taken looking north-east. The old castle keep can just be seen at the left of the picture. What is the town on the south bank of the river?

level bridges because they link the tops of the steep slopes. The central area of the city was planned and rebuilt in the early nineteenth century, though the fine sandstone buildings became blackened over the years.

Many of the poorer districts of Tyneside, like the rows of terrace brick houses in Gateshead which perch on the precipitous river banks, are being demolished. In north-east England, new towns have been built to try to solve the problem of overcrowding in the older towns. Aycliffe, Washington, Killingworth and Cramlington have all been built to house new industry, and to make homes for people from the older cities, while Peterlee was built largely to rehouse miners from abandoned mining areas.

167

Hull

Kingston-upon-Hull is built on very flat land, and the streets are certainly the flattest of any large city in Britain. A small river, the Hull, flows through this eastern edge of Yorkshire, and the flood-plain of the river forms the foundation of the city. It is not good building ground. In parts of the old city, buildings still rest on wooden supports. Today, steel piles are driven into the ground to support buildings.

The river Hull flows into the Humber where there is a northwards bend in the estuary. The water swinging towards the northern bank helps to make the estuary deep near Hull. The port of Hull originally was at the inlet formed by the small river where it entered the estuary.

Today the population of Hull is 300 000; but the city is surrounded by sparsely inhabited land—the nearest comparable town is Leeds, 80 kilometres away. No other large town is so remote from other centres of population.

Moreover Hull does not have good routeways connecting it with other parts of the country. In the days when most heavy traffic went by water, Hull was excellently placed, for the Humber drains the largest area of any estuary in Britain. The Trent, the Don, the Aire, and the Ouse, all flow into the Humber, and it was easy to send goods to places as distant as Nottingham and York. Today, however, not much traffic uses the rivers unless it is going to the smaller ports of Goole and Selby. No new motorway has yet been built linking Hull with places to the west. There is no road or rail bridge across the Humber, so to go south from Hull means going inland round the Humber inlet.

In spite of this disadvantage, Hull is a major port, serving especially the Yorkshire West Riding industrial area. There are several docks. The largest, King George dock, is equipped for handling grain in bulk. Another main import is wool. Much of Hull's trade is with European countries, especially Scandinavia, and a

Fig. 174 An oilseed crushing mill (Premier Oil and Cake Mills Limited) beside the River Hull. The lighters in the foreground are ready to deliver oilseed. The motor vessel is loading animal feeding stuffs for export.

great deal of timber is imported on small ships from the smaller harbours of Norway and Sweden. At the western end of Hull, two docks are reserved for trawlers, and Hull is the largest fishing port in Britain. The trawlers return with a catch of cod and haddock after about three weeks at sea. At the docks they undergo repairs and take on supplies such as ice. An ice factory is adjacent to the docks.

Hull is also a manufacturing town. Many of the manufacturing industries are along the river Hull. Although this is only a small river, it is packed with barges which carry goods from the docks. Flour milling and the production of vegetable oils are two of the most typical port industries.

Hull is not the only port on the Humber. Goole and Selby are ports much further inland. On the south shore, Grimsby is a fishing port, and Immingham imports ores for the steelworks at Scunthorpe. The towns along the south of the Humber have the largest frozen food industry in Britain. New oil refineries and chemical works have been built at Immingham. The south shore of the Humber is rapidly developing as an industrial region, and North Sea gas may help it even more. A bridge across the Humber, linking the two sides, would be a great advantage both to Hull and to the south shore of the estuary. The name 'Humberside' is already used, and a bridge would help to make a reality out of the idea. A single span bridge is planned for the 1970s.

9. Look at the map of Tyneside p. 165. (a) List the north bank and south bank towns. (b) List the new towns marked. (c) How long is the conurbation from west to east and north to south? (d) Compare the shape of the conurbation with that of Manchester. (e) Where is the lowest bridge across the Tyne? (f) Where are the main shipbuilding yards?

Fig. 175   British Fisheries.

10. *Passenger Movements* 1965
Total departures and arrivals

	Irish Republic	Europe and Mediterranean	Rest of world	Total
Liverpool	263 000	—	68 000	331 000
Tyne	—	154 000	—	154 000
Hull	—	26 000	—	26 000

Use this table to compare the ports of northern England as passenger ports. (a) What are the main differences between the east and west coast ports? (b) What advantages has the Tyne over Hull as a passenger port? (c) Where do most of the 'rest of the world' passengers come from? (d) Why do Manchester and the Tees have so few passengers that they are not included on the list?

11. *Some leading imports and exports in thousand tonnes*

		Food and drink	Timber	Ores and scrap	Chemi-cals	Textiles	Iron and steel	Machinery and trans. equipment
Liverpool	imports	4080	753	2070	167	93	103	75
	exports	374	6	24	1064	108	1006	217
Manchester	imports	1001	290	809	219	13	102	17
	exports	31	1	7	307	14	170	89
Tyne	imports	382	325	1224	43	1	11	13
	exports	10	—	8	28	5	18	23
Tees	imports	6	19	3642	489	—	28	7
	exports	12	—	25	570	6	429	27
Hull	imports	1634	640	103	143	1	178	22
	exports	1710	—	8	131	28	117	150

Study the table above then answer the following: (a) The Tees is a regional rather than a national port. What does this mean? (b) Liverpool leads in every commodity

except one. Which port takes second place in each commodity? Give reasons.
(c) Which port takes last place in each commodity? What does this show about
the hinterlands of the ports?

12. Draw a map of north-east England. Make the Cleveland Hills the approximate
southern boundary and the Pennines the approximate western boundary. Include
three rivers, four Tyneside towns, Sunderland, four Teesside towns. Shade the
coalfield and use symbols to show the location of the shipbuilding, chemical, iron
and steel, and engineering industries. Use the maps on pages 117, 130 and 165
to help you.

13. Write lists—as complete as possible—of what you would put in maps to
explain each of the following: (a) Hull is in an agricultural countryside and the
nearest large town is Leeds, 80 kilometres away. (b) The Humber drains the largest
area of any estuary in Britain. (c) Hull has difficult communications southwards.
(d) Most of Hull's trade is with Europe, whereas most of Liverpool's trade is
trans-Atlantic, or with tropical countries.

14. Draw two columns headed Liverpool and Hull. Compare the two towns,
using the headings: position, the port, communications, the hinterland, exports
and imports, manufacturing industries.

15. Study the table below. (a) What change took place in the tonnage of fish
caught between 1955 and 1965? (b) Why can both Hull and Grimsby claim to be
the largest fishing ports? (c) Using Fig. 175 draw a map to show the major fishing
ports of Britain, and draw bars beside each to represent the amount of fish caught.
[See p. 135 for a model of how to do it.]

Catch of fish in weight and value

	1955		1965	
	Kilogrammes	*£ value*	*Kilogrammes*	*£ value*
Fleetwood	63 960 603	4 010 810	4 842 307	4 423 694
Grimsby	198 484 439	11 030 170	174 684 030	14 445 804
Hull	270 017 087	11 879 049	196 821 704	13 774 765
Lowestoft	24 619 070	1 521 602	21 667 267	2 630 982
Milford Haven	20 920 151	1 457 551	8 581 339	772 924
North Shields	18 803 874	821 463	14 523 212	1 056 839

16. Read the following passage and look at the map (Fig. 175) and your atlas, then answer the questions below:

'The passively drifting or floating life of the sunlit surface waters we call the "plankton". This consists of some relatively large organisms such as jellyfish, but vastly more important are the smaller organisms, plant and animal, many of which are microscopic in size. The plankton form the true meadows of the sea. Nearly all the fish of the different levels of the water are nourished ultimately from the microscopic plant life of the sunlit surface waters.

For their nourishment the plants need light, water and carbonic acid gas but they also need supplies of nitrogen, phosphorous and certain other elements. Now the sea contains incalculable quantities of these, but the great bulk are in deep waters miles below the shallow illuminated zone where alone plants can live. It is not easy for the contents of the deep seas to pass upwards. In the tropical and temperate seas the warmer, upper layers float on the colder, denser water below and this prevents mixing. In the polar seas free mixing does occur, and hence the great productivity of these waters during the brief summer period. But in wide regions of shallow temperate seas where winter storms mix the water from top to bottom and rich currents flow in from the open ocean there is a similar fertility. It is such conditions which prevail around our coasts.'[1]

(a) Write a brief definition of plankton. (b) Why are the plants of the plankton only found in surface waters? (c) Much of the nitrogen, phosphorous, etc. is carried into the sea by rivers. Name four large rivers which flow into the shallow seas around Britain. (d) How does the mixing of water from top to bottom help the plant life of the sea? (e) Name the shallow seas which surround Britain. They are part of the 'Continental Shelf', which is a drowned part of the continental land mass. How deep is the water at the edge of the continental shelf? How deep is the shallowest part of the continental shelf? (f) Write a paragraph to explain why plankton are abundant in the shallow waters of the continental shelf. How does this affect the fisheries of Britain?

[1]Adapted from *British Marine Life* by C. M. Yonge (Collins 1944).

12. South Wales

There are two parts to South Wales: the coastal lowlands and the hills. The lowlands include the plain of Gwent, the Vale of Glamorgan, the Gower peninsula, and they extend westwards to Pembrokeshire. They are green undulating farmlands, in between crowded industrial cities. The rainfall here is around 1000 mm, much less than on the hills. The winters are mild, with up to nine months without frost on the western edge of Pembrokeshire.

It is mixed farming land, but dairy cattle are everywhere the most important enterprise, and the crops like oats and hay are grown for cattle. The mild damp climate is one advantage for dairy farming, and another is the market provided

Fig. 176. A sheep market in South Wales.

173

12. SOUTH WALES

Fig. 177   Carmarthen, a town in rural South Wales west of the industrial area. Draw a sketch of the photograph to show where Carmarthen is built in relation to the river. Add notes beside the sketch about the meanders, the flood plain, the bridges.

Fig. 178   The South Wales coast near Tenby, Pembrokeshire. Compare this photograph with the one of Cornwall on page 100. How are Cornwall and Pembrokeshire alike ?

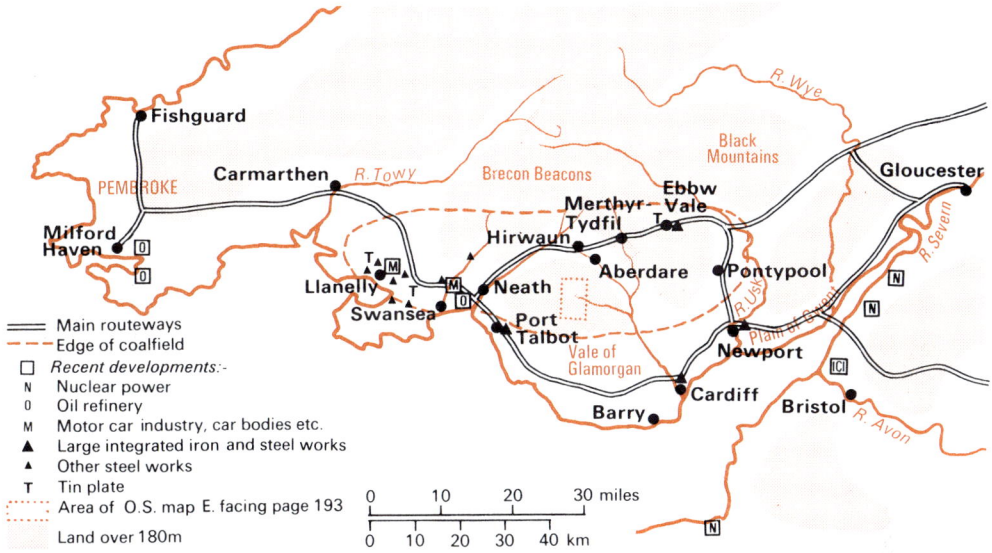

Fig. 179   South Wales and Severnside.

by the nearby industrial towns. The fields and hedgerows reach to a coast of bays and headlands, which is especially beautiful in the Gower peninsula and Pembrokeshire. Tenby, Mumbles and Porthcawl are some of the holiday resorts.

The hills of South Wales are cut into by very deep, steep-sided valleys, where rivers have eroded grooves in the land. Between the valleys are high moorlands which form lines of hills 450 m high but they hardly have a chance to broaden out into plateaux. The parallel valleys are so characteristic of South Wales that the hill region is known colloquially as 'The Valleys'. Here the climate is too wet and the ground too steep for much farming. Peat bogs and rough pasture cover the hillsides where sheep graze, and some pit ponies are still kept.

South Wales, however, is essentially an industrial area, and industry has depended largely on the coalfield. The South Wales coalfield is one of the richest

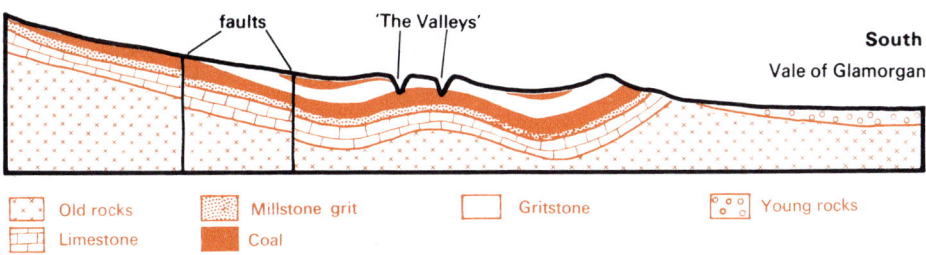

Fig. 180   Section across the South Wales coalfield. The valleys run from north-west to south-east.

Fig. 181 Cwm-parc, Glamorgan, looking eastwards. Notice the level hilltops beside the valley, the long rows of terrace houses in the valley.

in Britain, because it contains various kinds of coal, including good quality coking coal in the east, and anthracite in the west. Although broken by faults, it is fairly easy to mine especially at the northern end where the rocks dip gently. As the coalfield is cut by valleys, outcrops of coal are found on the valley sides. During

176

the nineteenth century there was a tremendous development of the coalfield. After 1850 the demand for coal suddenly grew, as railways, ships and steel industries all began to use large quantities of it. There was also a large demand for coal overseas. People crowded into the Welsh valleys as though it was a gold rush.

Ordnance Survey Map E, facing p. 193 shows one of the valleys, the Rhondda, which was completely changed by this boom in coal. Here the population grew from 4000 in 1861 to 163 000 in 1921. The coal mined in the Rhondda Valley was steam coal, used in ships and on railways. The railway line to Cardiff was opened in 1855, and Cardiff became one of the main coal exporting ports. A new port was opened at Barry later in the century. This sudden development of the coal exporting trade in Wales led to the pattern of roads, railways and towns squeezed into narrow elongated valleys which is still so characteristic of South Wales (Fig. 181). Coal is no longer exported, but coal mining is still a major industry, employing more people than any other in South Wales. Many of the smaller pits have now been closed, and only the large ones with good reserves remain open. This has resulted in much unemployment in the valleys. The population of the Rhondda Valley was only 95 000 in 1966.

Metal industries are, however, more important, and one-third of the coal mined goes into coke ovens for use in making iron and steel. Iron smelting is an old established industry in Wales. Before 1850, the towns at 'the heads of the valleys', from Hirwaun through Aberdare and Merthyr Tydfil to Ebbw Vale, grew as iron smelting towns. Rich bands of iron were found at the northern edge of the coalfield; there were also supplies of coal and limestone. By 1850, South Wales was the leading producer of iron in Britain.

But after 1850, when steel began to be made instead of iron, these towns were not so well placed. The local ores were nearly exhausted. Gradually the valley iron works died out, and enterprising firms moved their businesses to the coasts, where ore could be imported cheaply from abroad in returning coal ships. Another advantage on the coast was that the works did not have to be enclosed in such narrow cramped sites with poor east-west communications.

The movement to the coast continued, and today the coasts are far more important for iron and steel than the valleys. The only iron and steel works which remains in the valleys is at Ebbw Vale, and this was built here in 1938 by Richard Thomas and Baldwins, chiefly in order to bring jobs to an area where many people were out of work. This was part of government policy to aid the depressed areas. (See p. 131).

The growth of metal industries on the coasts has been so great that South Wales again took the lead in iron and steel production in the 1960s after being overtaken by the north-east region. The Steel Company of Wales plant at Port Talbot is the largest in Britain. It is surrounded by a region rich in metal smelting plant. The newest steel works is that of Richard Thomas and Baldwins (R.T.B.) at Newport—the Spencer Works—which was completed in 1962.

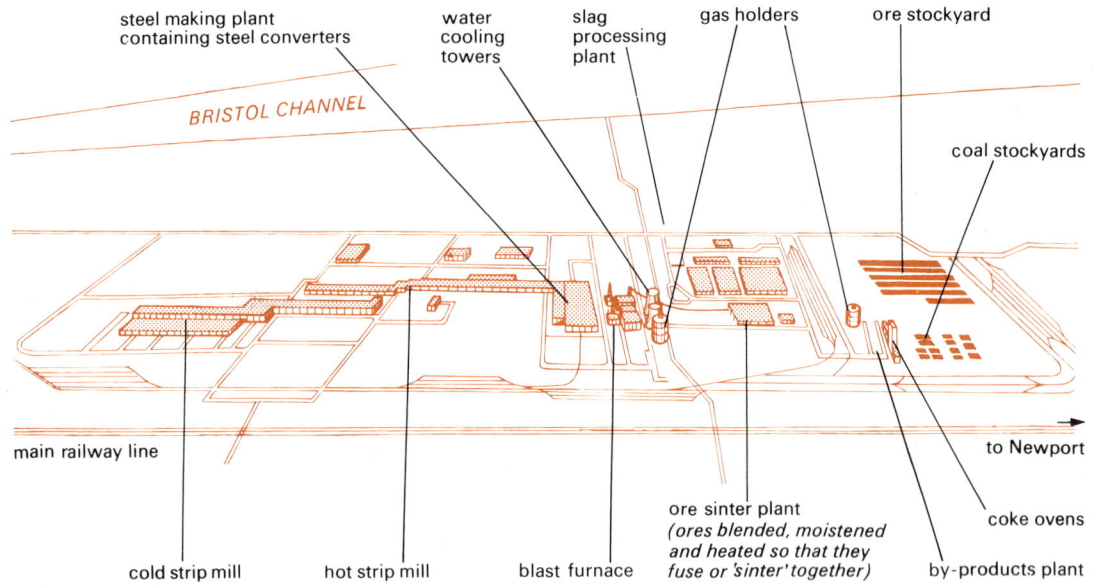

steel making plant
containing steel converters

water
cooling
towers

slag
processing
plant

gas holders

ore stockyard

coal stockyards

BRISTOL CHANNEL

main railway line

to Newport

cold strip mill

hot strip mill

blast furnace

ore sinter plant
*(ores blended, moistened
and heated so that they
fuse or 'sinter' together)*

by-products plant

coke ovens

Fig. 182   The Spencer steel works.

The Spencer Works

This is an integrated iron and steel works; that is, steel is made from iron at the plant in a continuous process. The Spencer Works employs (1967) about 8000 people.

Fig. 182 shows the layout of the works. The three main raw materials—coal, iron ore, and limestone—are brought in at the western end, closest to Newport. These are all processed before they are put in the blast furnace where iron is made.

Fig. 183 shows what happens inside the blast furnace. Hot air is blown in so that the mixture of coke, limestone and ore heats to 2000 °C. There are three large stoves beside the blast furnace which heat the air. The iron melts, and collects at the bottom of the furnace. It is let out through tap holes at the bottom. Tapping takes place every few hours. This is pig-iron, which got its name in earlier times when ore was poured into moulds lying side by side, resembling young pigs being suckled. The waste material of the blast furnaces is slag, which is cooled and used for road making.

The hot iron is poured into ladles and taken on a railway to the steel plant where it is poured, still hot, into the steel converter.

The three huge steel converters are the mainspring of the whole works, and the core of the mass of buildings and machinery which spread over the site. When iron leaves the blast furnaces, it contains various impurities, including 3 per cent to 5 per cent carbon, and smaller quantities of manganese, silicon and phosphorous. To make steel most of the impurities must be removed. They are driven off when they combine with oxygen at high temperatures. The iron is therefore heated again in an egg-shaped container called a converter, where it is changed into steel.

178

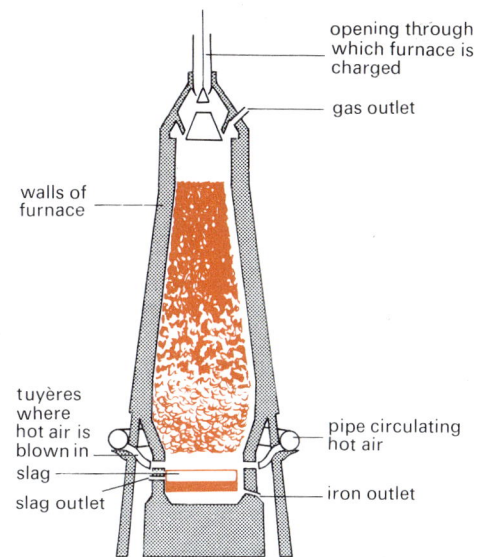

Fig. 183 The blast furnace, where ore, coke and limestone are heated to make pig-iron. Molten iron collects at the bottom and is tapped away every few hours.

The mixture poured into the converter is about 70 per cent iron and 30 per cent scrap. Much of the scrap comes from within the plant, from cuttings of ends of steel made when it is rolled.

The converters used at the Spencer Works are called L.D. (Linz Doenewitz), the name given to a process first used in the mid-1950s. Pure oxygen is blown into the converter. The molten iron reaches fierce temperatures and gives off such dazzling light that steel workers wear dark glasses to look at it. The steel is ready in about twenty minutes. Towards the end of this time the chemical composition of the steel is tested.

The finished steel must have exactly correct proportions of carbon, and other elements such as manganese. Different proportions give the steel different properties, making it harder, more flexible, more resistant to corrosion. Although nearly every process in the Spencer Works is automated, the job of the steel maker is not, and his work needs experience and skill.

The L.D. process is relatively new. Most steel was previously made by one of two methods. (1) The open hearth method—the iron is reheated by gases in a shallow basin and the varying amounts of iron, scrap, and other materials are added gradually, over a period (today) of about eight hours. It is a slow process, but the composition of the steel can be carefully controlled and the result is a good quality steel. (2) The Bessemer converter method (see p. 139)—air under great pressure is blown through molten iron. The oxygen in the air combines with the impurities in the iron which escape as gas. The Bessemer process works quickly, and hence the quality of the steel is difficult to control. Its use is limited because of the nitrogen in the air which is also blown through.

Fig. 184   A steel strip being rolled out in the hot strip mill at the Spencer steel works.

The L.D. process is an adaptation of the Bessemer process. By using pure oxygen, this disadvantage of the Bessemer process is overcome. This has only been possible in recent years, since oxygen has been produced in bulk. When the steel is ready it is cooled into blocks called 'ingots', and is rolled into thinner shapes in the hot strip mills. As the steel is rolled thinner, it becomes longer, until eventually it forms a strip about one and a half metres wide, 2·5 mm thick, and thousands of metres long, which shoots out between the rollers at a temperature of 1100 °C. It is further reduced in the cold rolling mills, and finishing processes make it smooth

Fig. 185   The iron and steel industry.

▲ Large integrated iron and steel
  works (capacity 1 million tonnes)

△ Other integrated iron and steel
  works (capacity below 1 million tonnes)

● Steel works
○ Blast furnaces

  Coalfields

  Jurassic iron ore deposits-supply
  97% of home produce

  Imports of ore-70% of ore used is imported
  Width of arrow shows relative size
  of imports into different regions

and malleable. Most of the long strips are coiled, but some are cut into smaller lengths called sheets.

There are many reasons why Newport was chosen as a site for this great new steel plant. One was that it was near Ebbw Vale, an iron and steel plant which is also part of R.T.B. A second was that it was near supplies of coking coal and limestone, which could be brought from the South Wales valleys. The low, level site also gave room to build, and to expand in the future. There was a water supply, for the works requires 264 million litres constantly circulating, chiefly to cool the hot machinery.

But the most important reason for choosing Newport was its position by the coast. Nearly all the iron ore which is used comes from abroad—from Sweden, Africa, and North and South America. Only a small amount comes from Oxfordshire. Moreover about 40 per cent of the finished steel is exported. The position on the coast and near Newport makes trade in raw materials and finished products easier. The company plans to build a new jetty to receive ore ships, and the ore will be carried to the plant directly by conveyer.

Newport has an advantage over Port Talbot, in that it is nearer to the Midlands and London markets. Fig. 186 shows why these markets are so important to steel producers. Except for the steel plating industry, nearly all the industries using steel are outside South Wales. Steel is the basis of manufacturing industry. It is used to make machinery, and in a great variety of products, as Fig. 186 shows.

Fig. 186 Where sheet steel is used in Britain. Compare this map with the one opposite (Fig. 185) showing where steel is made.

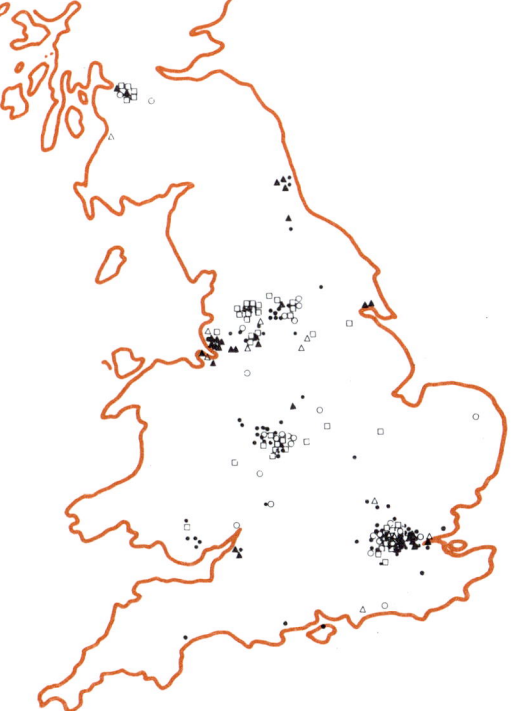

▲ Iron and steel kegs
• Steel furniture
△ Domestic refrigerators
▢ Washing and wringing machines
○ Motor vehicle bodies

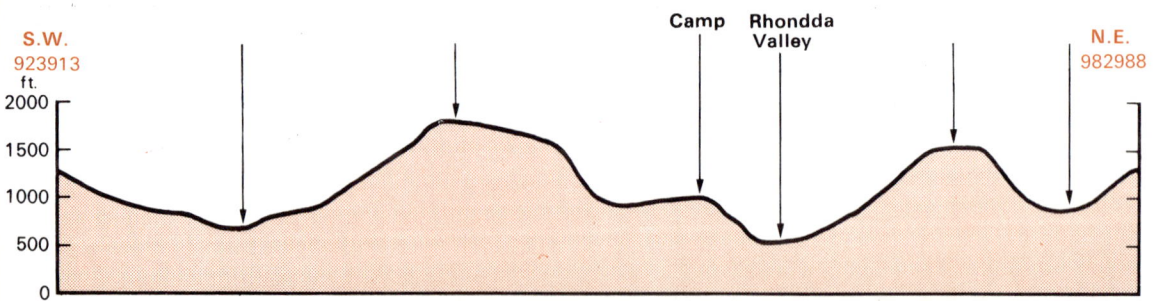

Fig. 187   The oil refinery at Milford Haven. The ria at Milford Haven has one of the most splendid harbours in Britain. What disadvantages has it as a port? Milford Haven is linked by oil pipeline to Llandarcy near Swansea where there is also an oil refinery.

Fig. 188   Section across Ordnance Survey Map E, facing p. 193 (see question 13).

Iron and steel are not the only metal industries in South Wales. Tin plating is also very important. Tin plate is steel sheet covered with a thin layer of tin. The tin coating is rust resistant, and tin plate is used in making cans and boxes. This is an industry which has grown a great deal, especially over the last 50 years, and continues to expand. Tin plating used to be fairly widespread in South Wales, but today it is concentrated in only three plants. Tin plating uses a great deal of the steel sheet produced in South Wales, and is one of the reasons why the steel industry has grown so much. The two depend on each other. Copper and nickel smelting have been important in the past, and galvanized iron is still produced (steel sheet coated with zinc). The area around Swansea and Llanelly is famous for metal smelting.

A majority of the people in South Wales are employed in the heavy industries of coal mining and metals. South Wales therefore was one of the regions which suffered much unemployment during the depression between the wars. However, more variety in industry has now come to the area. During the war, many factories were deliberately moved here to be less vulnerable to bombing. Several aluminium works were built, for example, and armaments factories were put up at Hirwaun and Bridgend.

Since the war it has been part of government policy to bring new growing industries to the development areas (see p. 131). Between 1945 and 1962 over 1000 new industries came to South Wales, many of them small light industries employing women. Two very large firms to bring variety to the area were British Nylon Spinners (now part of I.C.I.) who have a factory at Pontypool, and Hoover at Merthyr Tydfil.

On the whole, however, new industries have moved to the coast towns, which were already the largest centres of population. Cardiff is the largest town with a population of one-quarter of a million. In 1801, it was hardly more than a village, and with only 2000 people living there it was smaller than Merthyr Tydfil. It grew as a coal port and later added iron and steel industries. Today, it is also a centre of light industry, and is a city with many functions, as befits the capital of Wales. Swansea is a smaller town, but easily the largest of the group in the west of the coalfield where metal industries predominate. The agglomeration of industry is much greater around Swansea.

The coasts are favoured both for light and for heavy industry. This is likely to be increasingly the case. The new Severn road bridge has given South Wales a link with the Bristol area, which with new petro-chemical industries is likely to become much more industrial. 'Severnside' may be an industrial region before long.

The industrial development of South Wales can thus be summed up in four stages:
1. Growth of iron industries at the heads of the valleys.
2. Development of coal mining along the valleys.
3. Growth of coast towns with metal smelting industries.
4. More varied industry brought to region, but still with the greatest growth along the coast, and in the eastern half.

1. In what way is it true to say that there is little waste at the Spencer steel works? Which products can be re-used?

2. Describe what happens in (a) coke ovens, (b) blast furnace, (c) converter, (d) hot rolling mill.

3. The following table shows total U.K. steel output in million tonnes:

1920	9 036 406
1930	7 442 911
1950	16 553 383
1960	24 693 880
1965	27 442 160

Draw a graph to show change in steel output. How do you account for the drop in 1930, and the rapid increase since 1950?

4. Draw a bar graph to represent the following information:

1965 steel-output in million tonnes -

Open hearth	L.D. and Bessemer Converter	Electric arc	Others	Total
17 489 627	6 385 255	3 400 552	71 018	27 346 452

5. Write a list of the main industries found along the coast of South Wales and Severnside from Milford Haven to Bristol. [See also p. 114.]

6. How are Severnside and Humberside (a) alike, (b) different? [See also p. 114 ch. 8 and p. 169 ch. 9.]

7. The Government pays a grant of 40 per cent to industrialists who establish works in the Welsh valleys. The cost is about £1000 for each job created. What arguments would you use for and against this policy?

8. Look at Fig. 185. What facts does the map show about the difference between the iron and steel industry in South Wales and (a) Sheffield, (b) North-east England?

9. Using the Ordnance Survey map of the Rhondda Valley facing p. 193: Draw two rectangles the same size as the map. Mark on them the rivers and the 1000 ft. contour. On one, mark roads, railways, and mineral tracks. On the other mark built-up areas. Write paragraphs to explain the facts shown on each map.

10. Find Cwm-parc valley which extends through squares 9495 and 9596. Compare the map with the photograph of the valley on p. 176. Draw a sketch of the photograph, and label Cwm-parc, Cafn-y-Rhondda, Rhondda Valley, the A.4061, the mine, a coal tip.

11. Give the grid reference for the place where the photograph (Fig. 181) was taken from.

12. How does the route of the A.4107 (square 9295) differ from the routes taken by the other A roads? Where does a B road follow a similar route to the A.4107?

13. Fig. 188 has been drawn from south-west to north-east across the map. Copy the section and (a) Label the hills and valleys marked with arrows. (b) Add arrows pointing to the main roads. (c) What is the vertical scale used? (d) Draw a similar section from 922980 to 945000. Label the section and add a note about the shape of the valley.

13. The Midlands

Where are the Midlands? Geographers disagree over the answer to this question. This description takes for the boundary roughly the line of the long escarpments —the Cotswolds and Northampton heights—which cross central England. North of this line 'the local accents are of the northern kind; accents differ from town to town, but in the southern ear all vowels are unmistakably northern,' but further south, 'the local speech has a strong rustic flavour—if it has escaped the influence of London.'[1] It is probably best not to draw exact boundaries around a region which touches so many others.

The Midlands are an uneven country of hills and plains. The hilly lands are marked on Fig. 190 and include the Welsh borderland, which is a continuation of ancient rocks of the Welsh mountain mass. These have been eroded into a beautiful, varied scenery of hills, plains, and valleys. The Malvern Hills are a continuous ridge thrust straight up at the edge of the Severn Plain. Other areas of old, hard rock are the separated blocks of the Clent Hills, and Charnwood Forest.

The plains between the hills are composed of sedimentary rocks, red sandstones and clays, which have been more easily eroded to form lowlands. Many of the churches and cathedrals in the West Midlands are built of red stone, and the fields are often red where the plough has turned over the soil.

Coalfields are found around the edges of the hills. In the West Midlands these are scattered and rather small but they have helped in the industrial development of the region in the past. The coalfields of the East Midlands, however, are the most productive in the country.

Although the Midlands are primarily industrial, all the rural areas are intensively farmed. The Welsh borderlands are wet, with over 900 mm of rainfall, and most of the farmland is used for pasture and livestock. Hereford beef cattle, especially young cattle, are reared here, although they are often sent to counties further east for fattening. But dairy cattle are just as important, and easily take the lead in Shropshire in the plains around Shrewsbury. Sheep are also raised.

Almost as many hops are grown in Worcestershire and Herefordshire as in south-east England. This mild south-western corner of the Midlands produces a great deal of fruit, both small fruit and orchard fruit. The Vale of Evesham, where gravels beside the river Avon give well drained, sloping land, is especially famous.

[1] G. H. Dury: *The British Isles*. Heinemann 1964. p. 342.

13. THE MIDLANDS

Fig. 189   Hills and vales in Shropshire near Newcastle-under-Lyme.

The eastern areas of the Midlands are rather drier, and more of the land is used for arable farming than further west. A great many beef cattle are raised in Leicestershire. This is a traditional type of farming, for the pastures on the boulder clay soil are believed to be extremely nourishing and support a large number of cattle and sheep. Many of the cattle are bought in from farms further west for fattening.

The Midlands are a transitional region; in the west the land is used mostly for pasturing dairy cattle, in the east for arable farming and raising cattle for beef. The farm described on p. 53 is on the eastern edge of the Midlands, and the leading enterprise is arable farming.

Transport

The map, Fig. 191, shows that the Midlands are a cross-roads for man-made routes. Rivers flow away from the Midlands. The area is a watershed, and there is no one river linking the whole region together. But the rivers flowing away from the centre—the Severn, the Weaver and the Trent—lead to three different estuaries; and the headwaters of the Thames are only just outside the Midlands, leading to a fourth estuary. Parts of the Midlands, therefore, have always been linked with the ports, and much traffic has used the rivers in the past. The Severn, for example, was busy with traffic in iron ore from the Forest of Dean and coal from Shropshire, and Bewdley grew to be a great river port.

The canal network which was built to link the four river systems together, so that every part of the Midlands was served by water routes, was a great stimulus

186

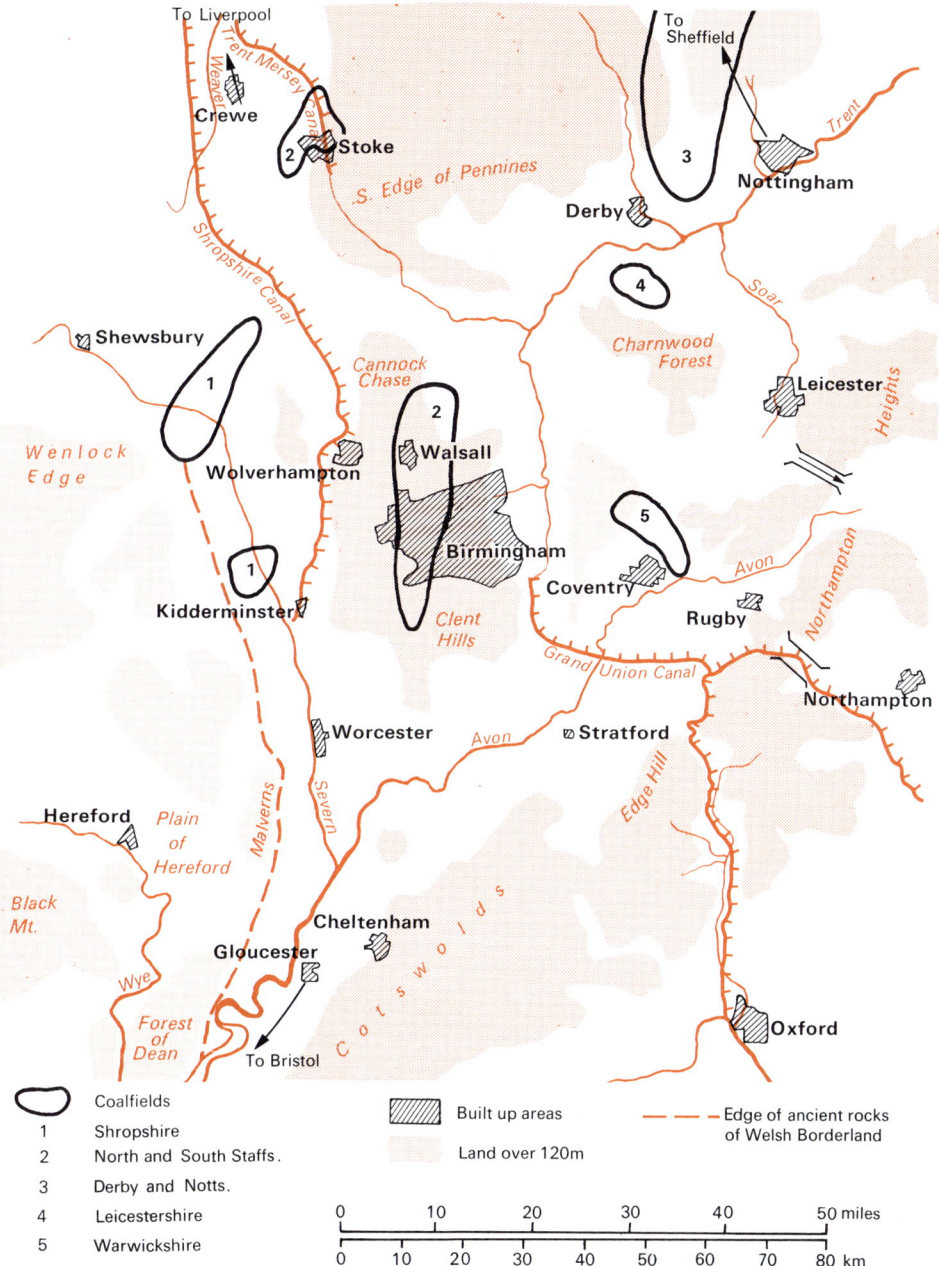

To Liverpool

Trent Mersey and

Weaver

Crewe

Stoke

2

S. Edge of Pennines

To Sheffield

3

Trent

Nottingham

Derby

Soar

Shropshire Canal

Shewsbury

1

Cannock Chase

Charnwood Forest

4

Leicester

Heights

Wenlock Edge

2

Walsall

Wolverhampton

Birmingham

5

Avon

Northampton Uplands

1

Clent Hills

Coventry

Kidderminster

Rugby

Grand Union Canal

Northampton

Worcester

Avon

Stratford

Malverns

Severn

Edge Hill

Hereford

Plain of Hereford

Black Mt.

Cheltenham

Cotswolds

Wye

Gloucester

Forest of Dean

Oxford

To Bristol

	Coalfields		Built up areas		Edge of ancient rocks of Welsh Borderland
1	Shropshire		Land over 120m		
2	North and South Staffs.				
3	Derby and Notts.				
4	Leicestershire				
5	Warwickshire				

0   10   20   30   40   50 miles

0 10 20 30 40 50 60 70 80 km

Fig. 190   The Midlands and Welsh borderlands.

187

to the growth of industry. The great canal building age lasted from 1757 to 1830. The engineers of the period, such as Telford, who later built the Menai Bridge, and Brindley, who built the Bridgewater Canal in Lancashire, learned much of their skill through constructing canals.

Most of the canals which were built with such enthusiasm are no longer used. They are too narrow and have too many locks. In the Midlands only a few still carry any goods, chiefly coal from the mines of south Staffordshire.

At the same time, the roads were greatly improved and became the envy of other countries. By 1830, the mail coaches averaged a speed of 16 km p.h., and it was possible to travel from London to Manchester in 18 hours. The cost of transport by canal, however, was only one-third that by road, and it was used for bulky or fragile cargoes, like coal and porcelain.

This cheap form of transport made an enormous difference to the trade of the country. These changes were described in 1782:

'The cottage, instead of being half covered with miserable thatch, is now covered with a substantial covering of tiles or slates brought from the distant hills of Wales or Cumberland. The fields, which before were barren, are now drained, and by the assistance of manure conveyed on the canal toll-free, are clothed with a beautiful verdure. Places which rarely knew the use of coal are plentifully supplied with that essential article upon reasonable terms; and, what is of still greater public utility, the monopolizers of corn are prevented from

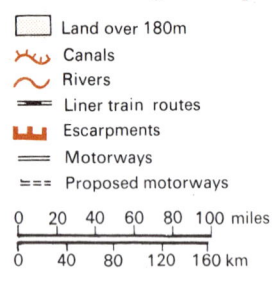

Land over 180m
Canals
Rivers
Liner train routes
Escarpments
Motorways
Proposed motorways

0   20   40   60   80 100 miles
0   40   80   120   160 km

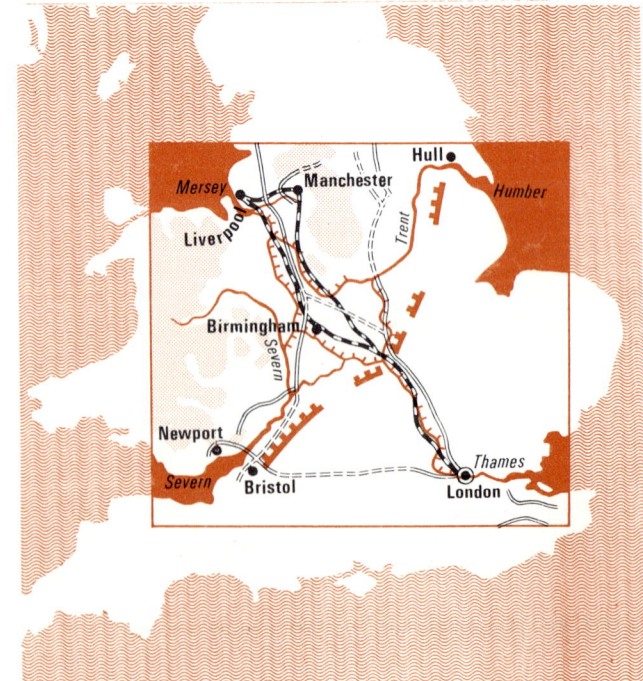

Fig. 191   The Midlands crossroads.

188

Fig. 192   The M.1 in the Midlands.

exercising their infamous trade; for communication being opened between Liverpool, Bristol and Hull, and the line of canal being through counties abundant in grain, it affords a conveyance of corn unknown in past ages.'[1]

However, both canal and road transport were overtaken in 1830 by the railways, which spread rapidly over the country after the commercial success of the first locomotive-drawn trains for passengers and goods in Lancashire. The first line to be completed across the country was that between London, Birmingham and Manchester. Railway lines soon covered the country with a dense network and because trains were fast and could carry large quantities of small goods, they certainly helped the growth of the small, light industries typical of the Midlands today. Some towns, like Crewe and Rugby, owed their growth to being chosen as railway junctions. But the cost of rail transport was greater than that of canal transport for bulky goods.

Throughout the last half of the nineteenth century and most of the first half of the twentieth, railways were used for carrying goods, and the canals gradually declined. Today much traffic still goes by rail, and the use of containers and development of freight liners may encourage manufacturers to use the railway more. But the railways have lost much of their trade to the roads, and road transport is used even over long distances and for bulky cargoes.

The great advantage of motor transport is that goods can be taken direct from door to door. The building of motorways is helping to speed up traffic. The motorways are designed for non-stop traffic including heavy lorries and bulk carriers. The first stretch of motorway which was completed in 1959 linked the Midlands to London. The map opposite shows that when the motorway system is complete, the Midlands will be well linked by road with other parts of the country.

[1] quoted in *English Social History* by G. M. Trevelyan

189

Fig. 193   Rugby. Compare this photograph with Ordnance Survey Map D, facing p. 193, and find where it was taken from. On the right of the picture is the large works of the Associated Electrical Industries, and beyond the gas works on the left is the factory of English Electric (now both merged in GEC). The cattle market is on the left by the railway.

Most of the questions below refer to Ordnance Survey Map D, facing p. 193 which shows Rugby, a town about 16 kilometres south-east of Coventry. Rugby has a population of 55 000. It is a main railway junction and, apart from being a major industrial town, it also has one of the largest cattle markets in the country. Many facts about the development of transport are illustrated in the map.

1. Follow the course of the river Avon from square 5277 to the point where it leaves the map in the west. Why is this part of the river unsuitable for navigation?

2. Describe the route followed by (a) the Oxford Canal and (b) the railway, from where they enter the map in the south (5268) to the point where they cross in square 5176. Where was it difficult to build them and how were the difficulties overcome?

3. What are: aqueduct, viaduct, underpass, lock? Find one of each on the map and give a grid reference for it. Why was each necessary?

190

4. Read pp. 186–9 then list the main types of routeway shown on the map in the order in which they were built. (The straight road in the north-east corner of the map is part of the Roman road Watling Street.) What are the advantages and disadvantages of each type of transport?

5. Compare (a) the pattern of roads and (b) the shape of the built-up area in Ordnance Survey Maps D and E facing p. 193. How was each influenced by relief?

6. Find examples on the map of: (a) nucleated settlement—settlement clustered round one main centre, (b) ribbon development—houses strung out along a road, (c) urban sprawl—haphazard spread of houses over the countryside.

7. What arguments would you use (a) in favour of, (b) against: bringing the canals back into use; sending all heavy freight by rail.

8. Write an essay to explain one of these statements: (a) Farming in the Midlands is transitional, (b) The Midlands lie at the cross-roads of England.

The industrial regions

There are three industrial regions in the Midlands, each with a distinctive combination of manufactures. (1) The West Midlands, which includes Birmingham, Coventry and the Black Country; (2) The Potteries, in and around Stoke-on-Trent; (3) The East Midlands, centred on the three towns of Nottingham, Leicester and Derby.

The West Midlands

The map below shows Coalbrookdale, which is a little removed from the main area of the West Midlands. It was here that coal was first used to smelt iron

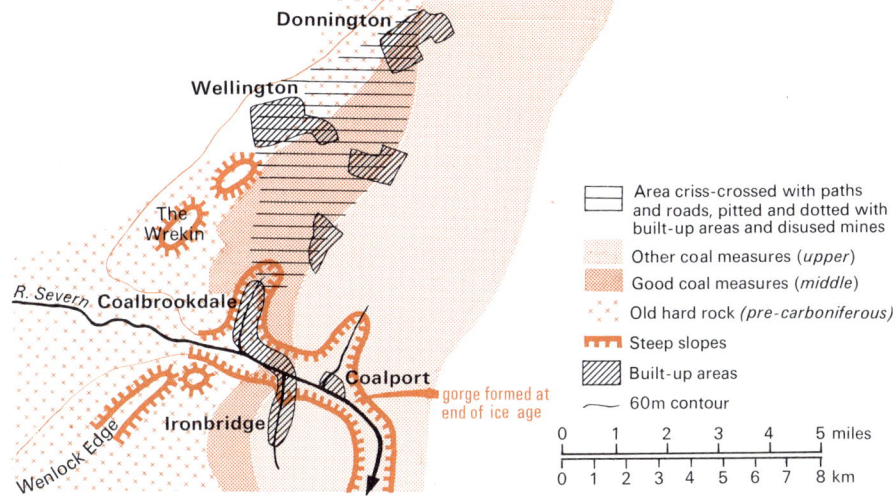

Fig. 194   Coalbrookdale and the Shropshire coalfield.

191

successfully, the process which more than anything else started the industrial revolution. The first iron bridge built in Europe remains as a monument across the Severn.

Thriving iron industries grew on the small coalfields of Shropshire and Staffordshire. Hundreds of blast furnaces, coal and iron mines made the West Midlands one of the smokiest, most pitted landscapes in Britain, hence the name 'Black Country' given to part of the region.

Today, the whole character of industry in the West Midlands has changed. The two outstandingly important industries are engineering, especially the manufacture of small metal goods, and the motor car industry. Both these industries depend on good communications. The small metal goods must be sent to the builders and engineers who need them, and the motor car industry must gather a great variety of products at the assembly plants. Thus the central position of the Midlands, and the development of transport, greatly helped the industries most typical of the Midlands today to grow.

The following is a description of a factory typical of the Birmingham area.

An engineering factory

G.K.N. Screws and Fasteners Limited is situated in Smethwick on the borders of Birmingham and the Black Country. Here 5000 people are employed making small metal goods. For example, 15 000 different sizes of screw are made. Another speciality of the factory is the production of pushrods for the motor car industry. (Pushrods open the valves on the type of engine used in most cars.)

Fig. 195   An old iron ore mine in the Forest of Dean. Find the Forest of Dean on the map on page 187, and the route up the Severn to Coalbrookdale.

Map C, Kettlewell and Conistone Moor, Yorkshire (one inch represents one mile).

The raw material for this factory arrives in the form of steel rod and wire. The wire may be up to 13 mm in diameter. It is brought by road from steel works at Cardiff and Scunthorpe. On the shop floor are hundreds of machines, which cut and shape the steel. The machines are set to make whichever shape and size is required. One man may work five machines. The incessant hammering of the machine tools makes an engineering factory one of the noisiest places to work in.

This factory was built in the middle of the nineteenth century close to a canal, where coal could easily be brought to provide the steam power by which the machines were originally run. The factory turned over to electric power in the 1920s. The canal is no longer used even to take the finished product to the railway. Nearly all the products are sent by road, and there are regular deliveries of lorry loads especially to London and the motor car factories.

This description of a west midlands factory gives some idea of the variety of products made in the area. It is also typical in that it depends largely on South Wales for supplies of raw material, and it shows the way that means of transport and power have changed over the decades.

Birmingham, the 'city of a thousand trades', is a great engineering workshop. A metal goods wholesaler in Birmingham stocks thousands of products, including

Fig. 196 Birmingham has a very large building programme. Much of the Victorian city remains—streets of red brick two-storey terrace houses and small factories and workshops. Near the centre whole areas have been bulldozed, the streets replanned and high blocks of flats built. The old Bull Ring is overlooked by a round tower which houses offices, and nearby there is a covered market and bus station built on several floors linked by escalators.

large machine tools, tiny tools for the jewellery and clock trades, and a whole range of screws, nails, nuts, bolts, washers, hinges and locks. These goods are expensive in proportion to their small size and weight. Manufacturers can afford to transport them long distances. As Birmingham is at the centre of the country it is well placed for distributing small but vital equipment.

A characteristic industry of Birmingham is the making of jewellery. This trade is concentrated in 130 hectares of small, congested houses and workshops called the jewellery quarter. Each firm employs fewer than ten people.

North of Birmingham and continuous with it, are the towns of the Black Country, shown on the map below. The name is out of date, for today there is almost no heavy industry, and most of the remaining smoke comes from the electric power stations. As in Birmingham, a variety of goods are made, but metal goods are far more important than anything else. They range from quite simple things like baths and buckets to complicated products such as machine tools or switch gear. There is little heavy industry left apart from iron and steel smelting at Bilston.

The Black Country has lost some of the advantages which originally made it an industrial region. The best coal seams and the iron ore have been used up. The region has turned to the manufacture of smaller goods, because the cost of transporting bulky raw materials to this inland area would be too great.

Coventry was an important mediaeval town, but modern manufacturing industry came to it rather late, and it has grown most rapidly in this century. The population, now 300 000, has doubled since 1930. It is one of the most prosperous cities today because it has so many different kinds of engineering industries which employ nearly half the people.

Fig. 197   The centre of Coventry, rebuilt after devastation during World War II.

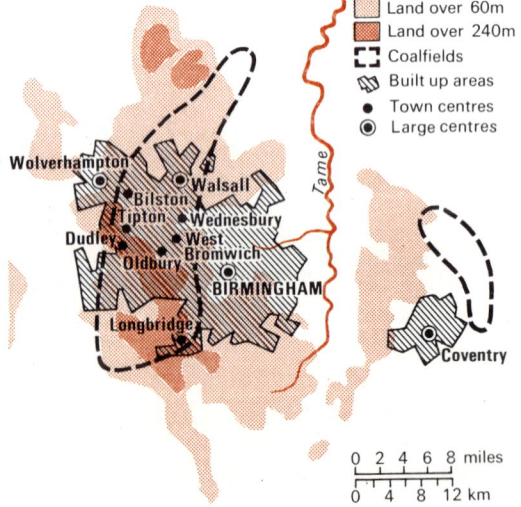

Fig. 198   The Black Country—the group of tow spreads out north-west of Birmingham.

The motor car industry

The greatest employer in both Birmingham and Coventry is the motor car industry. The motor car industry is one of the most important to Britain, because motor cars are our greatest single export. Commercial vehicles and tractors are in second place. The motor car industry is a growth industry. The demand for motor cars is growing and during the first half of the 1960s, the leading manufacturers all increased their production. In order to do this, they had to build more factories. Fig. 201 shows where the main motor car factories are, and which ones were built after 1960. Besides building new factories on new sites, most of the older factories were expanded and reorganized.

The largest car firm is British Leyland and Fig. 199 shows the location of some of their factories. British Motor Corporation was formed in 1952 when the Austin Motor Company joined the Nuffield organization, making one vast concern. The makes of vehicle produced by the joint firm included Austin, Morris, M.G., Riley and Wolseley. In 1966 B.M.C. merged with Jaguar cars of Coventry and in 1968 with Leyland Motors. This is one of several large scale mergers which have taken place in the motor car industry.

The motor car industry is a masterpiece of organization. There are over 10 000 pieces in a motor car, and these must all be collected at the assembly plant and fitted together. British Leyland have factories which specialize in making certain parts, such as radiators or engines. Some of the smaller parts are made in machine shops at the assembly plants. Most of the car bodies are made by the Pressed Steel works at Oxford or Llanelly, and the separate pieces of shaped steel are welded together. The bodies arrive at the factory 'in the white', that is, unpainted.

Many parts are not made by British Leyland but by other companies which specialize in making certain goods for motor cars. These components include electrical equipment (starters, lamps, instruments), hardware (door handles, locks, nameplates) trim (seat cushion frames, imitation leather), glass and rubber.

At the assembly plant, the body is painted and the different parts are fitted to it. It is placed on a moving conveyor. Each man working on the assembly of the car has a special job to do, such as fitting in electrical equipment or windows. A separate conveyor carries the engine, which is fitted in to the body. Usually a man does not spend his entire time at one job, but gains experience of many different jobs. British Leyland's Longbridge factory can produce over 120 cars per hour.

A large proportion of motor car and component factories are situated in the Midlands, with a special concentration in the Birmingham-Coventry area. One reason for this, is that the Midlands produce such a large variety of goods, especially metal goods, that it has been easier to assemble motor cars here than in other parts of the country. The same is largely true in the London area, the other chief centre of the industry. Individual men, however, like Herbert Austin who founded the Austin works at Longbridge in 1905, were just as important as natural advantages in deciding where the factories were built.

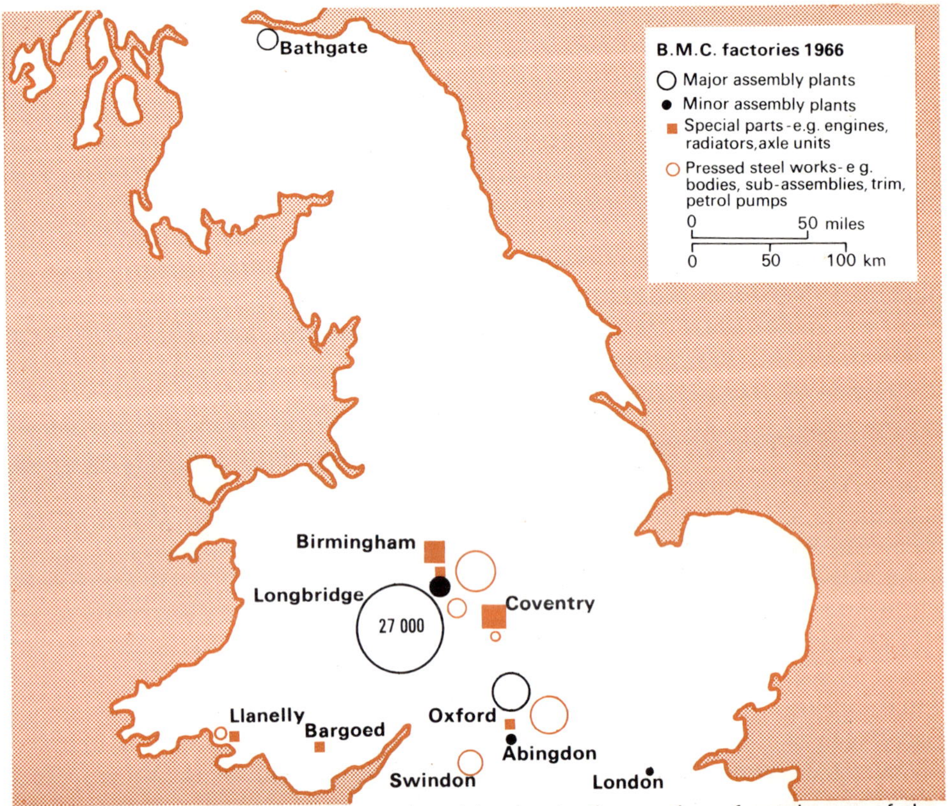

Fig. 199 Rings and squares proportioned in size to the number of employees of the British Motor Corporation. B.M.C. is now part of British-Leyland.

B.M.C. factories 1966
○ Major assembly plants
● Minor assembly plants
■ Special parts - e.g. engines, radiators, axle units
◯ Pressed steel works - e.g. bodies, sub-assemblies, trim, petrol pumps

Bathgate
Birmingham
Longbridge
27 000
Coventry
Llanelly
Bargoed
Oxford
Swindon
Abingdon
London

Fig. 200 The British Motor Holdings assembly line at Longbridge.

196

Bathgate
Linwood

Halewood
Speke
Ellesmere Port

Birmingham
Longbridge • Coventry

Oxford • Luton
Abingdon Dagenham

● Existing in 1959
○ Built from 1960

Fig. 201   Location of motor-car assembly plants.

When the time came for building new factories in the 1960s, these were not built in the prosperous Midland and London areas. Instead, they were deliberately sited elsewhere, because of government policy to bring new growth to the development areas. Thus large new works were built by Ford, Vauxhall, and the Rootes group on Merseyside, and B.M.C. and Leyland Motors built their new factories in Scotland.

The Potteries

The pottery towns form one of the most interesting industrial landscapes in the country. Stoke-on-Trent is built on the headwaters of the river Trent where they cut steeply into the edge of the Pennines. It is hard to go any distance without a view over the deep valley of the Fowlea Brook which flows through the centre of the town.

'To the eye, the place is a perpetual shock and challenge, with its surrealistic swirl of tips, ovens, streets, odd patches of green, canals, old buildings, new buildings.'[1] In the centre of the town there are clay pits and coal mines, and one

[1] John Wain: Portrait of Stoke-on-Trent. Geog. Mag. 1960. p. 39.

third of the central area has been made derelict by dumps from the mines, tips of broken pottery from the kilns, disused clay workings, and subsidence.

Stoke-on-Trent, although comparatively small (population 250 000), is a conurbation. The six towns which joined together—Tunstall, Burslem, Hanley, Fenton, Longton and Stoke—amalgamated officially in 1910. This is perhaps our most self-conscious conurbation, for whereas in London, Birmingham or Manchester the city has spread out from the centre to absorb the smaller towns and villages, in Stoke-on-Trent the towns were rivals of equal importance.

Curiously, the equally close neighbour Newcastle-under-Lyme has not become part of the conurbation. It is different from the other towns, for it is not concerned with the pottery industry.

Stoke-on-Trent is unique in its concentration on one particular industry. More than half (57 000) of the productive working population are employed in the pottery industry. The making of fine porcelain dates only from the eighteenth century when Josiah Wedgwood founded his factory and started to transport china clay from Cornwall along the newly constructed Trent-Mersey canal.

The local clay was used for centuries before this to make coarser pottery, and it is still dug to make earthenware, drain pipes and tiles. The ovens where the pottery is fired now burn continuously using gas, electricity or oil. There are still a few score of the bottle-shaped kilns which gave the potteries their strange smoky skyline, but these are gradually being pulled down. Apart from the pottery industry, the largest employers are the quarries and the mines, but in spite of the growth of engineering industries, the making of pottery is still the main function of Stoke-on-Trent.

Fig. 202   A view over the Potteries.

Fig. 203   The Stoke-on-Trent conurbation.

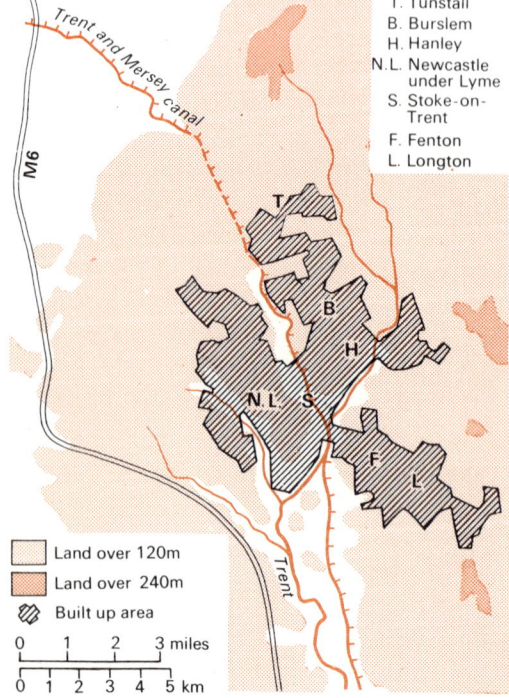

T. Tunstall
B. Burslem
H. Hanley
N.L. Newcastle under Lyme
S. Stoke-on-Trent
F. Fenton
L. Longton

Land over 120m
Land over 240m
Built up area

0   1   2   3 miles
0   1   2   3   4   5 km

9. Use Fig. 190 and your atlas, and the information given below, to draw sketch maps of these four county towns. Add notes beside your map.

Gloucester

Until the Severn road bridge was built in the 1960s, Gloucester was at the lowest road crossing of the river Severn. It was a flourishing Roman town. It is still a cathedral and market town, and a major centre for road and rail routes. Manufactures include railway carriages, synthetic fibres, and food processing (e.g. Walls Ice Cream).

Shrewsbury

Built inside the curve of a meander on the river Severn, and almost surrounded by it. In early times this was a good defensive site. Routes from Shrewsbury lead into central and North Wales, via the Severn and Dee Valleys, and it is sometimes called the 'unofficial' capital of Wales. It is a market town for the region and has a large live-stock market. It also has an increasing number of engineering industries.

Hereford

On the river Wye in the centre of an uneven lowland, which is partly enclosed by the Malvern Hills, Black Mountains, Shropshire Hills and Forest of Dean. An ancient cathedral and market town, surrounded by agri-cultural land. Many food processing industries-e.g. brewing, cider manufacture, flourmilling, fruit and vegetable canning.

Worcester

On the river Severn in centre of rich agricultural lowland. It is a cathedral and market town. Famous local indus-tries include glove making and pottery, but it also has many new expanding engineering industries.

10. Read pp. 190–194 and make summaries like those above for Birmingham, Coventry and Rugby.

11. Look at the map on p. 191. (a) Name two advantages of this area for the early growth of an iron industry. (b) How did the towns along the Severn get their names? (c) How is the area between Donnington and Coalbrookdale like the Black

Country and how is it different? (d) Look at your atlas and notice the Severn meandering in a broad valley above the gorge at Coalbrookdale. There is a great contrast in the valley shape here, believed to have been caused by water pouring from a lake at the end of the ice age.

12. It is only when we look at a more detailed list of statistics than the one printed below that we can see that motor cars are Britain's most valuable single export. Generalized export figures show the following:

Exports **1965**

	in £ million		
Total	4723·8		
Food and live animals	154·8		
Drink and tobacco	143·2		
Inedible raw materials	144·3		
Mineral fuels, lubricants	133·4		
Animal and vegetable oils	6·7		
Chemicals	439·1		
Manufactured goods, e.g. textiles, iron and steel	1210·8	Machinery, other than electric	930·6
Machinery and transport equipment	1985·6	Electric machinery	330·9
		Transport equipment	724·1
Others	506·0		

Draw a divided bar graph to represent these figures. [See p. 137 for an example of how to do it.]

13. Figure 204 opposite shows the sub-divisions of the West Midlands used as a basis for regional planning in 1968. (a) Use your atlas and the maps in this chapter and name the towns of the West Midlands conurbation and north Staffordshire. (b) What counties are in the rural west? (c) Use the figures below to draw a map to show population distribution. (Use dots to represent population. A good scale would be one dot represents 25 000 people.) (d) Which region has the highest density and which the lowest?

	1961 *Population census*	*Per cent of total*
West Midlands conurbation	2 340 700	49·4
Coventry belt	583 000	12·3
Rest of Central Division	1 042 100	21·9
North Staffordshire	468 000	9·9
Rural West	309 400	6·5

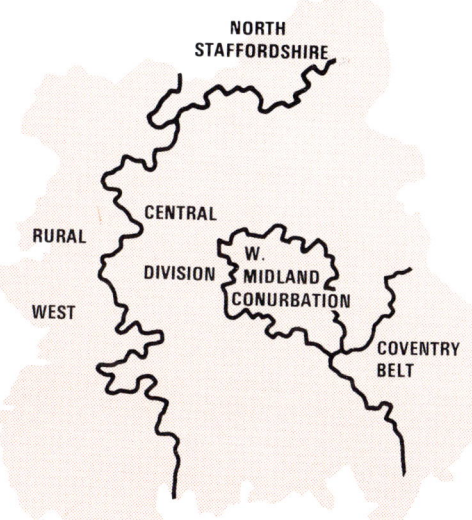

Fig. 204   The West Midlands.

The East Midlands

The river Trent changes in character about 40 kilometres below the Potteries. The valley of the river Trent between Burton and Newark, and its tributary the Soar below Leicester, is shown on Fig. 206. The Trent here meanders through a broad flood plain 2 or 3 kilometres wide. The slopes rise at the edge of the flood plain fairly sharply to a height of about 75 m. In places where the river flows against the edges of the valley there are quite steep river cliffs.

The flood plain is correctly named, for the river Trent has flooded regularly in the past. But the tributary rivers have been cleared of cluttering plants, some stretches have been straightened and the river bed has been dredged to help carry the water away more easily. These preventive measures seem to have lessened the danger of flooding. Most of the villages along the river are built on the rising ground away from the flood plain, although parts of the larger towns have spread into the flat land.

It is clear from the map that the Trent valley has a great many uses. This is one of the main areas in Britain for the extraction of gravel. Much more gravel is now dug than formerly, for since World War II it has been increasingly used in making concrete, now a major building material. Gravel is dug from pits beside the river, and there are many artificially formed lakes where abandoned pits have filled with water. Gypsum, also, is produced in large quantities. Gypsum is a crystalline mineral which occurs in the clays of this region, in large masses or as thin white veins. Gypsum, again, is increasingly used in building, for it is used to make plaster and plasterboard. Fireclay, used for making drainpipes, is found in the south Derbyshire and Leicestershire coalfields, and in Nottinghamshire small quantities of oil are obtained.

201

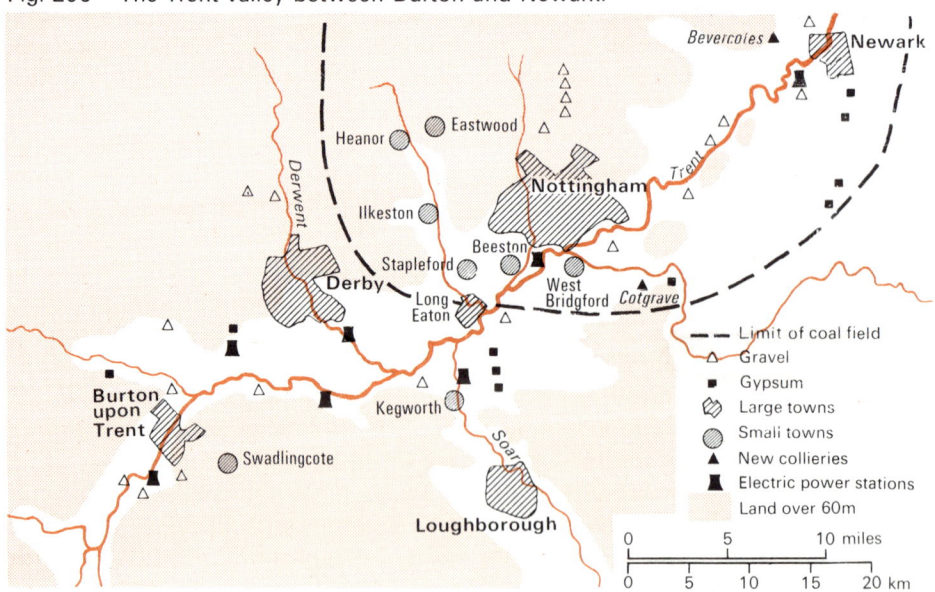

Fig. 205   High Marnham Power Station on the River Trent.
Fig. 206   The Trent valley between Burton and Newark.

Bevercoles ▲
Newark
Heanor ● Eastwood
Derwent
Nottingham
Ilkeston ●
Trent
Stapleford
Beeston
Derby
Long Eaton
West Bridgford
Cotgrave
— — Limit of coal field
△ Gravel
■ Gypsum
▨ Large towns
● Small towns
▲ New collieries
⬛ Electric power stations
Land over 60m
Burton upon Trent
Kegworth
Soar
● Swadlingcote
Loughborough

0		5		10 miles

| 0 | 5 | 10 | 15 | 20 km |

13. THE MIDLANDS

The East Midlands coalfield, which forms the southern half of the large Yorks-Derby-Notts. field, is the most productive in Britain. Two new collieries, opened on the eastern, concealed part of the coalfield, show that here the coal mining industry is certainly not declining. Much of the coal goes straight to the electric power stations which line the Trent. The river provides plenty of water for cooling. Most of the power stations shown on the map were built after 1950, and the huge works with six or eight cooling towers dominate the landscape of this fairly low countryside. About half the power generated here is fed into the national grid, and is actually 'exported' from the region.

The exceptional variety of industry makes this one of the most prosperous parts of the county. Three main cities are the core of this intensely industrial region. Nottingham, Leicester and Derby, to put them in order of size, are all ancient cities built at crossing points of rivers. They were already thriving market towns at the beginning of the industrial revolution and textile manufactures were firmly established in all three.

Several inventions of machines by local men helped these towns to become the chief manufacturers of stockings and socks, knitwear of all kinds and lace. Footwear is another main product, which perhaps grew because of the traditional cattle farming of the area which made leather available. Today almost all the leather used is imported. Engineering is a major industry throughout the region.

Leicester is surrounded by rich agricultural land and grew as a market for wool, corn and cattle. Today it is the main centre of the hosiery, knitwear and footwear industries, but also manufactures a great variety of engineering products, including hosiery machinery, typewriters and instruments.

Derby grew largely during the railway building era. It is at the southern tip of the Pennines, and commands the route up the Derwent Valley to Manchester, so it is a natural focus of routes. It was chosen as the headquarters of the Midland Railway company in 1844 and the making of railway waggons and engines became the leading industry of the town in the nineteenth century. Today, there are still large railway engineering works. Textiles, too, are still a major industry, though in a different form. British Celanese (Courtaulds) have a large works for the production of man-made fibres at Spondon just outside Derby.

The aircraft industry

By far the largest number of people in Derby—over 20 000 (1970)—work for Rolls Royce, which built factories in Derby early in this century. Cars are no longer made in Derby, and most of the work is devoted to the design and manufacture of aero engines. The first Rolls Royce aero engine was made in 1914, and since then the firm has produced many famous engines including the Merlin, which powered most of the aircraft used in World War II. More recently the firm has pioneered the vertical take off engine. Rolls Royce engines are used in many different kinds of aircraft in different parts of the world.

Obviously the manufacture of aircraft is largely a matter of assembly. Far more is risked in the manufacture of an aircraft than for instance of a motor car, because it is so large and expensive. Cancellation of orders can result in millions of pounds of loss and sometimes the waste of years of research. This is particularly true of very large aircraft. Many of the aircraft made in Britain, however, are relatively small. Much of Britain's export trade is in small aircraft.

The aircraft industry is scattered as widely as the motor car industry and is not confined to the Midlands. Availability of skilled labour is even more essential. Derby is only one centre of the industry. Others include Bristol, where Bristol Siddeley engines are made, and where the supersonic Concorde is being (1968) designed and developed in collaboration with the French. Several towns outside London have aircraft industries; at Weybridge the VC10 is produced. Coventry also has a large aircraft industry, and there is a cluster of aircraft works on the south coast in the neighbourhood of the Solent.

The largest of the three great East Midlands cities is Nottingham. It was built on a crossing point of the Trent, just south of Sherwood Forest. A high sandstone cliff standing back about 1500 m from the river overlooks the valley, and after the Norman conquest a castle was built here.

Boats coming up the Trent could not go above Nottingham, because the river is here blocked by gravels, so the town also grew as a river port. Today there is still some river trade, chiefly in timber, grain, pulp and petroleum. During the canal building age, the Beeston canal was built around the shallow part of the Trent.

For many years Nottingham could claim the largest market place in England where the annual goose fair was held. It is a good example of a town built at the junction of highland and lowland. Goods could easily be exchanged here from the plains of the Trent to the east and the Pennine hills to the west.

Besides being a commercial centre, Nottingham is also a large industrial town, again with a great variety of industry. The extractive industries employ about 4000 people, and there is one coal mine actually within the city boundaries. Delicate lace textiles are still produced and supplied to warehouses in the crowded streets of a quarter called the lace market. Many of the lace factories have now moved to Long Eaton just outside Nottingham. Many people also work in factories which make children's clothing.

A few well-known firms, however, are the largest employers in Nottingham: Player's tobacco and Raleigh bicycles, while Boots pharmaceuticals have moved their works to a site in the neighbouring town of Beeston. The older part of the University was built largely with money provided by Sir Jesse Boot. Nottingham is known to many as 'Queen of the Midlands'.

14. Look at Fig. 14 and write a list of the extractive industries of the East Midlands.

15. Draw maps to show the advantages of (a) Derby as a route centre, (b) Nottingham as a market town.

16. How do you account for the fact that (a) there are many electric power stations along the middle reaches of the Trent but few along the middle reaches of the Thames, (b) many coal mines are being closed in west Derbyshire while others are being opened east of Nottingham. [See also p. 132.]

17. Using the figures below and the accounts on pages 195 and 203, write a comparison of the motor car and aircraft industries under the headings: raw materials used, where the factories are, numbers employed, size, price and numbers of product made.

	1965	
	Numbers employed	Value of exports £ million
Motor cars	499 000	250·9
Aircraft	260 000	80·9

18. Figure 207 below shows the divisions of the East Midlands used as a basis for regional planning (1968). Which two sub-regions have been omitted from the

Fig. 207   The East Midlands.

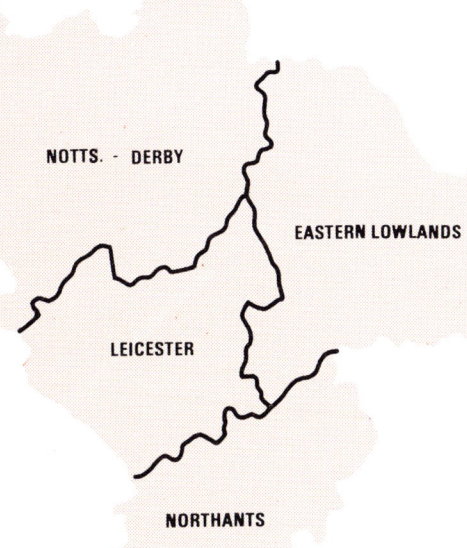

NOTTS. - DERBY

EASTERN LOWLANDS

LEICESTER

NORTHANTS

13. THE MIDLANDS

account in this chapter? Look at the figures below. What do they show about differences between (a) the four divisions of the East Midlands and (b) the West and East Midlands?

Employment in 1963 (Percentage of employees)

	Notts. Derby	Leicester	Northants	Eastern Lowlands	East Midlands	West Midlands
Agriculture, forestry, fishing	1·3	1·6	2·4	15·4	3·1	1·9
Mining and quarrying	13·2	4·8	—	—	8·3	2·3
Manu-facturing	40·7	53·4	51·4	26·9	43·5	52·6
Construction	6·3	6·6	7·3	7·2	6·6	6·1
Service Industries	38·5	33·6	37·9	49·6	38·5	36·6
Number of employees	728 000	324 000	169 900	155 600	1 380 600	2 254 600

14. The Glaciated Highlands

Many of the features of the landscape of the Scottish Highlands, the Southern Uplands, the Lake District, and the Welsh Mountains were formed during the Ice Age. About two million years ago the climate of Britain became much colder than it is today. Snow that fell during the winter months was not completely melted away in the summer, and it began to accumulate. This happened first in the mountain areas which were colder and received more snow than the lowlands.

The snow first collected in hollows as it cannot lie on steep slopes. During the day the sun warmed the surface layers of snow, which melted. The melted water seeped into the air spaces in the snow and froze there at night. Thus each layer of snow became more like ice.

As each year's snowfall was added, a great weight of snow built up in the hollows, pressing on the lower layers, which became compact. Eventually the weight and pressure of accumulated snow caused the bottom layers of ice to slip and move out from the hollows as tongues of ice. These tongues of ice, or 'glaciers', moved down valleys in the mountains. As snow continued to accumulate, the glaciers thickened, forming an almost complete cover with only the steep mountain tops showing above the ice. The ice also spread out in sheets over the surrounding lowlands. The map overleaf shows the area of the British Isles that was covered by ice during the Ice Age.

The movement of ice in the hollows deepened and enlarged them, steepening the walls of the back and sides, and creating a lip at the point where the tongue of ice left the hollow (Fig. 208). These deepened hollows are common in our

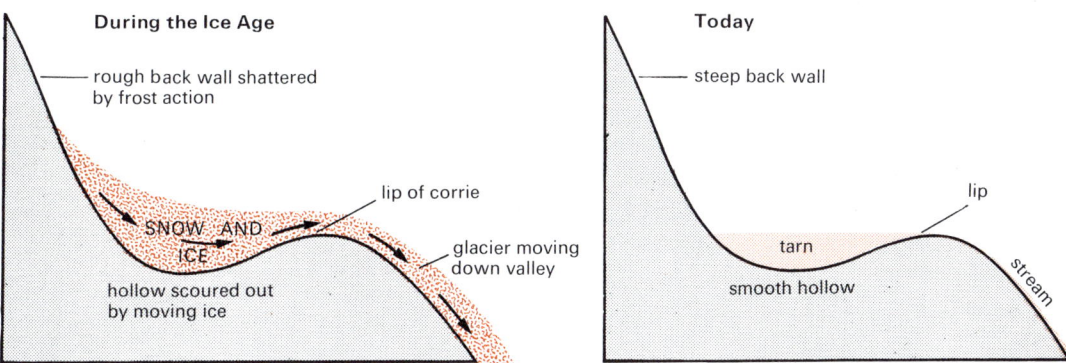

Fig. 208   Section through a corrie.

mountain regions and are called corries, cwms or cirques. Many of them now contain small round lakes or 'tarns'.

Often ice from several corries collected in one valley, forming a large glacier. The glaciers which filled the main valleys of the Highlands during the Ice Age were large and powerful. Many in Britain were over 300 m deep and 600 m wide. As a glacier moved through the valley, it scraped the sides as well as the floor of the valley. It changed the valley shape from the V-shape of a river-worn valley, to a U-shape. A glaciated valley is today characterised by its wide flat floor and steep sides.

Since ice is rigid, it cannot round a bend as easily as water does. A valley glacier therefore wore away projecting spurs of land forming 'truncated spurs'; it also wore away the lower parts of tributary valleys. Part of a tributary valley was then left at a higher level than the main valley, 'hanging' above the valley side. The streams which today drain the hanging valleys descend steeply into the main valley. There is often a gorge-like valley section where there is a series of small waterfalls.

Fig. 209 Llyn Cau below Cader Idris, Central Wales. This corrie lake is marked on Ordnance Survey Map F, opposite. Compare the photograph with the map. How high are the summits? How high is the lake?

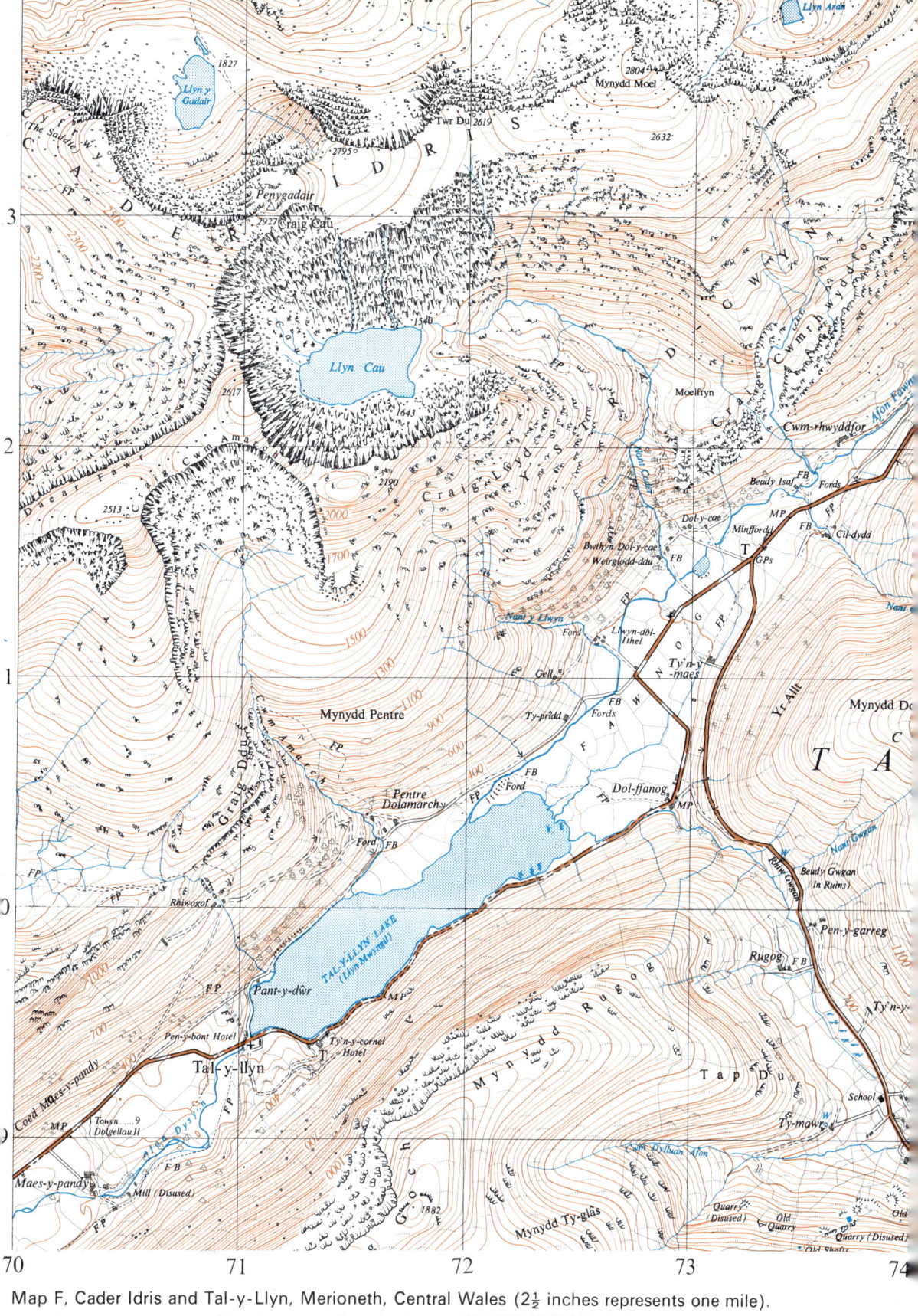

Map F, Cader Idris and Tal-y-Llyn, Merioneth, Central Wales (2½ inches represents one mile).

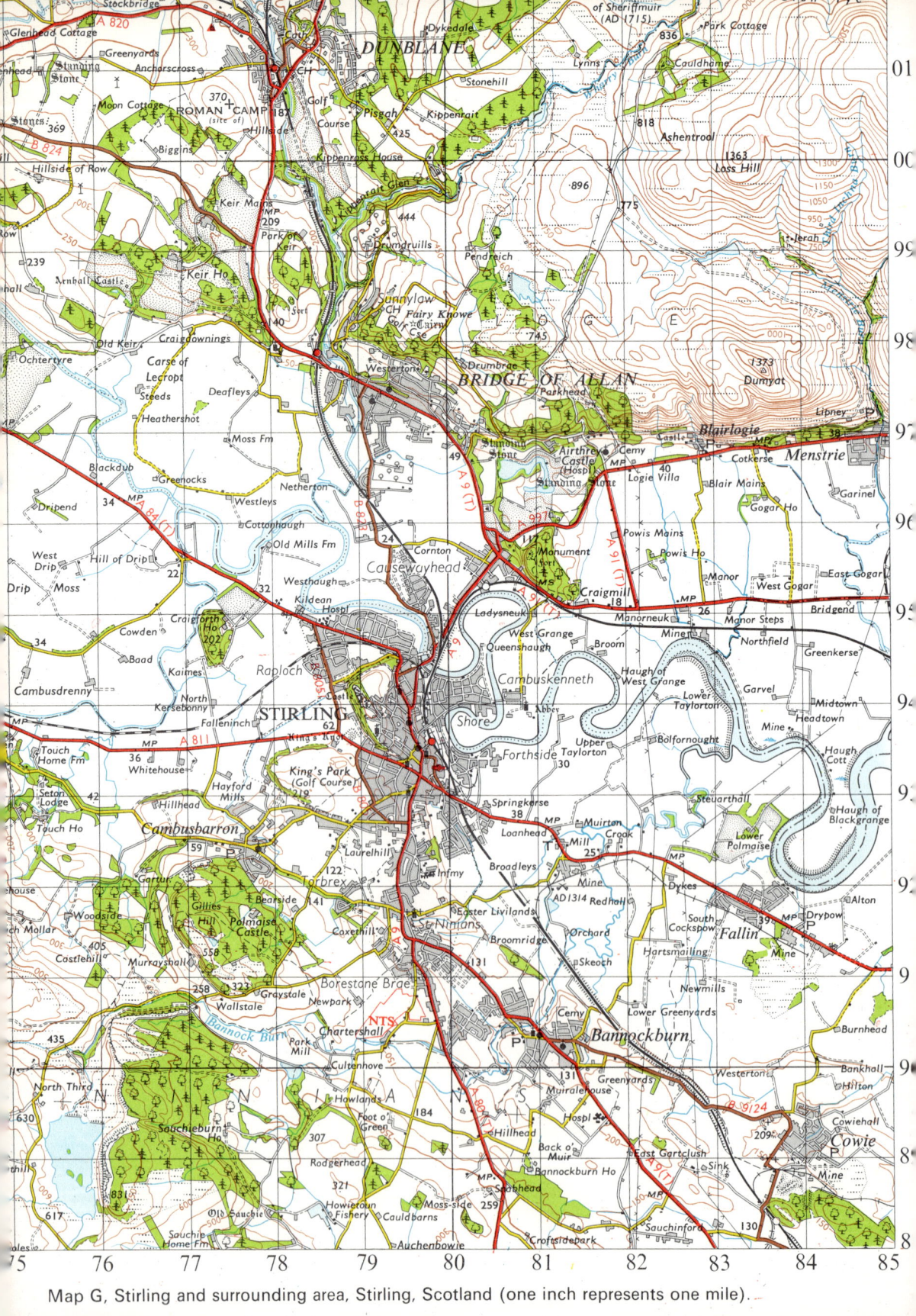

Map G, Stirling and surrounding area, Stirling, Scotland (one inch represents one mile).

14. THE GLACIATED HIGHLANDS

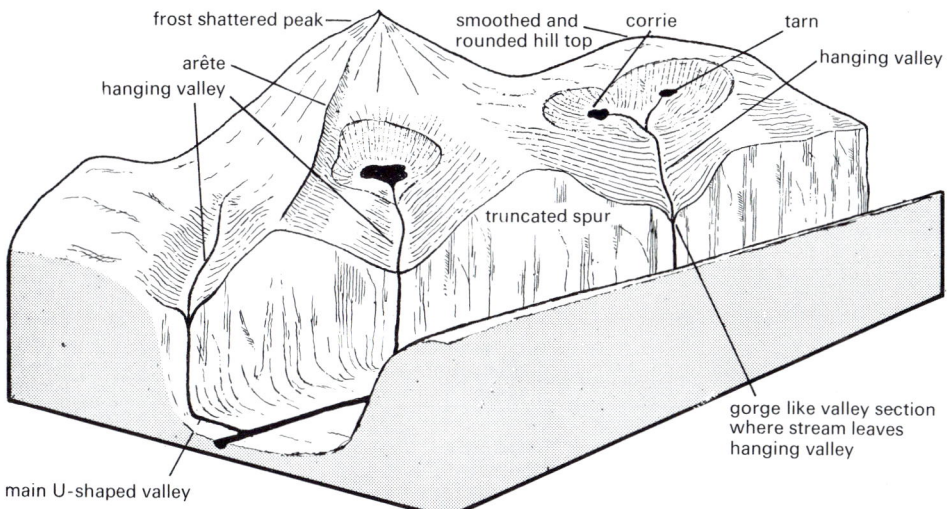

frost shattered peak

smoothed and
rounded hill top

corrie

tarn

arête

hanging valley

hanging valley

truncated spur

gorge like valley section
where stream leaves
hanging valley

main U-shaped valley

Fig. 210   Diagram of glaciated mountain scenery.

Fig. 211   The extent of the ice which covered Britain during the Ice Age.

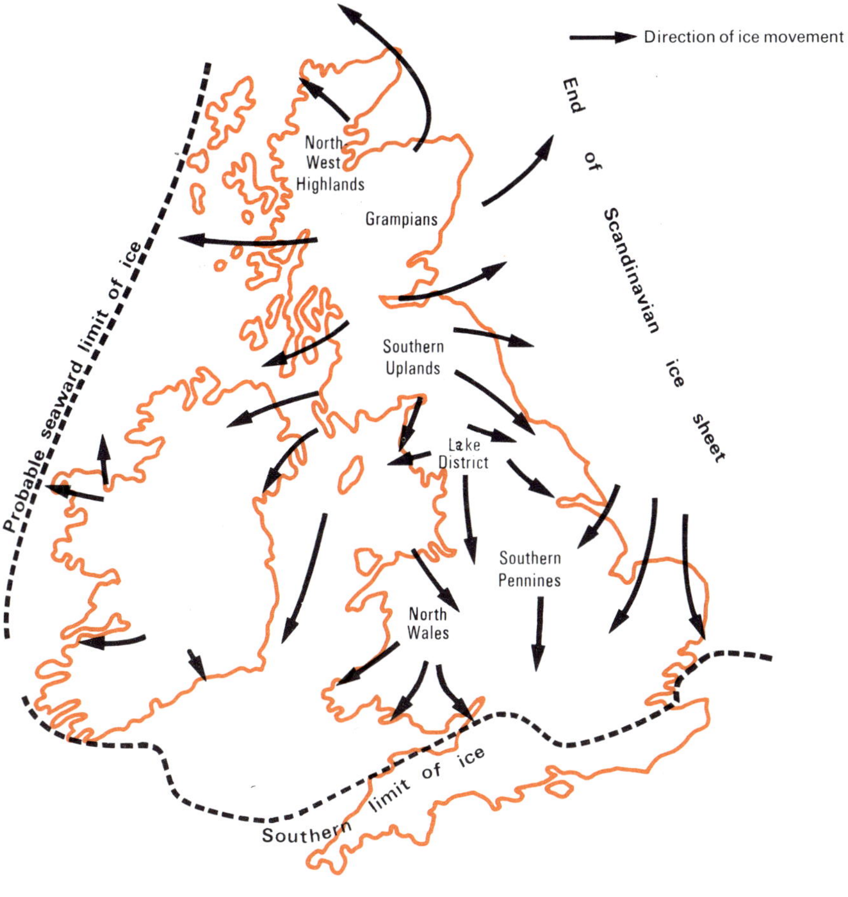

Direction of ice movement

North
West
Highlands

Grampians

End   of   Scandinavian   ice   sheet

Probable seaward limit of ice

Southern
Uplands

Lake
District

Southern
Pennines

North
Wales

Southern   limit   of   ice

Fig. 212   The ribbon lake in the foreground is Tal-y-Llyn south of Cader Idris in Central Wales. It is shown on the Ordnance Survey Map F, facing p. 208. The camera is pointing towards the south-west. Compare the photograph with the map, and identify (with names or grid references) as many features as you can.

Most glaciated valleys were deepened as well as re-shaped. In places, the ice in the valley glacier was able to scoop out deep hollows in the valley floor. Parts of the valley floor become 'over-deepened', and a glaciated valley usually descends in steps. The over-deepened hollows which were scooped out during the Ice Age are today often filled with water. Long, narrow ribbon-shaped lakes, partly filling the bottom of the U-shaped valleys, are typical in glaciated mountain regions. The map of the English Lake District (Fig. 216b) shows many of these ribbon lakes.

Although ice sheets and glaciers no longer cover this country, they have altered the shape of the land over which they passed. The ice eroded and re-shaped the land in two ways. The underside of a glacier freezes on to the surface over which it passes. If the rock has many joints the ice may succeed in tearing out pieces as it moves on down the valley. This rock is carried away, frozen into the underside of the ice. The process is called 'plucking'.

Because ice picks up material by freezing on to it, the underside of the glacier is rough and scrapes the rocks it passes over. This scraping action, called 'abrasion', wears down the underlying rocks. The ice swept away soil from the mountain

210

Fig. 213 Surfaces of bare rock and rounded summits near Loch Avon in the Cairngorms.

areas, which is one of the reasons why the soils are now thin, and there are many surfaces of bare rock. Many of the mountain summits in the glaciated highlands have been smoothed and rounded because ice has passed over the tops of them.

The peaks which stood out above the ice were not smoothed but were shattered by frost action. When temperatures are above freezing, snow and ice melt, and water can enter cracks and crevices in the rocks. When the temperature drops below freezing point the water in the cracks freezes and expands. The expansion forces the cracks a little wider apart and eventually pieces of rock break away. Alternate freezing and thawing attacked the back walls of corries and the higher slopes of the valley sides where they projected above the snow, making them rough and jagged. Where a ridge was attacked on both sides by freeze and thaw it was worn back until only a sharp-edged dividing wall was left. These sharp ridges are called arêtes.

The pieces of rock detached by freeze and thaw ranged from small fragments to quite large blocks. They fell on to the moving ice and were carried away by it.

211

Other rocks were picked up underneath the ice. When the glacier reached a warmer area it melted and dropped the material it had been carrying with it. This material collected in an uneven heap along the edge of the ice and is called a terminal or end moraine. Much of the material which the glacier picked up in the mountain regions was carried away to the lowlands where it formed widespread deposits of glacial drift. (See p. 85.)

The action of freeze and thaw is still strong in our mountain areas where the temperature often varies from above freezing during the day to below freezing at night. There are many bare rock surfaces exposed to its attack, and 'screes' of loose rock collect at the foot of the steep slopes.

The Cader Idris area in Central Wales is shown in Ordnance Survey Map F facing p. 208. It is an area in which snow and ice accumulated. There are several corries marked. The biggest one shown in Fig. 209, contains a small lake called Llyn Cau (7112). The walls of this corrie are so steep that they are shown by cliff symbols. To the south-west and north there are other smaller corries also with very steep back walls. Only a narrow ridge of land is now left between the corries, and arêtes are developing on the north-west, west and south-west of the Llyn Cau corrie.

The stream leaving Llyn Cau, the Nant Cader, joins the Afon Fawnog. The Fawnog valley, shown in Fig. 212, has the flat floor, steep sides and narrow lake which are typical of glaciated valleys. At the outlet of the Lake Tal-y-Llyn is a barrier of higher ground. This is probably a 'rock barrier' at the end of an over-deepened section of valley in which the lake has collected. Where the Afon Dysyon leaves the lake it has cut down through the barrier lowering the level of the lake, so that it no longer fills the whole valley. The rivers which flow into the lake also bring down material which they deposit in the lake. Silt brought by rivers is gradually filling up the lake from its upstream end, and also from the north side where the Cwm Amarch stream enters the lake.

1. Look at the NW. section of the map which shows the mountain Cader Idris. There are several summits to this mountain. Find the summits at these points and write a list of the heights of the summits: 704133, 711130, 720134, 727137, 710122, 799117, 714118.

2. Draw a square to represent the NW. corner of the map. Mark in the square the mountain summits listed above. Join the summits together with lines to show the highest land between the hollows. Draw Llyn Cau and Llyn-y-Gadair. Now draw lines to show the precipitous slopes. Make the lines follow the direction of the slope downhill. (Imagine you were rolling a stone from the top into the lake— which way would it go?)

3. Look at the long profile (Fig. 214) drawn from the highest to lowest points shown on the map along the line of the Nant Cader and Afon Dysyon. Find on the map the points labelled on the section. Copy the section and add the following notes: *frost-shattered* rear wall of corrie; level floor of valley filled with alluvium

14. THE GLACIATED HIGHLANDS

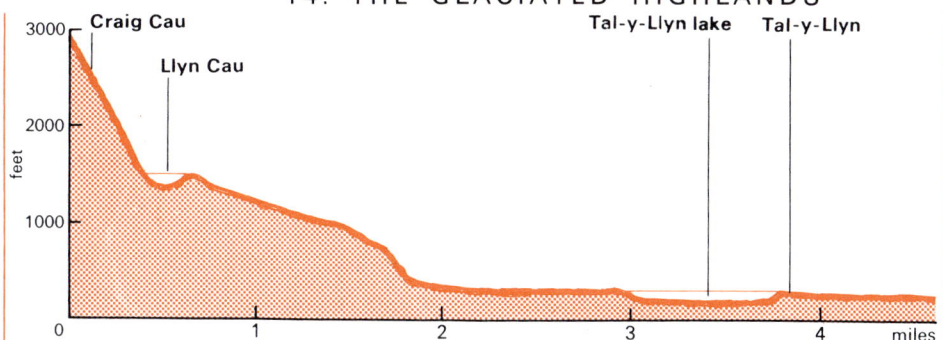

Fig. 214   Long profile of a glaciated valley, Nant Cader and Afon Dysyon.

brought by rivers; *ribbon lake*; *hanging valley* above main valley; gorge-like valley section as stream enters main valley; *rock-barrier*.

4. Compare this section with that of the river valley shown on p. 101. Why are there more steps in a glaciated valley? Why is the vertical scale used in the two sections different?

5. Explain the meaning of the words italicised in question 3.

6. Use Ordnance Survey Map F, facing p. 208 to answer the following: Draw two sections across the Tal-y-Llyn valley (a) from 720110 to 730100, (b) from 706100 to 714090. Describe the differences in shape between the two parts of the valley. Explain these differences.

7. Make a list of the changes that have occurred in mountain valleys like the Fawnog valley due to glaciation.

Occupations in the highlands

The glaciated highlands in Britain are sparsely populated regions. The tourist industry, quarrying, hydro-electric power stations, and forestry provide some jobs, but most people work on farms. A hill farm, typical of the mountain districts is described below.

Seathwaite farm

Seathwaite farm lies at the head of the glaciated Borrowdale valley in the English Lake District. Its position is shown on Fig. 216b.

2600 sheep are kept on Seathwaite farm. They are mainly Herdwicks, a Lake District breed which are not kept anywhere else. Most mountain areas keep to their own traditional breed of sheep. In Wales the Welsh mountain sheep predominate, in the Scottish Highlands, the Scottish Blackface, and in the Southern Uplands, the Cheviot. The wool produced by Herdwicks is rather coarse and is mainly used for carpeting and felting. They are small wiry sheep and so do not produce as much meat as many other breeds, but they are very hardy and can survive the severe winters of the Lakeland mountains. A few Swaledale sheep, a Yorkshire breed, are also kept.

213

The sheep stay out on the mountains all year, except for the year's new lambs which are not strong enough to weather their first winter on the mountains. These lambs are sent away in October to be 'boarded out' with farmers on the lowlands of west Cumberland or the Solway. They are brought back the following April and are then able to live the rest of their lives on the mountain slopes, or fells, surrounding Seathwaite.

Approximately 550 lambs are born each year of which fifty males are sold as fat lambs in September. Since 1965 these fat lambs have been bought directly from the farmer and collected at the farm by the Fat Stock Marketing Corporation. Some rams are kept until they are three years old. They are then known as 'wethers' and are sold at the October Ram Fairs in Cockermouth.

The sheep have to be brought down from the mountain pastures or fells several times during the year. Lambing begins about April 20th, so the ewes are brought down a week before that. All the sheep are brought down again in June for shearing except the ewes with lambs which are not sheared until July. At the end of August they are brought down again for the fat lambs to be sold. At the end of September some of the ewes are sold for mutton. The end of October, as well as April, is the time for dipping, so the animals must be brought down on all these occasions and again in mid-November when the ewes are mated. The farmer loses between thirty and forty animals a year on the mountains through accidents.

32 of the 1214 hectares which make up the farm, lie in the floor of the valley. The land here is quite flat and the soils are stony and gravelly, composed of material deposited by the river Derwent and the many tributaries which it receives from the mountain sides. Most of the soils are too stony to be ploughed.

The fields are kept under permanent pasture. This land at the head of the valley is less liable to flood than some of the flatter land further down, which at one time was an extension of Derwentwater. However, stone drains have been laid under the fields to help carry the water away. The valley pastures are also lightened by adding basic slag (the waste product of iron making) and lime, which are strongly alkaline and neutralize the acid nature of the soils. 2500 kg per hectare of lime and basic slag is applied to the fields every three years. After this time the heavy rain has washed it out of the soil and more must be applied. Some manure is also added to these fields every three years.

These measures give a much better growth of grass, and the treated pastures are known as 'improved pastures' as opposed to the untouched and therefore unimproved pasture of the fells.

Ten hectares of the improved land produces hay and several cuttings can be made each year. This is important as the cattle kept on the farm have to remain inside for six months of the year, so a large quantity of fodder is required. To supplement the hay and give a balanced diet, the farmer buys beet pulp—the residue left after sugar has been extracted from the sugar beet—and brewers grains—the residue left after barley has been malted to make beer.

Each year about twenty 18-month old bullocks are sold off as 'stores' to be fattened for beef on the lowland farms of Yorkshire and Lancashire.

The farmer has about fifty cows and calves on the farm at any one time. Most of the milk goes to feed the young calves. The extra milk is used on the farm itself, so there is no dairying. In the summer, which is the peak producing time for milk, the farm sells teas to holiday-makers who come to walk over the beautiful mountain country which surrounds Borrowdale, or who drive up the valley from Keswick.

The farm buildings (Fig. 215) are used to house the cattle in the winter and to store their fodder, and the farm implements. There is also a dipping pen for the sheep. Not many implements are required on a farm of this type and until 1945 all the work was done by horses. Now there are two tractors on the farm, a machine for spreading manure and a tedder which tosses the cut hay and so helps to dry it out before it is baled.

The farm and its outbuildings are all made of local stone and roofed with slate which is quarried a short distance down the valley. The farm itself is about 300 years old; the date 1663 is carved on one of the beams in the living room, and the outbuildings have been added gradually over the years. The farm is now rented from the National Trust which bought it in 1943 and which owns most of the land in this valley.

The field walls are also made of local stone and built without mortar. These dry stone walls are strong and can withstand high winds and flooding streams. They

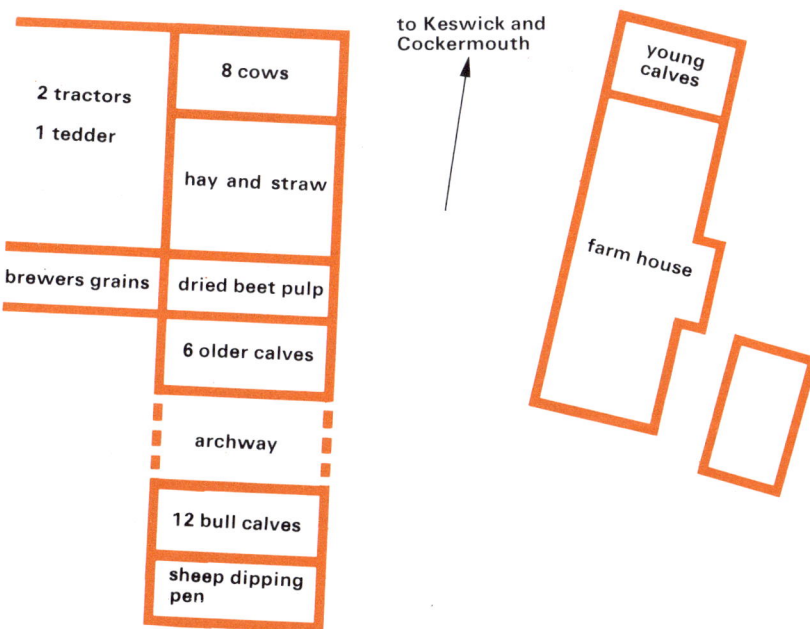

Fig. 215   Plan of farm buildings, Seathwaite farm.

need repair only after severe winters when the base of the walls may heave with frost action on the ground. The walls run up the fells to about 450 m and provide a certain amount of shelter from winter storms for the sheep.

Keeping sheep and breeding store cattle is not a very profitable type of farming, but it is important in a country like Britain, where the better quality land is over-crowded, to make the best possible use of the less productive regions, and farmers receive a subsidy from the Government to make it worth their while.

Most farms in the mountain areas of Wales and Scotland are similar to Seathwaite farm, but along the edges of the highlands farming changes. More land is ploughed up for oats and root crops, and cattle are more important than sheep. In some places they are fattened for beef, but if there is a town nearby, or if the communications to a large town are good, dairy cattle are kept and the milk is sent to the towns.

As farming in the bleak surroundings and harsh climate of the highlands is difficult and often unrewarding, many farms have been abandoned, and deserted cottages are a common sight.

There is little alternative to farming and the other activities do not provide enough jobs. As there is little work, many people, particularly young people, have left. The glaciated highlands are areas of depopulation.

The wild beauty of the mountain areas makes them attractive to holiday-makers, and more people visit them every year. Walkers and climbers come for weekends as well as for longer holidays. In Scotland, fishing, shooting and winter sports attract many others.

1. The Lake District

The lakes lie in valleys which radiate from a central core of mountains. They are easy to reach in cars and coaches as well as on bicycles or on foot. The M.6 motor-way passes 8 kilometres east of Kendal, bringing the Lake District within three hours driving time for over five million people in the cities of Lancashire, west Yorkshire and the Midlands.

The Lake District is therefore the most accessible mountain area in Britain and popular with climbers, walkers and tourists. Many people would like to build holiday cottages there, but building and land use are carefully controlled, as the Lake District is a National Park. New buildings have to be of local materials, and car parks and camp sites must be approved by the National Parks Commission, in order to preserve the natural beauty of the area.

The tourist centres are the small towns of Ambleside, Windermere, Kendal and Keswick. Keswick also has a pencil making industry. Graphite which makes the 'lead' for pencils used to be mined in Borrowdale, but is now imported from Ceylon.

2. The Welsh Mountains

The glaciated highlands are made of ancient rocks and these provide some useful materials. In North Wales slate is quarried.

14. THE GLACIATED HIGHLANDS

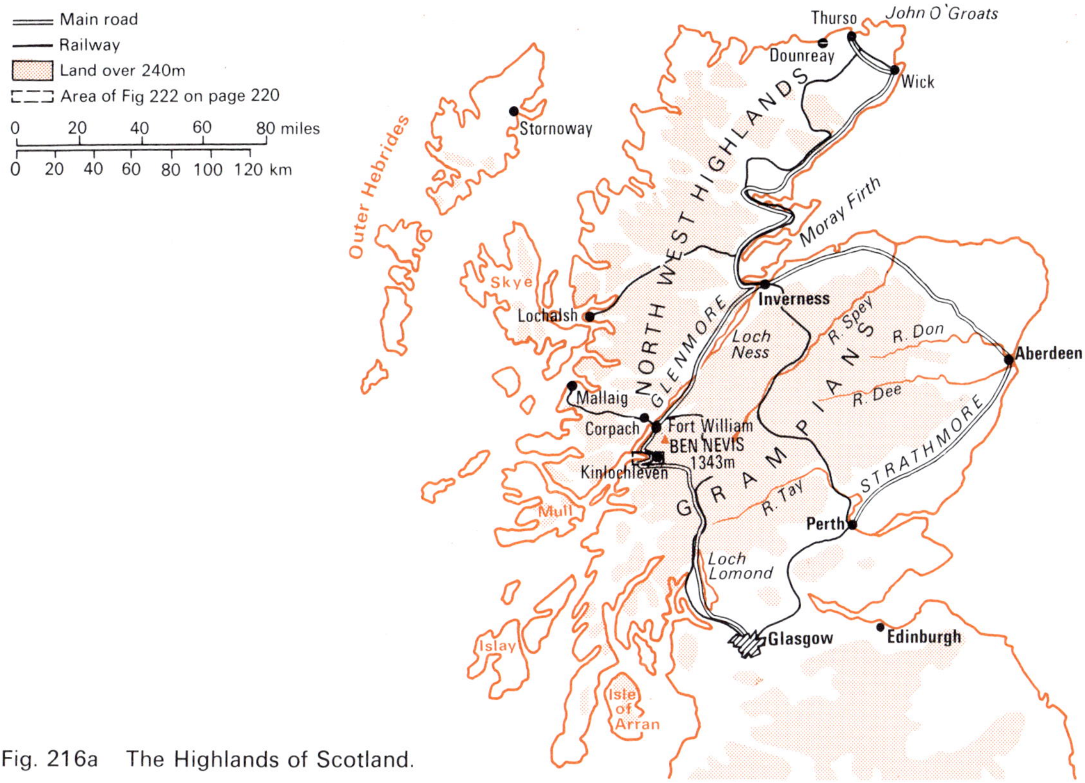

Fig. 216a   The Highlands of Scotland.

Fig. 216b   The Lake District.

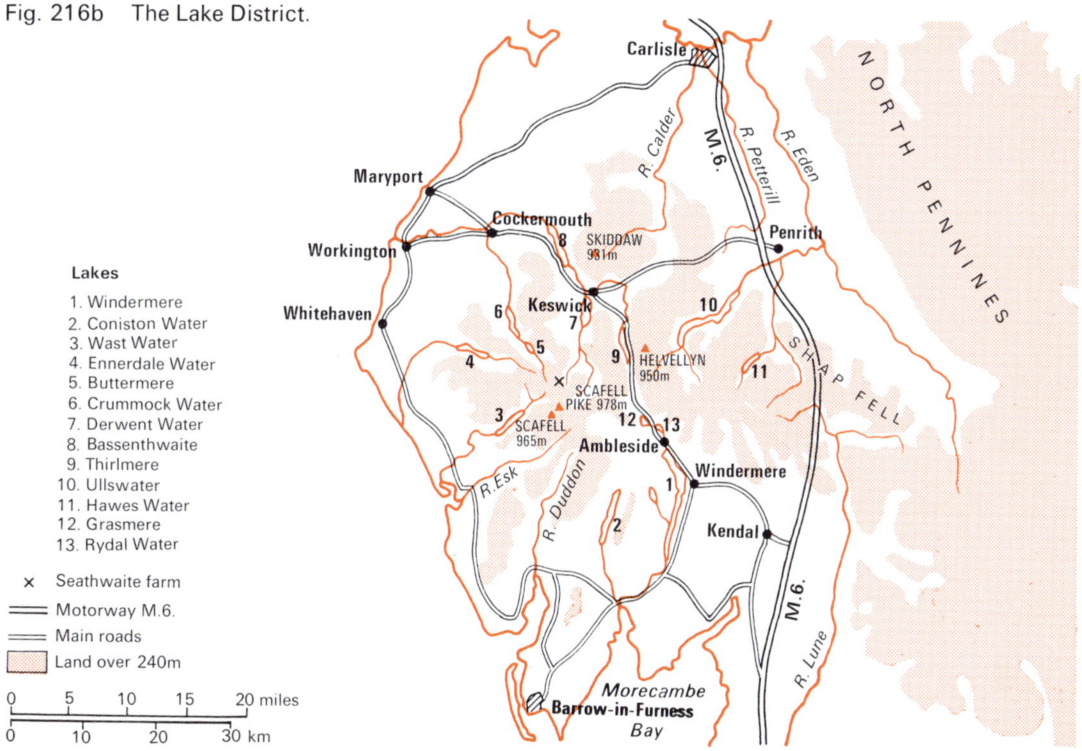

Lakes

1. Windermere
2. Coniston Water
3. Wast Water
4. Ennerdale Water
5. Buttermere
6. Crummock Water
7. Derwent Water
8. Bassenthwaite
9. Thirlmere
10. Ullswater
11. Hawes Water
12. Grasmere
13. Rydal Water

✕   Seathwaite farm

═══ Motorway M.6.

─── Main roads

▨   Land over 240m

Fig. 217 Splitting a large block of slate at the Penrhyn quarries.

Fig. 218 Farm on the north slopes of Cader Idris, Central Wales. Draw a sketch of the photograph, and label, frost-shattered bare rock surface, scree slopes, and limit of grazing land.

I R I S H   S E A

Holyhead
ANGLESEY
Menai Bridge
Bangor
B
Caernarvon
L
SNOWDON
BL

Llandudno
Birkenhead
Liverpool
Rhyl
Flint
Chester
Denbigh
Alwen resv.
Wrexham
Conway
Chwd
Dee
Bala Lake
L. Vyrnwy (resv.)
Wnion
Vyrnwy
Shrewsbury

Cardigan
Bay

CADER IDRIS
Dovey
PLYNLIMON
Severn
Aberystwyth
Rheidol
Ystwith
Elan Valley resvs.
Claerwen resvs.
Teme
Lugg
Severn
Wye
Hereford
Cardigan
Fishguard
Teifi
BRECON BEACONS
Brecon resvs
Usk
Wye
Towy
Tawe
Neath
MONMOUTH-SHIRE
Swansea
Taff
Newport
Cardiff

Areas in which slate is quarried
Land above 180m
Border between Wales and England
County boundary of Monmouthshire
Area of O.S. map F facing p. 208
▲ Slate mining centres
B.   Bethesda
L.   Llanberis
B.L. Blaenau Ffestiniog

0   10   20   30   40   50 miles
0 10 20 30 40 50 60 70 80 km

Fig. 219 The Welsh Mountains.

Fig. 220   Elan Valley Reservoir, Central Wales.

The photograph (Fig. 217) shows the Penrhyn quarries near Bethesda. The slate is blasted out along huge terraces. It is then cut into blocks and split until it is thin enough to be trimmed or 'dressed' for roofing slate. Much of the slate cannot be split finely enough, or is flawed, so there is much waste, and there are huge spoil heaps near the quarry.

Slate is also quarried at Blaenau Ffestiniog and Llanberis, but the amount of slate quarried is much less than it used to be because newer roofing materials such as tiles are much cheaper.

One of the main natural resources of Wales is water; reservoirs (shown on Fig. 219) supply water which is piped to large industrial towns many miles away.

Dams have been fairly easy to build as they have a foundation of hard rock, and the U-shape of the valleys means that a narrow dam can create a large reservoir (Fig. 221). In some cases the level of a natural lake has been raised by a dam at its outlet, and new lakes have been created by damming rivers.

Liverpool, 105 kilometres away, is supplied from Lake Vrynwy, and Birmingham, 117 kilometres away, from a series of reservoirs in the Elan valley and the Claerwen reservoir. The Alwen reservoir at Hiraetog supplies Birkenhead, and reservoirs in the Brecknock area supply the South Wales towns.

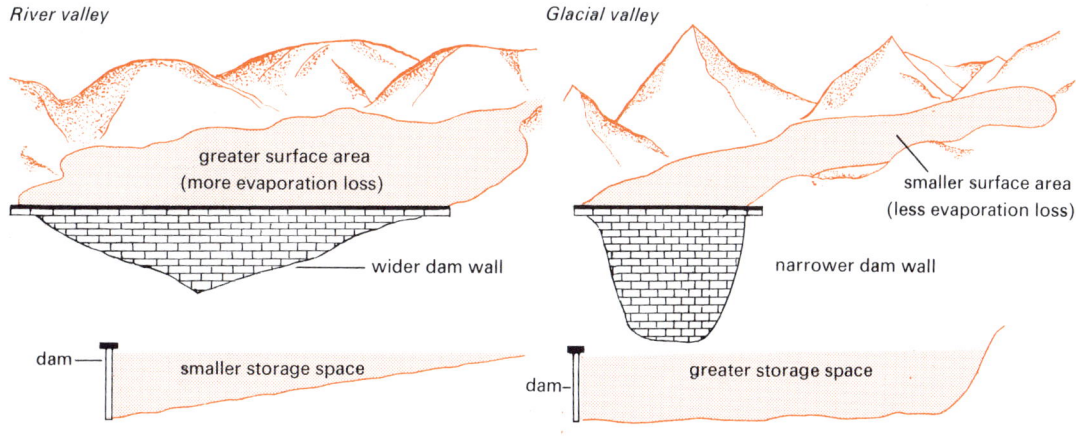

Fig. 221   Reservoirs.

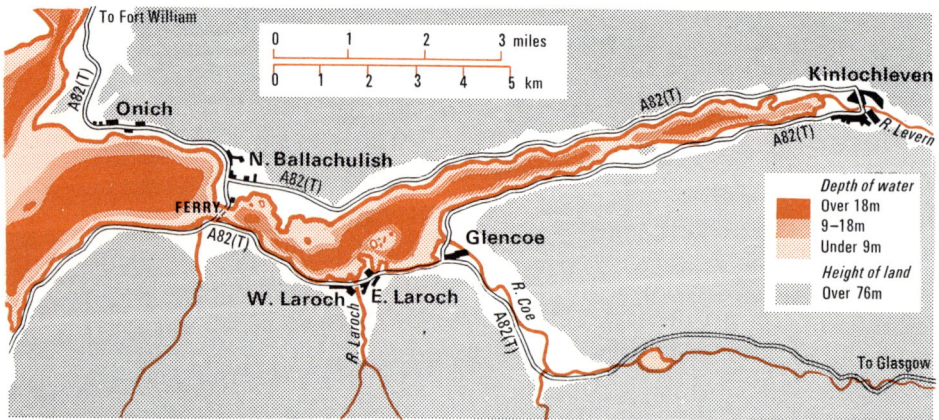

Fig. 222   Loch Leven, part of the main road route from Glasgow to the north-west Highlands. How long is the road round the Loch? How much longer is it than the ferry route? Look at the shape of Loch Leven. What evidence is there in its shape to show that it is a glaciated valley?

3. The Highlands of Scotland

Along the west coast of the Scottish Highlands, communications are extremely difficult. There are hundreds of islands, large and small, and these are the remotest, most inaccessible parts of Britain. Many of the glaciated valleys on the mainland have been flooded by the sea. They form long narrow steep-sided inlets called 'fiords', or in Scotland, sea lochs. Loch Leven (Fig. 222) is a typical fiord.

These long inlets hinder communications along the west coast. Road traffic has either to make a long detour round each loch or cross it by a ferry. Inland from the coast the roads have to climb the steep gradients of the mountains. There are few roads, and only two railways penetrate the Highlands, neither reaching the North-west. People live a long way from a main route and often 10 kilometres or more from the nearest shop. Under these conditions it is necessary to be as self-sufficient as possible, and in the more remote parts of the west Highlands and Islands an old farming system, called crofting, still survives.

The crofter keeps sheep, poultry and perhaps a couple of dairy cows to provide milk for the family. He grows oats and potatoes for his own food, and hay and turnips for his animals' winter feed. He only occasionally sells a calf or some lambs for money. Crofting is not very profitable and most crofters combine crofting with some other occupation, such as fishing, forestry, or shepherding or gamekeeping on one of the large estates.

Trees do not grow well on the islands and the exposed west coast because of the strong salt-laden westerly winds coming off the ocean. However, large areas of forest are found in the glens and lower parts of the rest of the Highlands. The Forestry Commission has planted most of these forests within the last fifty years. Our natural forests were nearly all cleared before then. All the planted forests are

220

of coniferous trees, producing softwood which matures in fifty to eighty years, so some of the wood is nearing maturity. Deciduous trees grow more slowly and produce hardwood.

The trees are planted close together but have to be thinned out at regular intervals to give the best trees more space. The wood from the thinnings forms half the total yield of the plantation and it is sawn for fencing and pit props at a number of small saw mills.

The Highlands make a poor site for most industries, because of the difficulty of bringing in raw materials and sending out finished goods. The industries which are found in the Highlands are either traditional, such as the making of Harris tweed in the Outer Hebrides, the hand knitting of the Shetlands and the distilling of whisky which is carried out all over the Highlands, or are industries for which the Highlands offer special advantages.

Atomic energy works are kept remote from centres of population. Dounreay on the north coast of Caithness is therefore an excellent site for a nuclear reactor.

The pulp and paper industry uses huge quantities of wood and water. The mill at Corpach, near Fort William, uses 1000 tonnes of wood and 100 million litres of

Fig. 223   The site of Corpach.

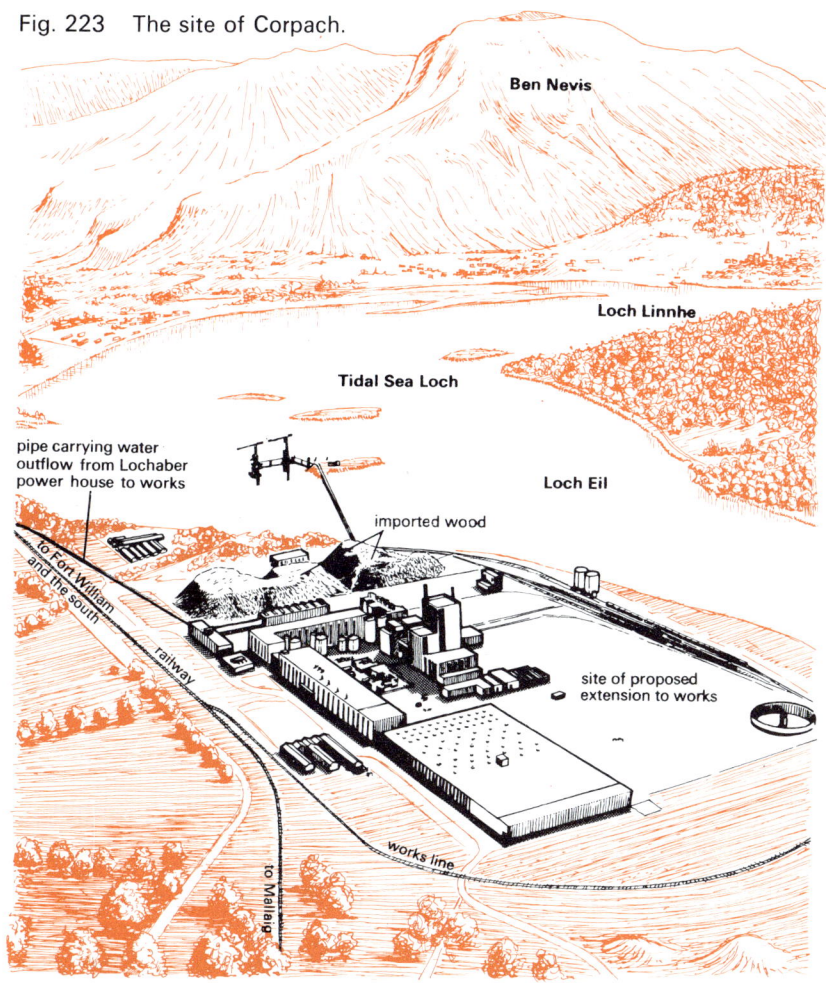

Ben Nevis

Loch Linnhe

Tidal Sea Loch

pipe carrying water
outflow from Lochaber
power house to works

Loch Eil

imported wood

to Fort William
and the south

railway

site of proposed
extension to works

works line

to Mallaig

water a day, and must dispose of a large amount of effluent every day. At present most of the timber is imported from Canada, but much locally grown timber will eventually be used.

Another major industry of the Highlands is the production of aluminium. An enormous supply of electric power is needed and can be generated cheaply from the abundant water of the area. Aluminium is produced at Fort William, one of the few growing towns in the Highlands.

The raw material of the aluminium works is alumina which is manufactured from bauxite ore in Burntisland, Fifeshire. At Fort William the alumina is converted into aluminium in an electrically heated furnace, cast into ingots and distributed to processing plants in other parts of the country. Aluminium is also produced at a similar site in Kinlochleven, about 16 kilometres south-east of Fort William.

8. Using the description of Seathwaite farm, p. 213, list the difficulties of farming in the mountain areas under the headings: physical features, climate, soil, markets.

9. List the work done in Seathwaite farm throughout the year in connection with the animals. What other work is done?

10. What are improved pastures, fells, fat lambs, wethers, stores?

11. What are the differences in size, use of land, equipment and markets between Seathwaite farm and the Northamptonshire farm described on page 53?

12. Farming on the 'edges of the highlands' is described on page 216. Find the lowlands along the edges of the highlands (a) in Wales (Fig. 219, p. 218), (b) in the Lake District (Fig. 216b, p. 217), (c) in the Highlands of Scotland (Fig. 216a, p. 217). Draw a map of one of these regions, and shade the highlands, and the edges of the highlands. Write notes beside your map to describe the farming in each area.

Fig. 224 Lochaber hydro-electric power station and aluminium works, Fort William. The water is pumped 32 kilometres from Loch Spean and Loch Treig.

13. What would you include on maps to show each of the following: (a) The Lake District is a centre for tourists, (b) The lakes of Wales supply water to many large cities in England, (c) The glaciated highlands are regions of depopulation.

14. What arguments would you use for and against: (a) damming more valleys in the mountain districts to supply water; (b) planting large areas of hillside with coniferous trees; (c) building motorways through the mountain districts.

15. Using Fig. 221, compare river valleys and glaciated valleys as sites for reservoirs.

16. Using Fig. 223, make a list of advantages of the site of Corpach for pulp and paper manufacture.

The Southern Uplands

In the Southern Uplands the effects of glaciation have been less dramatic than in the other highlands. These uplands were completely covered by ice which has smoothed and rounded both hills and valleys, and deposited glacial drift over a large area. There are fewer corries, lakes and bare rock surfaces, although valleys are U-shaped. Bronze-green grassy slopes, broken here and there by plantations of coniferous trees, are characteristic of the uplands.

The higher parts of the uplands are used entirely for sheep farming and the Southern Uplands have the highest density of sheep population in Britain; the county of Roxburgh has an average of 125 sheep per square kilometre, or about 1 sheep per hectare. However the farming of the valleys varies from west to east.

The western counties are wetter and in Dumfries the rainfall is 1256 mm a year. Glacial drift deposits have formed undulating lowlands along the coast between Solway Firth and Stranraer. These lowlands, and the valleys of the rivers which flow south from the hills, are rich green pasturelands where dairy cattle graze. A local breed of beef cattle, the Galloway, is also reared. In the eastern counties, especially in the Tweed valley, the climate is drier. The rainfall in Kelso is 692 mm

Fig. 225   The Southern Uplands.

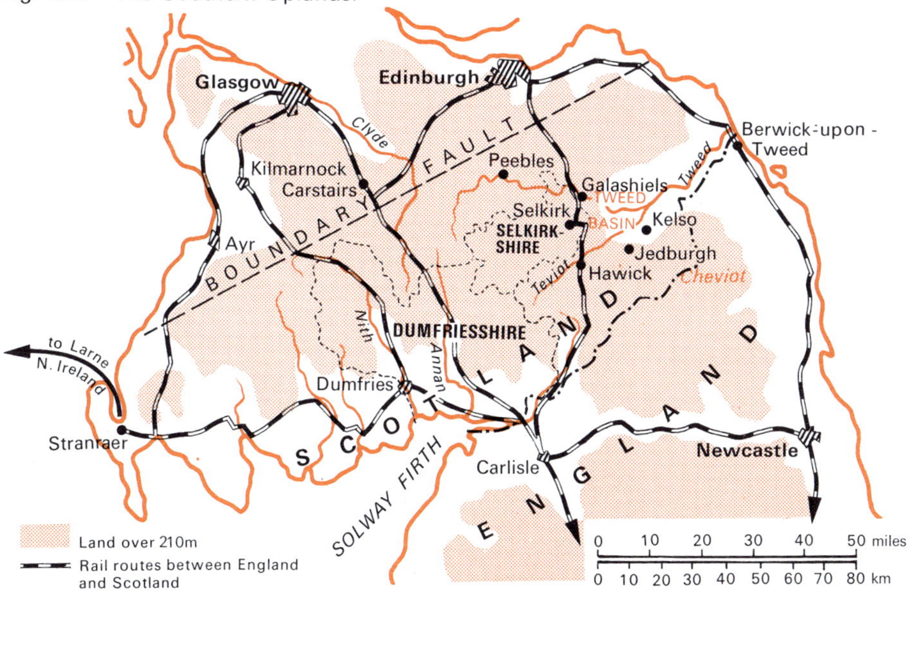

a year. Four times more land is used for arable farming in the east than in the west, and crops of barley, oats and potatoes are grown. Going higher up towards the edges of the Tweed valley, the land is used for fattening sheep and cattle; on the highest parts, only sheep can graze.

There is also a contrast between west and east in manufacturing industry. The western towns are market towns and processing centres for the surrounding agricultural areas. They have creameries, grain mills and factories which make agricultural machinery. Dumfries (27 000) also has a rubber factory and wool textile industry.

The wool industry is far more developed in the towns of the Tweed Basin. In an area with so many sheep the spinning and weaving of wool has been a local industry for many centuries. When steam power was introduced into the manufacture of textiles the Tweed valley having no coal resources was at a disadvantage, and fell behind the Yorkshire area. In order to compete the industry began to specialize in high quality, expensive knitwear and tweeds for which it is still famous. The small towns of Hawick (population 16 000), centre of the industry, Galashiels, Peebles, Selkirk all have wool textile industries.

The Southern Upland valleys carry several main lines of communication between England and Scotland. In the west the rivers draining south to the Solway provide valley routes linking with the Clyde and Ayrshire rivers. In the east the river valleys are tributary to the east-flowing Tweed, and north-south routes are more difficult except along the coast and over Teviothead.

17. Look at the statistics below and Fig. 225.

Numbers of Livestock per square km:

	Sheep	Pigs	Cattle
Dumfriesshire	97	7	53
Selkirkshire	124	1	15

(a) What are the differences in the number of sheep and cattle reared? Give reasons for the differences. (b) Why are more pigs reared in Dumfriesshire than in Selkirkshire?

18. In the Southern Uplands there is a contrast in climate and farming between the west and the east. Name some other regions where there are similar contrasts.

19. Look at Fig. 225. (a) Name the rivers which flow south, east and north from the Southern Uplands. (b) Which valleys and lowlands are used by rail routes? (c) Draw a map to show land use. Shade three areas: (i) sheep-grazing land; (ii) mainly pastureland for dairy cattle; (iii) 40 per cent of land used for arable farming.

15. The Lowlands of Scotland

Most of the lowland of Scotland is in the Central Valley, and four million people, 80 per cent of the Scottish population, live there. It contains the best agricultural land in Scotland, and nearly all the manufacturing industry.

The industrial wealth of Scotland, like the north of England, is based on coal and the industries which grew during the industrial revolution. Of the five coal-fields in the Central Valley, the Lanarkshire or Central coalfield, which underlies the Clyde Valley, is the largest. Iron ore was found next to the coal seams, and by

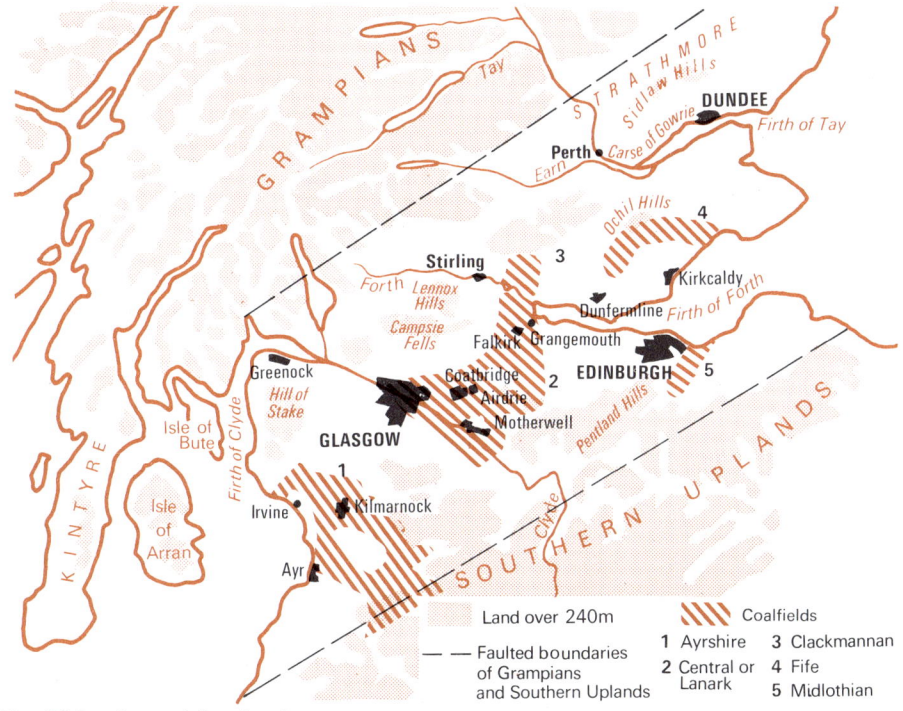

Fig. 226   Central Scotland.

the middle of the nineteenth century the Clyde Valley was the leading iron producing region in Britain. Heavy engineering industries, using iron and steel, were
firmly established and producing such things as ships, bridges, locomotives,
boilers, ships' engines, cranes, mining and earth-moving equipment.

The towns of the Clyde Valley—Airdrie, Coatbridge, Motherwell, Wishaw,
Hamilton and Glasgow—are engaged in heavy industry. Local iron ore is now
exhausted and ore is imported from Sweden, North Africa and eastern Canada to
the Clyde. Nor is local coal any longer sufficient to supply the iron and steel works.
The best seams of the Central coalfield have been worked out and the bulk of
Scottish coal is now mined in the eastern fields of Fife and Midlothian. This coal
is transported to the Clyde Valley and coking coal is also imported from Durham.

Although the local raw materials are exhausted, the iron and steel industry has
remained, because of the huge demand for steel in the area. Integrated steel works
have been established, the newest of which is the Ravenscraig works at Motherwell. The steel works make steel tubes, steel sheet for motor cars, and steel plate
(sections of thick and rigid steel) for use in shipbuilding, construction and other
forms of heavy engineering. But the industry for which Clydeside is most famous
is shipbuilding. One third of Britain's shipping, by tonnage, is launched from
Clyde shipyards and 20 000 people are employed in the industry.

A Clyde shipyard

Fairfields shipyard lies on the upper Clyde at Govan and is one of the most
modern yards in Britain. Five ships can be built at any one time. The building
berths range in length from 180 m to 300 m and many types of ship are built
including naval vessels. Fairfields employ about 3000 people, although numbers
fluctuate.

The work of building a ship begins in the office of the naval architect. He must
plan not only the shape of the ship's hull, but every detail of the fittings before
work can begin on fabricating the ship, to allow for all the cables and pipes which
go in later.

Each piece of the ship is cut out of steel plate by an electronic burning machine.
The steel plates are brought by lorry from the Ravenscraig steel works. Sections
of the ship, for example the stern section, are then fitted together, and lifted by
giant cranes when they are needed. All this work is done under cover in huge sheds.

Outside, a wooden frame, called a berth, is made, on which the ship is assembled.
First the keel of the ship is laid on the berth. The ship is flat-bottomed and the
bottom is laid in sections on the keel. Next come the side plates, the bulkheads
(cross-plates, dividing the ship into compartments), the decks and finally the bow
and the stern units. The ship is then painted and ready to be launched.

Launching blocks have been built under the ship, and well lubricated with thick
oil, so that the ship can slip down easily into the water.

Fig. 227   Part of the docks on the Clyde at Glasgow.

At launching, the ship will probably have been under construction for two years, but is far from ready to go to sea. It is taken immediately to the 'fitting-out basin'. Here the engines are fitted. These are designed by the constructional engineer at Fairfields but are made by another firm specializing in marine engines. All the electrical work for heating and ventilating the ship, the plumbing, carpentry and furnishing are done in the fitting-out basin.

The ship is then ready to go on its sea trials. If it passes it is given a certificate by Lloyds, the shipping insurance organization. Only then is the ship handed over to the owners.

Shipbuilding began to grow on Clydeside in the 1840s. Glasgow shipbuilders were great pioneers. They built the first steam powered ship and the first steel ship. Glasgow engineers, many of whom were also shipbuilders, pioneered the development of ship's engines, and the workers of Clydeside became skilled in the crafts of shipbuilding. Many shipping firms had offices in Glasgow or used the Clyde ports, so ship buyers were on the doorstep, and Clyde-built ships quickly earned a world-wide reputation for quality.

227

15. THE LOWLANDS OF SCOTLAND

The diagrams below show that the shipbuilding industry is much less prosperous at present than it was at the beginning of the century. They also show that
before 1939 there were great fluctuations in the amount of shipping that was
launched. In the years when very little was built, there was serious unemployment.
The tonnage of ships launched on the Clyde, and in the whole United Kingdom
is remaining static at present while world production is increasing. Britain is
supplying a much smaller proportion of the world's shipping and has been overtaken by Japan, West Germany and Sweden. Britain's competitors, particularly

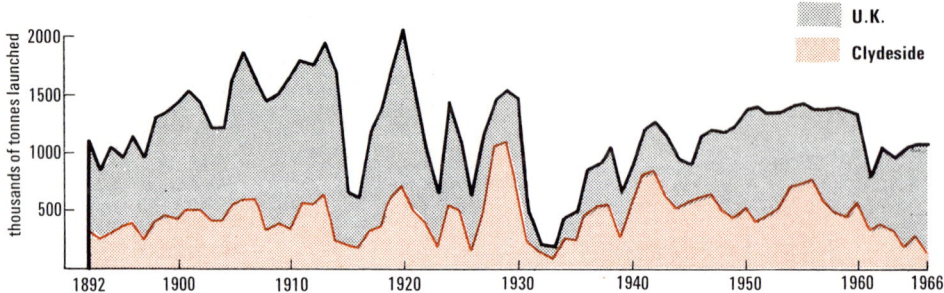

Fig. 228a   Shipbuilding in (1) The United Kingdom, (2) Clydeside.

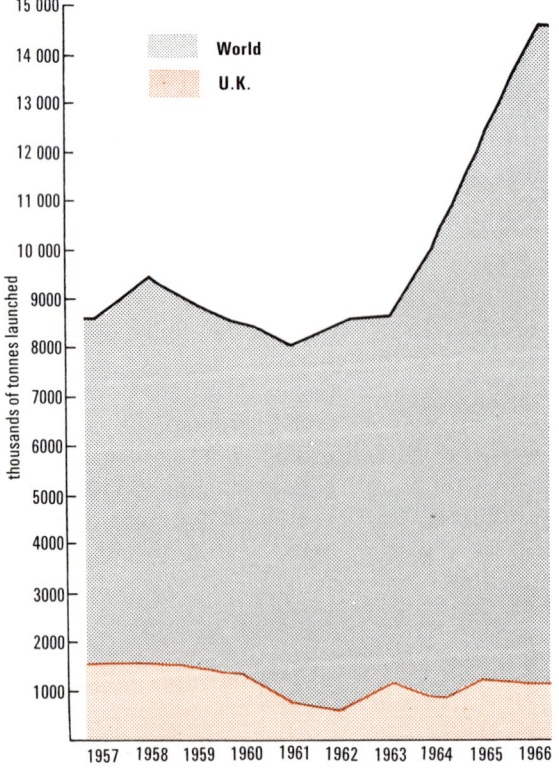

Fig. 228b   Shipping launched in
(1) the world, (2) the United
Kingdom.

Japan, produce ships more cheaply, give buyers a longer time to pay and at a lower rate of interest. As the cost of a ship is millions of pounds this may mean a big saving. Since 1945 world demand has been for bulk carriers, such as oil tankers. These ships weigh up to 250 000 tonnes, measure up to 300 m in length and need a depth of 15 to 25 m of water. Japanese shipyards are deep enough to build ships of this size. British shipyards, however, were founded in the days of smaller ships. The river Clyde is not deep enough or wide enough to launch that size of ship, although smaller bulk carriers have been built.

Clydeside, although building a great variety of ships, specializes in passenger and cargo liners. The famous Cunard liners—the Queen Mary, Queen Elizabeth and Queen Elizabeth II were all built in John Brown's shipyards at Clydebank; but this type of ship is no longer in great demand.

There is a limit to the number and size of bulk carriers which can be used for world shipping, as only a few ports can berth such large ships. Bulk carriers are only suitable for carrying a single commodity, like oil or wheat. For a mixed cargo a new type of ship is being developed. It is called a container ship, as its cargo is packed in containers of a standard size before it reaches the port. The containers are then slotted into the ships' holds, making loading and unloading very much quicker. Container ships are smaller than tankers and Clydeside is well suited to building them.

Because shipbuilding involves a variety of skills, members of up to twenty Trades Unions may be employed on one ship. In 1965 it was recommended that

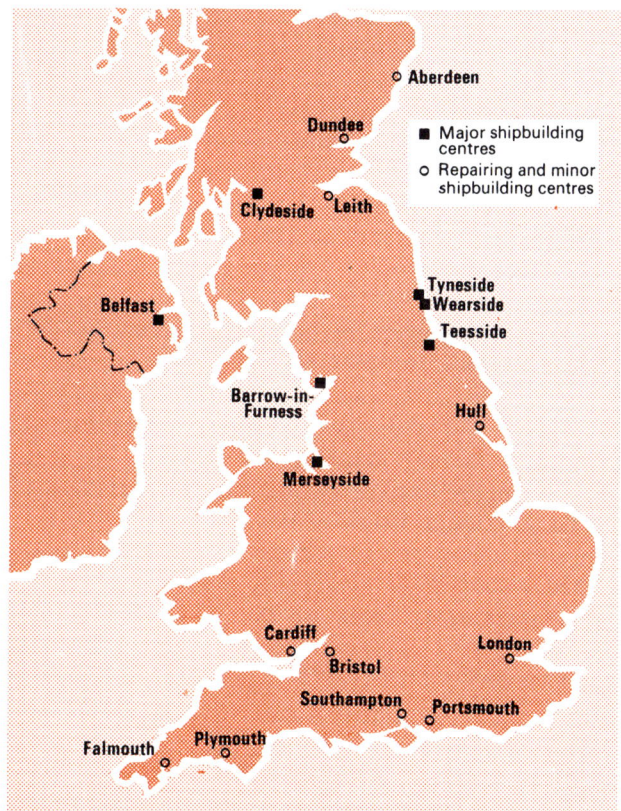

Fig. 229 Shipbuilding in Britain.

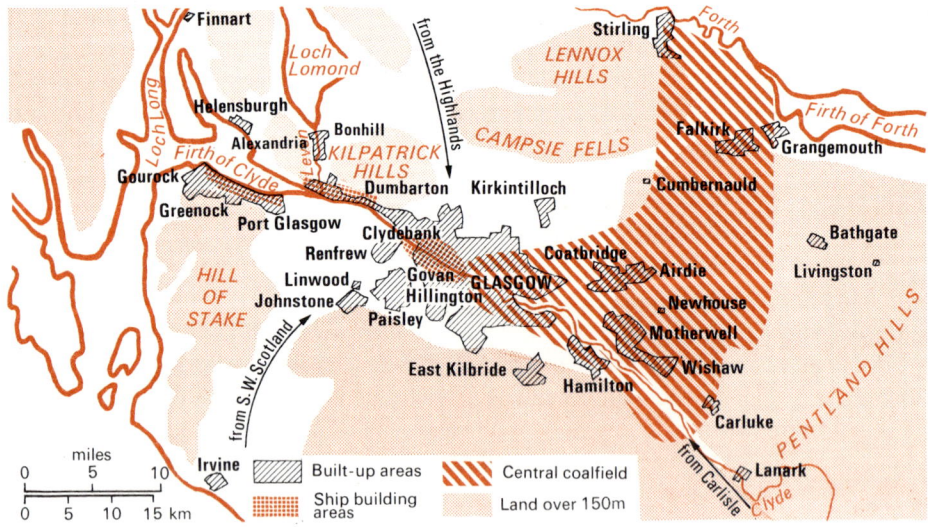

Fig. 230   Glasgow and the Clyde Valley.

the unions involved in shipbuilding be amalgamated into five, and that the ship-yards be reorganized into four major groups, to make the shipbuilding industry more competitive. Firms would be amalgamated to pool their resources and organize their work more efficiently. The groups are:

1. Lower Clyde (4 firms)
2. Upper Clyde (5 firms)
3. Wearside (5 firms)
4. Tyneside (5 firms)

These and other shipbuilding centres are shown on the map. The industry in Merseyside and Belfast is dominated by the single firms of Cammell Laird and Harland and Wolff, so amalgamation is not necessary.

During the nineteenth century when transport was developing throughout the world, ships, locomotives, bridges and all the products of Clydeside were in great demand. When money is in short supply in the world, construction work is the first to stop. Demand for heavy engineering goods falls, and people working in these industries are unemployed. This happened during the depression of the 1930s and the Clyde Valley like Tyneside suffered from very high unemployment. Since then industrial estates have been established and new industries encouraged to set up, especially those producing goods for which demand is increasing and those which are less affected by economic conditions in the rest of the world.

The description below of the approach to Glasgow by air tells of some of the new industries which have begun to change this part of Scotland.

'The aircraft loses height and fields appear, mistily green in a shade that is Scotland's own. There are the pyramids of colliery spoil and the gantries of

230

Fig. 231 A tanker berthing at Finnart, Loch Long, which is a fiord. Why can tankers berth here, but not at Grangemouth on the Firth of Forth, Fig. 233?

Clyde Shipbuilding. Then the sun catches spheres glittering over to the east. That is Grangemouth, the chemicals centre. That factory must be B.M.C.'s Bathgate plant. A further circuit and fields full of bright coloured cars flash under the wing. The Scottish car, the Hillman Imp, is coming from the new production line in its thousands'.[1]

Many of the new industries are metal and engineering industries but they are much more varied than formerly and many are expanding, such as aero-engines (Rolls-Royce) at Hillington, motor cars (Rootes) at Linwood, heavy vehicles (British Leyland) at Bathgate, business machines at Glasgow, electronics at Cumbernauld, East Kilbride and Newhouse.

Fig. 230 shows the Clyde Valley industrial area based on the Central coalfield. On the eastern side of this region is Falkirk, which was the home of the first iron works in Scotland— the Carron Works. Now aluminium processing is more important and kitchen ware and tinfoil are manufactured. Grangemouth is the centre of the expanding oil and chemical industries. Oil tankers are too big to berth at Grangemouth, and have to berth at Finnart on Loch Long. This is on the west coast, but can accommodate the largest vessels. The oil is piped to the refineries and a new petro-chemical plant at Grangemouth. Grangemouth is the most rapidly expanding port in Scotland. It exports refined oil and oil products and is the eastern outlet for iron and steel and cars from the Clyde Valley. Most of its trade is with Scandinavia from which timber and wood pulp are imported.

Glasgow, with a population of over one million, is the centre of the whole Clydeside region. It lies at the lowest bridging point of the river Clyde, which makes it a focus of routes. It is the commercial centre for the west of Scotland and provides services such as shopping, entertainment and hospital treatment for an

[1] Supplement to *The Times* on Aspects of Scotland—3rd September, 1964.

Fig. 232   Gorbals–Hutchensontown area of Glasgow. Tenements line the streets on the left. At the top of the photograph, the ground has been cleared for new blocks of flats.

area which extends as far as the Western Highlands and Islands. 'The very first journey of many a new-born Hebridean is a homeward flight from Glasgow'.[1]

Iron and steel manufacture, and all forms of engineering are found within the city. Consumer goods, including furniture, confectionery, biscuits and hosiery are manufactured.

The city did not begin to grow until the eighteenth century when trade with America increased; then its site on the widest estuary on the west coast, facing America, became an advantage. The river was too shallow for ships to get right up to Glasgow and outports at Greenock and Port Glasgow were used. The bed of the Clyde estuary, however, was easily dredged and now a 11 m deep channel carries ocean going ships into the centre of Glasgow. No dock gates are needed as the tidal range is very small, and the approaches to the port are sheltered from all directions, but the river must be continually dredged to keep the port open. Exports are of machinery, whisky and iron and steel goods whereas imports are of less valuable and bulky goods, chiefly iron ore and grain. The port has new handling facilities for the iron ore, although the biggest ore-carriers cannot be used, and grain is milled and stored in elevators at the quayside (Fig. 227). Much of the Clyde trade is with the Americas and sugar is refined at Greenock, tobacco processed in Glasgow and cotton spun into thread at Paisley.

Glasgow became a Victorian boom town with the growth of heavy industry in

[1] Molsley: *Glasgow's Spheres of Influence* in *The Glasgow Region* edited Miller and Tivy, Constable 1958.

Fig. 233   Oil refinery at Grangemouth. Note the mud banks in the Firth of Forth.

the nineteenth century. People flocked into the city to find work—from the surrounding lowlands, from Ireland and the Scottish Highlands. Close-packed tenements were built to house the people. These are three or four storey blocks, containing between eight and twelve one- or two-roomed flats, opening off a common staircase. These stone-built tenements, now encrusted with the smoke and grime of nearly a century, are the main type of housing in the centre of Glasgow. As each tenement houses many people and tenements and industrial works were built side by side, with few open spaces, the central districts of Glasgow are badly overcrowded.

After the era of prosperity and building came the First World War and the depression when few new buildings were erected. The old tenements fell into a state of disrepair and now Glasgow faces the worst housing problem in the country. The tenements are being demolished and replaced by new blocks of flats in glass and concrete, but fewer people can be rehoused in these areas if they are not to be overcrowded again. New housing estates are being built to house the extra people who have had to move away, but there is not much building land left as Glasgow is hemmed in by high moorland and much of the low land near the Clyde is liable to flood. Old coal workings make other areas unsafe for building as there is the danger of subsidence. Glasgow has therefore had to look beyond the city limits for places to house its people.

Four new towns in Central Scotland cater largely for Glasgow people. These are East Kilbride, Cumbernauld, Irvine and Livingston. A fifth new town, Glenrothes, in Fife, has also absorbed a number of people from Glasgow. Several older towns such as Kirkintilloch, Hamilton and Johnstone are also expanding to house

Glasgow people. Industry is moving to these new centres and many of the expanding industries have set up here.

1. What are: steel plate, building berths, bulkheads, launching blocks, fitting-out basin?

2. What are the differences between bulk carriers and container ships? Mention size, the harbours and docks they can use, types of cargo they can carry.

3. What advantages did Clydeside have which enabled it to become the leading shipbuilding area of the world during the nineteenth century? What disadvantages does it have today?

4. How is Glasgow (a) like and (b) different from Liverpool? Write your answer under the headings: position, the port, industries, recent developments. [See also p. 158.]

5. Look at Fig. 230. (a) What facts about Glasgow's position have helped it to be a focus of routes? (b) Write a sentence about each of the following towns to describe its position: Motherwell, Govan, Grangemouth, Linwood, Cumbernauld, Finnart. (c) Which of the above towns do you associate with each of the following: port and large oil refineries, new town, port for large oil tankers, Ravenscraig iron and steel works, Hillman Imp, Fairfields shipyards.

6. Use the information on p. 235 and Fig. 234: (a) List the textiles produced today in Scotland. (b) What local fibres were originally used? (c) What fibres are today imported? (d) What other industries are associated with the textiles? (e) Where else in Scotland are textiles made? [See ch. 14, p. 224.]

Fig. 234   Textiles and associated industries.

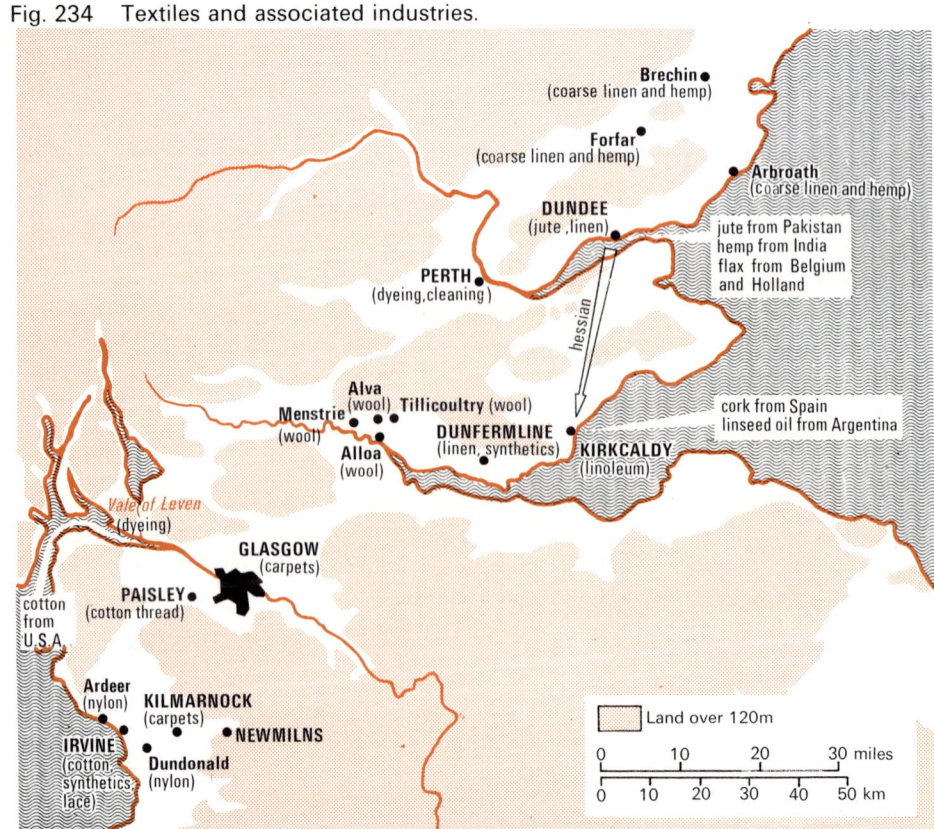

Textiles

Throughout Central Scotland local wool was made into twill and local flax into linen, until the eighteenth century. Cotton was introduced to the west at that time, and as in Lancashire this new fibre replaced the older wools and linens. The cotton industry declined later when heavy industry developed. Relics of it are found in the manufacture of cotton thread in Paisley and the dyeing, bleaching and printing of fabrics in the Vale of Leven. The wool industry has become specialized in heavy goods such as carpets, made in Glasgow and Kilmarnock, although knitwear is manufactured in Alloa and at Alva, Menstrie, and Tillicoultry—small towns at the foot of the Ochil Hills.

In the eastern towns linen remained important. In Angus coarse and heavy materials such as canvas and tarpaulins are made. Flax and hemp were imported from Europe for these industries and in the 1830s the coarsest fibre of all, jute, was introduced. Dundee became the centre of jute manufacture as it was the town in which the problems of spinning and weaving this fibre were first solved. Sacking, twine and hessian are the main products. Much hessian cloth is sent to Kirkaldy where it is used as a backing for linoleum and other floor coverings produced in the city.

In Fife the concentration was on fine linens, but this branch of the industry has changed to manufacturing synthetics. Nylon is also produced at Ardeer and Dundonald in Ayrshire.

Towns in the East

Unlike the west side of the Central Valley which has one large conurbation, the east side has several separate towns. There are two large cities, Edinburgh with a population of nearly half a million, and Dundee with 200 000.

Edinburgh is the capital of Scotland. The old heart of the city clusters round Castle rock—the steep-sided remnant of an old volcano. This was an easy site to defend and guarded the main lowland route into Scotland at its narrowest point between the Pentland Hills and the Firth of Forth. The site of the city was cramped, and in the eighteenth century it was built out northwards. The 'New Town' was planned on a rectangular pattern of wide streets with parks and squares and large stone-built houses. The city spread beyond the old and new towns during the nineteenth century in Victorian tenements, terraced houses and villas.

Edinburgh houses government offices and an old and famous university. The demands of a capital and university city for paper, books, journals and other publications have given rise to paper-making, printing, publishing and book-binding industries. The paper works along the banks of the river Esk use the soft water of the river. Other industries are concerned with food processing (see Fig. 236) and now with the electronics industry which employs more people than any other.

Leith, the port of Edinburgh, to which it is now joined, is situated on the wide

Fig. 235 Stirling. The old part of the town is built round the castle. The newer part, shown by a more regular pattern of streets, is built nearer the river. Compare this photograph with Ordnance Survey Map G, facing p. 209. In which direction was the camera pointing?

Forth estuary. Its docks have been greatly extended and improved. Its industries are largely those of processing imports.

Dundee lies on the north bank of the Tay. It controls the routes east-west between the Sidlaw Hills and the estuary and south across the Firth. Its main industry is jute manufacturing, which employs one out of every five workers.

Although the rail bridges over the Firth of Forth and Firth of Tay were built in the 1890s, goods moving by road along the east side of Scotland had until 1963 to make long detours round the firths. In 1963 the Forth Road Bridge was opened, and in 1966 the Tay Road Bridge. These have made the journey between Edinburgh and Dundee up to two hours shorter.

Because roads have improved so much, many new industries have been attracted to eastern Scotland, especially Fife, which is between the two long firths. These are industries producing light goods of high value such as transistors, telecommunications equipment and calculating machines. They do not require large quantities of raw materials and can use road transport to bring in materials and to distribute their products.

Some of the new factories have been built in the new towns of Glenrothes and Livingston (in West Lothian) but industrial estates have also been established at Donibristle, Leven and Cowdenbeath. Several older industrial towns such as Kirkcaldy and Dunfermline have extended their range of industries and even the more traditional Scottish industries have expanded. A new woollen mill, for example, has been opened at Rosyth.

236

The map (Fig. 226) shows that the Central Valley of Scotland is not the valley of a single river or drainage basin. It is an uneven lowland drained by several rivers. The Central Valley was not formed by erosion but by earth movements.

When pressure is exerted on the rocks which form the surface layers of the earth they may break. Rocks slip along the line of the break, which is called a fault. Where there are large faults the rocks may eventually, bit by bit, slip hundreds of feet. The movement of layers of rock along faults is one of the main causes of earthquakes.

The north and south boundaries of the Central Valley are fault lines. Two parallel faults are found at the southern edge of the Scottish Highlands and the northern edge of the Southern Uplands. The land between them has sunk down, forming the central valley. This is called a rift valley.

Most of the Central Valley is formed of sandstones and limestones, but there are also volcanic rocks made of solidified lava from old volcanoes. The volcanic rocks are resistant to erosion, so they form the hill ranges of the Central Valley. Rivers flow through gaps between the hills, and towns are built in the gaps. One of the gaps is shown on Ordnance Survey Map G, facing p. 209.

Stirling lies on the river Forth in the gap between the Campsie Fells and the Ochil Hills. Stirling Castle was built to guard the gap which formed an easy line of attack. From the Ordnance Survey map, it can be seen that the castle (789941) is built on a small, but steep-sided hill. This hill is the remnant of an old volcano and as it is steep-sided and craggy was an easy site to defend. A settlement grew up round the castle for protection.

It was easy to build a bridge over the river Forth at Stirling, because higher land comes close to the river on both sides. It was also the furthest point downstream at which the Forth could be crossed, until the Forth rail bridge was opened in 1890. Routes converged on Stirling. It controlled the main route north via Strathallan to Perth and the Highlands and the easy east-west route through the Forth Valley. With the coming of the railways in the nineteenth century, Stirling expanded as a market town and service centre for the surrounding farm lands. Industries processing farm produce grew up, coal was mined nearby and metal and engineering industries were established.

Perth, in the gap between the Ochil and Sidlaw Hills occupies a similar position and has a similar history. Whereas Stirling lost some of its importance as a route centre with the building of the bridges over the Firth of Forth, Perth has retained its importance. Traffic going north to the Highlands and Aberdeen still goes through Perth although much now uses the new Tay bridge via Dundee.

Most of the following questions refer to the Ordnance Survey map of Stirling, Map G, facing p. 209.

7. Draw a rectangle half the size of the Ordnance Survey map to represent it. Draw in the 50 ft. contour and the river Forth. Use your atlas to name the hill

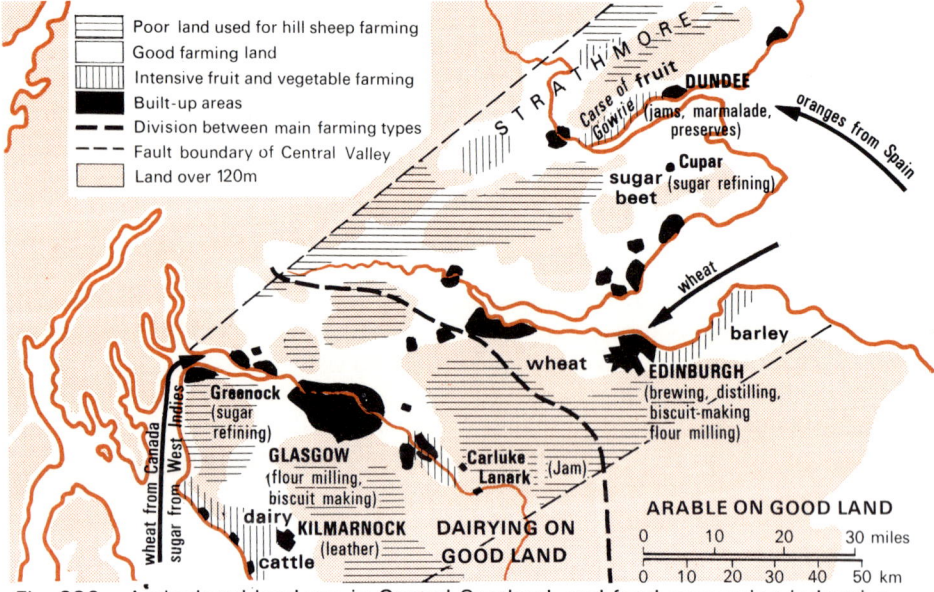

Fig. 236   Agricultural land use in Central Scotland, and food-processing industries.

ranges in the north-east and south-west. Shade the built-up area of Stirling and draw the route of the A.9 and the main north-south railway. Add notes to your map to explain the position of Stirling as a gap town.

8. Use your sketch drawn for question 7 and mark in all the coal mines shown on the map. Shade all the area beneath which coal is found. Use Fig. 226 and name the coalfield.

9. How is the route of the A.9 (a) like and (b) different from the route of the north-south railway?

10. Describe the course of the river and the shape of the valley of (a) the Forth and (b) the Bannockburn.

11. Describe the site, and the shape of the built-up area of Bridge of Allan. How have they been influenced by relief and drainage?

12. Draw a sketch of the photograph of Stirling (Fig. 235) and label the meandering river Forth, the valley floor, remnant of an old volcano, built-up area, main railway.

Agriculture

The Central Valley is the richest farming region of Scotland. There is more flat and easily cultivated land, the softer rocks form deep fertile soils, and the lowlands are warmer and drier than the rest of Scotland.

On Fig. 236 showing land use in the Central Valley a line is marked south of the river Forth, dividing the valley into two parts. In the west, the good farming land mainly grows grass, and dairy cattle are kept to provide milk for the large towns.

238

Butter and cheese are made in areas further away from the conurbation of Glasgow and the Clyde Valley. In the east, the good farming land is mainly arable but livestock, both cattle and sheep, are fattened. They are reared locally or in the Highland valleys, and young cattle are also imported from Ireland, through Glasgow, to be fattened. Strathmore is the main area for fattening beef cattle. Wheat and barley are grown, especially in the south-east and sugar beet in Fifeshire, near the refinery at Cupar.

Although not part of the Central Valley, lowland extends, in patches, along the east coast of Scotland right to John O'Groats. Farming on these lowlands is like that of the 'highland edges' described in ch. 14, p. 216. Grain crops are grown and sheep and cattle reared and fattened.

The lowlands widen out in three areas. Each of these is centred on a market town which serves the land around it. In the extreme north are the lowlands of Caithness, centred on Wick and Thurso. Further south are the Moray Firth lowlands, centred on Inverness, and the Aberdeen lowlands, centred on Aberdeen. Inverness and Aberdeen are also major route centres.

Aberdeen lies between the mouths of the rivers Dee and Don, and is an old university city. It is the leading fishing port of Scotland, landing herring, cod, hake, haddock and plaice. Its industries are listed below.

Industries of Aberdeen

Type of Industry		Products
Engineering	(1) Heavy	Ships Agricultural machinery
	(2) Light	Electrical goods
Textiles		Woollen hosiery and overcoating Linen
Timber		Paper and sawn timber

Aberdeen is the third largest city of Scotland. Known as the 'granite city' most of its buildings are faced with the high quality granite which is still quarried nearby.

13. What is (a) a fault, (b) a rift valley, (c) a volcanic rock?

14. Look at Fig. 236. (a) Name three areas in the Central Valley where sheep are raised. (b) Why is there more arable farming in the east and dairying in the west? (c) Name the areas where market gardening is important. Which are in sheltered positions, on south-facing slopes, near large built-up areas? (d) Which locally produced agricultural products are used in local processing industries?

15. Draw sketch maps to show the position and communications of (a) Inverness and (b) Perth.

16. Look at the map and table below, and find the towns listed on your atlas map.

Thousand tonnes 1965

	Total foreign trade	*Total coastwise trade*
Ayr	57	915
Ardrossan	405	1006
Clyde	10 411	1971
Stornoway	1	76
Inverness	11	177
Aberdeen	463	802
Dundee	328	136
Methil	152	728
Grangemouth	2596	1638
Granton	180	294
Leith	1124	721

(a) Which ports have more coastwise than foreign trade? (b) Which four ports have more foreign than coastwise trade? The following sentences refer to these four ports; name the port each sentence refers to:

Textile fibres are the leading import.

Over two-thirds of the total trade is in oil.

Imports of food and raw materials are more than 4 million tonnes and exports

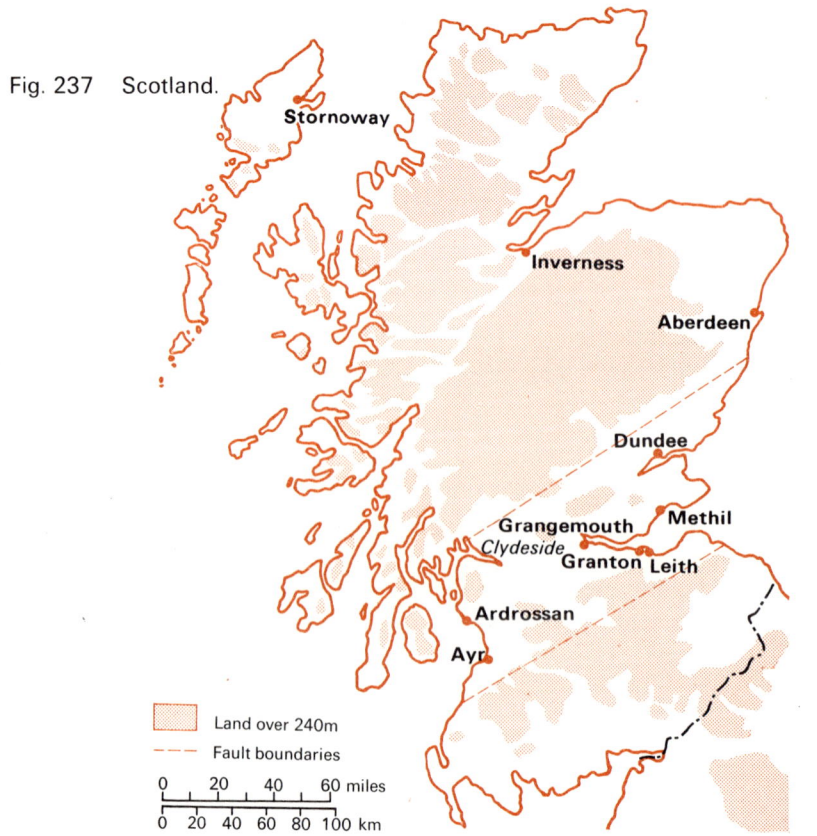

Fig. 237 Scotland.

Stornoway

Inverness

Aberdeen

Dundee

Grangemouth Methil
Clydeside
Granton Leith

Ardrossan

Ayr

Land over 240m
Fault boundaries

0   20   40   60 miles
0   20 40 60 80 100 km

of manufactured goods are more than 1 million tonnes.

15 per cent of imports are timber and pulp products.

(c) Ayr and Methil both have a high proportion of outward traffic in coal. From which coalfields is the coal mined? (d) Why is 99 per cent of Stornoway's trade in imports? What goods are probably exported? [See also p. 220.]

17. Write an essay to explain why three-quarters of Scotland's population live in the Central Valley.

Port of Leith

Imports

Timber	
Wood pulp	For paper making in Edinburgh
Grain	Milled into flour at Leith
Phosphate rock	Manufactured into fertilizer at Leith
Food stuffs, mainly dairy products	To supply the industrial towns of Central Scotland

Exports

Coal	To be distributed round the coast to other British ports

---

Manufacturing Industries of Dundee (other than Jute)

Types of Industry	Products
Food-processing	Jam, preserves and marmalade. Sweets, chocolates, confectionery 'Dundee cakes'.
Engineering (1) Heavy	Shipbuilding Machinery
(2) Light	Clocks and watches
Electronics	Calculating machines

Older Industrial towns in Fifeshire

Town	Original Industry	New Industries
Kirkcaldy	Linen Linoleum	Chemicals Furniture Engineering Floor coverings in new materials
Dunfermline	Linen	Synthetics Engineering

16. Northern Ireland

From 1800 to 1921 the whole of Ireland formed part of the United Kingdom of Great Britain and Ireland. It was governed from London and its position was like that of Scotland or Wales today. In 1921, after years of trouble and rebellion, Ireland was given independence. The Irish Free State was created, with its own Government in Dublin. It became the Republic of Ireland in 1949.

Basalt

County boundaries

Boundary with the
Republic of Ireland

Land over 120m

242

16. NORTHERN IRELAND

The six north-eastern counties of Ireland—Antrim, Down, Armagh, Tyrone, Fermanagh and Londonderry—decided not to join the Irish Free State, but to form the state of Northern Ireland, and remain part of the United Kingdom. There were several reasons for this. The first was the difference in religion between the two parts of Ireland. Many Scottish and English people settled in the north-east in the sixteenth and seventeenth centuries. They were Protestants and the majority of the people here are still Protestant, whereas the people of the rest of Ireland are mostly Roman Catholics.

The six counties were the most prosperous in Ireland, and contained nearly all the manufacturing industries. But these industries depended on Great Britain for their raw materials and markets. The people in the North therefore felt they would fare better as part of a United Kingdom with no barriers to trade with Great Britain. The Government of the Irish Free State wanted to encourage the use of the Irish language, but few people in the six counties could speak it.

Northern Ireland became a self-governing state of the United Kingdom, having its own Parliament at Stormont near Belfast. Twelve representatives are also sent to Westminster which deals with the external affairs of the whole United Kingdom.

Ireland is therefore divided by an international boundary and the border and customs house must be passed on the roads between the Republic and the North. Some international boundaries follow lines which naturally divide people, such as ranges of hills or mountains, swamps, or deserts. The boundary between Northern Ireland and the Republic does not do this. It follows the line of the county boundaries and is often inconvenient.

The map shows clearly that the highlands and lowlands of Northern Ireland are not divided into neat zones but are interspersed. The highlands are open moorlands covered with coarse grass, heather and peat bog. They provide rough grazing for sheep, but cultivation is not possible and the only improved land lies in the valleys below 240 m. There are no trees except in a few areas where coniferous trees have been planted (Fig. 242). All the highlands have been smoothed and their valleys widened and deepened by the action of ice.

Although similar in appearance, the highland areas are made of different rocks. The Antrim Plateau is made of black solidified lava called basalt. About sixty million years ago this lava poured out over the surface of north-east Ireland and the west of Scotland, which were joined at that time. The basalt is geologically speaking quite a young rock. Being fluid the lava formed level surfaces as it solidified. Since then the land between Scotland and Ireland has sunk beneath the sea, forming the North Channel. The land west of the present Antrim Plateau also sank, to form the hollow now filled by Lough Neagh and the valley of the river Bann. As Fig. 238 shows, the basalt extends west of the river Bann into County Londonderry. Its edge forms a steep escarpment overlooking the valley of the river Roe. The edge of the basalt also forms a steep wall north of Belfast, where it rises 200 m sheer from the Lagan valley (Fig. 248).

16. NORTHERN IRELAND

Fig. 239   The Sperrin mountains. Find these on the map. How high are they? How has glaciation affected the shape of them?

The Sperrin mountains are made of very old, hard rocks similar to those of the Scottish Highlands. The mountains of Mourne are made of granite and contain the highest mountain in Northern Ireland, Slieve Donard, 852 m. A large reservoir in Silent Valley provides Belfast with its water.

1. Look at Fig. 238, p. 242. (a) Which way does the river Erne drain? (b) Where is it cut by the boundary? (c) What difficulties does this create for both countries?

2. Which two rivers form part of the boundary? Suggest why it may be difficult to use a river as an international boundary.

3. Londonderry and Strabane are two market towns just inside the boundary. What difficulties arise from this position?

4. How are the highlands of Northern Ireland (a) like, (b) different from the highlands of Scotland? Think of height, extent, glaciation, land use, climate, communications.

5. Which rivers flow into and out of Lough Neagh, and into Belfast Lough?

6. Lough Neagh is the biggest lake in the United Kingdom. How long and how wide is it? Compare its size with Loch Lomond, Lake Windermere. Suggest why it is a different shape.

7. How big is the lowland centred on Lough Neagh from north to south, and east to west? Describe the position of the three lowlands which are separate from this main lowland.

The lowlands are covered by glacial drift up to 60 m thick. In the Lagan Valley and along the south shore of Belfast Lough the glacial drift is sand and

244

Fig. 240 Drumlins in Strangford Lough. Find it on the map, page 242. Draw a sketch of the photograph and add notes to indicate length, width, and height of the drumlins.

Fig. 241 Horses grazing on drumlin slopes with the Mourne Mountains in the background.

gravel and the country is flat. But most of the drift is boulder clay. In many places the boulder clay has been shaped by ice into small rounded hills called 'drumlins'. They are between 15 and 30 m high, about a kilometre long by half a kilometre wide. They occur in swarms extending over many square kilometres. Between the drumlins are boggy hollows which have mostly been drained. In Strangford Lough, and the Loughs Erne there are hundreds of drumlins rising above the shallow water (Fig. 240).

245

Fig. 242   Afforestation in the Mourne Mountains. The farm gateposts are typical of Co. Down.

The drumlins provide the best sites in the lowlands for farms, which are built there to avoid the boggier land of the hollows. In the highlands the farms are built on the sides of the valleys, above the land liable to be flooded in winter, and below the steep slopes of mountains. Highland farms are usually strip-shaped to give each farmer a section of both improved land and rough pasture.

Farms in Northern Ireland are mostly small. 60 per cent of them consist of 12 hectares or less. This means that most farms can be worked by the farmer and his family with no hired help. Nowadays, with many more machines available to help the farmer it is possible for one man to manage much more than 12 hectares. Some farmers have bought another farm and run the two as one large unit. Fields are small and bounded by thick hedges of hawthorn and fuschia which take up a lot of land. The farms are low, white-painted single-storeyed buildings and the entrances to them are marked by fat white gateposts.

The two maps opposite show farming country in County Down. In map (a) the farms and their outbuildings are grouped together into a small hamlet or

246

'clachan'. In map (b) the farms are scattered evenly over the area. A hundred years ago most of the farms of Northern Ireland were grouped into clachans. The families living in the farms were usually related, and often had the same name. Many clachans take their name from the families who lived in them, with the addition of 'town' or the Irish word 'Bally'. The clachan in Fig. 243(a) for example, is called Kearnystown and originally Kearnys owned several of the farms.

Near the clachan was a large unfenced field divided into strips. Each year several strips were allotted to each farmer for the year and these were scattered over the field. On them he grew oats and potatoes to feed his family and his animals. Beyond the cultivated field was rough pasture land where animals from any of the farms could graze. Each man was also allotted a section of bogland. From this he could cut peat or turfs, which were then dried out and burnt as fuel.

As the population of Ireland increased, the cultivated land had to be divided among many more people. Allotments of land became fewer for each family and many could hardly exist. The years 1845, 1846 and 1847 were disastrous. In these three successive years the potato crop, on which people depended for food, failed. Thousands of people starved to death and thousands more emigrated to the U.S.A., Canada and Britain. The land was redistributed so that each farmer's land was joined into one unit. New farmhouses were built on these holdings and many clachans were abandoned. Thus the pattern of scattered farms developed.

Until the last century there were no large towns in Northern Ireland. Neither the Romans, who founded towns in England, nor the Anglo-Saxons who established the large villages of south and east England, settled in Ireland. The Normans built strongholds in the east, such as Carrickfergus Castle, on Belfast Lough but had little success in settling the country, where the pattern of small hamlets remained.

Fig. 243 Types of settlement.

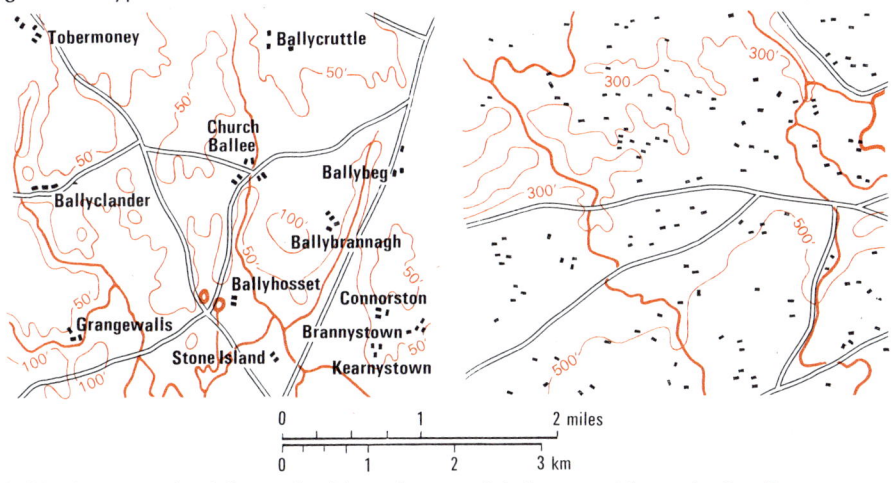

(a) Clachans south of Strangford Lough. (b) Scattered farms in Co. Down.

247

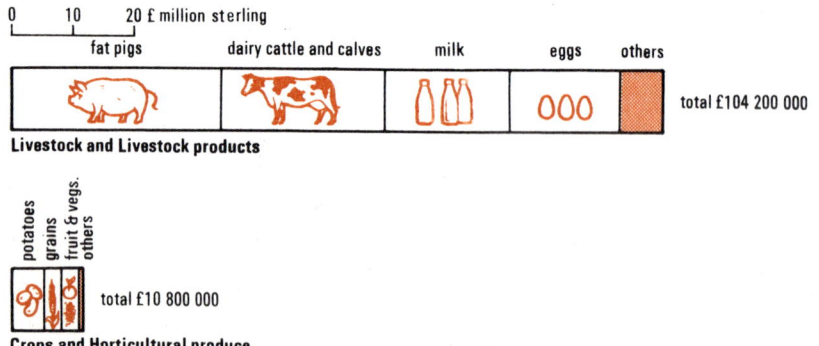

Fig. 244   Cutting peat near Kilrea, Co. Tyrone. How deep is the peat cutting? Why are the turfs left in piles near the cutting?

Fig. 245   Value of agricultural produce in Northern Ireland, 1966.

In the sixteenth and seventeenth centuries when English and Scottish people were given grants of land in Northern Ireland by the Government, they founded many small settlements. Many never grew beyond a small group of houses at a cross-roads or lining a street, but some grew into the present towns of Northern Ireland. These were the towns well situated as market centres, or where the linen industry became established.

248

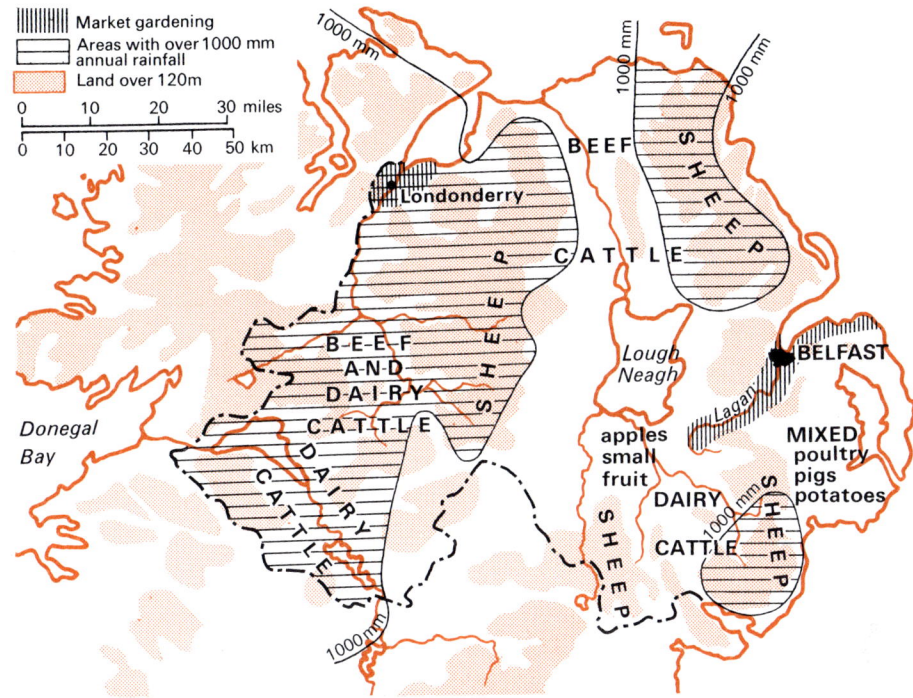

Fig. 246 Farming.

8. What are clachans? What types of land did each farmer from the clachan have and what did he use them for? What changes took place in Northern Ireland after 1845?

9. Using the bar graph opposite, (a) Write in figures the value in £ sterling of production of dairy cattle and calves; pigs; grain crops. (b) Why are pigs often raised where there is also a great deal of dairying? (c) Suggest reasons why live-stock is more important than arable farming in Northern Ireland.

10. Look at Fig. 246. (a) Where are most of the sheep raised? (b) 80 per cent of the improved land is used for grass. Where is most of this land? (c) Find the three areas where dairy cattle are raised. In Fermanagh, they are raised chiefly for butter and cream, but in the other two areas they are raised for milk. Suggest reasons for this. (d) What type of soils are there in the Lagan valley? What other advantages has this valley for market gardening? Where else is there market gardening?

The linen industry

Linen has been spun and woven in people's homes from locally grown flax for centuries. This crop is not grown anywhere else in Britain. Flax looks like a cereal crop and grows to about 1 m high. It has blue flowers. The flax stem provides the fibre from which linen is manufactured. The flax is pulled by hand so that the fibres are as long as possible. To loosen the fibres flax must be soaked or 'retted'.

249

This is done in streams or ponds on the farms. It must then be beaten or 'scutched' to get rid of the pulp and obtain the fibrous core. Hardly any flax is grown now as on a small farm it involves too much work.

In 1685 groups of refugees from France who were skilled workers of fine linen settled in Northern Ireland. They established their trades at Lurgan, Portadown and Banbridge, towns still important today for linen working. The quality of Irish linen improved and the industry expanded greatly in the eighteenth century. There was no longer enough local flax to supply the industry and flax was imported from Russia. It now comes from Belgium and Holland. Linen is creamy brown when it is spun and woven and must be bleached white. The bleaching was done in Belfast which became the market for the finished cloth. It became the centre of spinning and weaving also when the industry was mechanized.

Linen, especially fine linen, was a difficult cloth to make by machine, as the thread does not stretch and so is very liable to break. The first spinning machine did not come into operation in Belfast until 1828 and the yarn was still woven on hand looms until 1914. A power loom was made in 1850, and linen weaving gradually became a factory industry. Most factories were built near the port of Belfast because coal to drive the machines and flax could easily be imported here, and the finished linen exported. Belfast thus grew rapidly during the nineteenth century as the centre of the linen industry.

Three-quarters of all the linen mills now lie within 48 kilometres of Belfast, although towns throughout the country are concerned in some way with the linen industry, many of them in clothing—manufacturing shirts, handkerchiefs and other linen goods. Northern Ireland makes nearly one-third of the world's linen. Three-quarters of it is exported, mainly to the U.S.A. However, the linen industry has contracted in recent years. Competition from rival linen-producing countries (Belgium, France, Germany and Japan) and from high quality cotton goods and synthetic fibres has hastened the decline. Linen also is a less fashionable fabric than it once was, so demand for it has fallen.

Shipbuilding

In 1853 shipyards were established in Belfast. Northern Ireland has neither coal nor iron which are used in large quantities in this industry. However, both could be easily imported by sea from the west of Scotland and the fact that wages were lower in Ireland off-set the extra cost to the shipbuilders of importing these things. This is no longer the case, however, as wages in shipbuilding and engineering are standardized throughout the country, and shipbuilding has contracted in Belfast as it has in all parts of the country. The Belfast shipbuilding industry is dominated by one very large firm, Harland and Wolff, which employs about 10 000 people, although when there are enough orders it can provide work for as many as 30 000. Belfast is particularly noted for tankers and aircraft carriers as they can be launched in the deep water of Belfast Lough.

The other main manufacturing industries are the aircraft industry, which has also contracted, and the food processing industries. These process local agricultural produce and include ham and bacon curing, vegetable canning and the making of dried milk, butter and cheese.

Because Northern Ireland depended so heavily on the two main industries of shipbuilding and linen, which have both declined, it has suffered severely from unemployment, which is still much higher than anywhere else in the United Kingdom.

Much has been done in recent years to encourage firms to establish factories in Northern Ireland, particularly firms engaged in the new, expanding industries which can employ people from the old contracting ones. Of these, light engineering, synthetic fibres and chemicals are the most important. Many expanding firms who found it difficult to obtain labour where they were, have come to Northern Ireland. The light engineering includes the making of radios, vacuum cleaners, cutlery and precision tools. Chemicals are represented in the artificial rubber plant at Londonderry. The tyre industry has set up there also, using the artificial rubber, and a new oil refinery was opened in Belfast in 1964.

The synthetic fibres industries form the group which has expanded most rapidly in Northern Ireland. Linen-making machinery is fairly easily adapted to making synthetic fibres and many plants have changed to making synthetic or linen and synthetic mixtures. Several new factories have also been built.

Town	Industry
Carrickfergus	Rayon
Antrim	Nylon
Coleraine	Acrilan
Kilroot	Terylene
Carnmoney	Elura-stretch yarn
Ballymena	Soflon: nylon stockings
Newtownards	Weaving synthetic
Dungannon	Glass yarn and fibre
Londonderry	Orlon
Ballyclare Doagh Saintfield	Linen and synthetic mixture fabrics

Belfast with a population of half a million contains one-third of the people of Northern Ireland. Belfast grew very rapidly in the late nineteenth century with the development of the linen and shipbuilding industries. During the famine years of 1845–7 also many people left the land and went to Belfast in search of work. The city is composed of small terraced workers' houses and more spacious Victorian mansions, all built of red brick. It is hemmed in to the north-west by the steep edge of the Antrim Plateau, but new suburbs have been built along the Lagan Valley and the shores of Belfast Lough. The area from which Belfast draws its workpeople extends to Lisburn, Bangor and Carrickfergus.

The port of Belfast handles three-quarters of the trade of Northern Ireland. It has the advantages of being sheltered and having a low tidal range (3 m) making the construction of docks unnecessary. The straight deep-water channel, called Victoria Channel, was dredged in 1837 and 'Queens Island' was created from the dredged material. This peninsula is now the site of the aircraft works and part of the shipyards. Belfast is a collection and distribution centre for the whole of Northern Ireland.

Londonderry (52 000) is the only other large town in Northern Ireland. It was founded in 1633 by a group of London merchants, who prefixed London to the Irish name Derry. It was originally a walled city and the old walls are well preserved although the city now spreads far beyond them. Londonderry stands at the head of Lough Foyle. It is the second port of Northern Ireland, but is far behind Belfast in its volume of trade. It is the centre of the shirt-making industry, using

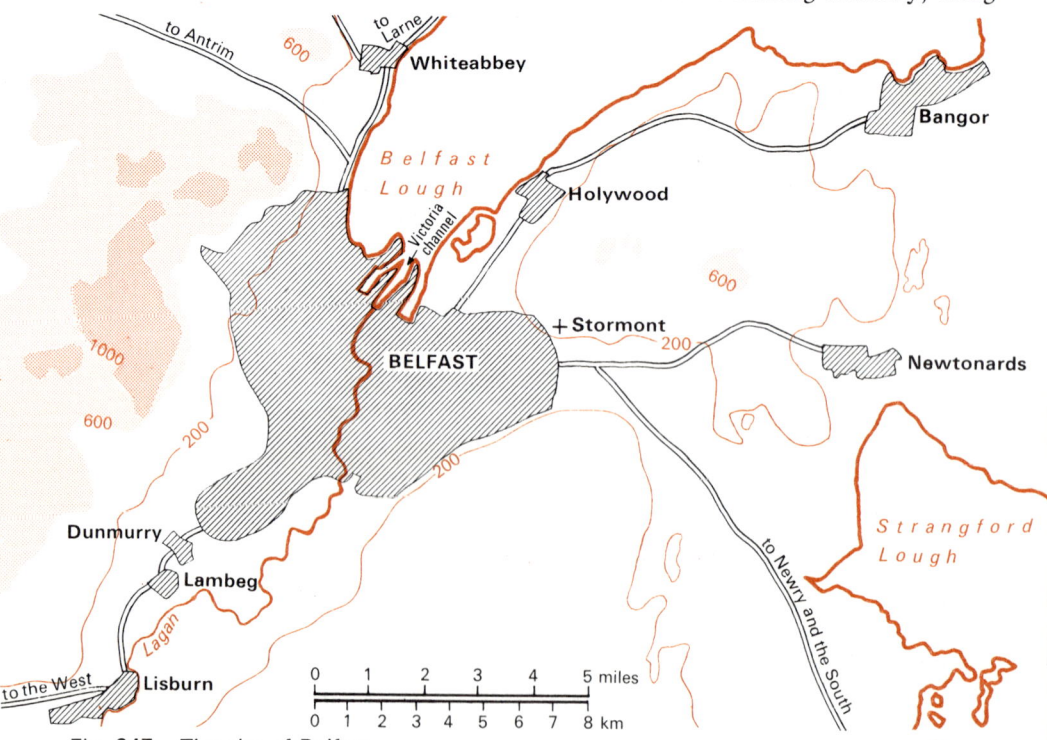

Fig. 247   The site of Belfast.

Fig. 248   Port of Belfast. Part of the Antrim plateau is in the background. The steep edge of a layer of basalt can be seen. Coal is being unloaded in the foreground.

Fig. 249   Harland and Wolff's shipyards, Belfast Lough.

not only locally made linen and synthetic fabrics, but importing cotton cloth from Lancashire to be made into shirts. This industry mainly employs women, but there was not much employment for men. The opening of the artificial rubber and tyre works, and the proposed orlon factory due to open in 1968 is providing more work for men.

11.   Compare the recent changes in the linen industry of Northern Ireland and the cotton industry of Lancashire. [See also page 151.]

12.   Draw a map to show the routes between Northern Ireland and Great Britain, and the commodities carried.

Main ferry routes:
    Larne–Stranraer
    Belfast–Heysham
    Belfast–Liverpool.

Main trade routes:

Livestock and foodstuffs	from Belfast to Liverpool
Coal	from Ardrossan to Belfast
Steel	from Glasgow to Belfast.

13.   What advantages does Belfast have over Londonderry?

14.   Compare shipbuilding in Belfast with shipbuilding on Clydeside (p. 228). Think of (a) site of the shipyards, (b) size of the estuary, (c) sources of raw materials, (d) number of firms.

Index

254

sugar beet, 51, 57, 239
Sunderland, 165
Swansea, 183
Swindon, 34
syncline, 35, 36

Tal-y-Llyn, 210, 212
tarn, 208
Taunton, 106
Tay, Firth of, 236
Team Valley Estate, 166
Teesside, 137, 140, 141, 143, 158, 170
temperature, 48
terraces (*see* river terraces)
textile manufacturing, 146–154
    cotton, 151–153, 158, 161, 232, 235
    hosiery, 203
    jute, 236
    lace, 204
    man-made fibres, 153–154, 203, 251
    wool, 84, 147–151, 224, 235
Thame, River, 21
Thames, 12, 20, 33, 61
Thomas & Gilchrist steel, 140
thunder, 38, 39
Thurso, 239
Tillicoultry, 235
tin, 110–111
tin plate, 182
tobacco, 113, 204, 232
tor, 108
Torquay, 105
tourist industry, 105, 216
Trafford Park, 156, *163*
Tranmere, 160
Trent, River, 186, 201
    Vale of, 117, 128
Tunbridge Wells, 33

Tweed, River, 224
Tyne gap, 129
Tyneside, 141, 144, 164–167, 170, 230

U-shaped valleys, 208–210
unemployment, 131

Vale of York, 117, 128
V-shaped valleys, 16

Washington, 167
water table, 27, 121
water vapour, 46
wave-cut platform, 93
Weald, The, 32, 138
weathering, 15, 21, 33, 212
Weaver, River, 142, 186
Welsh Mountains, 216–219
Weybridge, 204
wheat farming, 50, 53, *56*, 57
Whin Sill, 124
Wharfedale, 121, 124
Wick, 239
Widnes, 143, 162
Wilton, 143, 144
wind gap, 24
Winsford, 142
wool manufacturing, 84, 147–151, 224, 235
Worcester, 199
Worsted, 148

Yarmouth, 90
York, 129
Yorkshire:
    Hull, 158, 168–169, 170, 171
    textiles, 146–151
    Vale of York, 117, 128
    Wolds, 25